Human Rights in World Histo[

Defended by a host of passionate advocates and organizations, certain standard human rights have come to represent a quintessential component of global citizenship. There are, however, a number of societies that dissent from this orthodoxy, either in general or on particular issues, on the basis of political necessity, cultural tradition, or group interest.

Human Rights in World History takes a global historical perspective to examine the emergence of this dilemma and its constituent concepts. Beginning with premodern features compatible with a human rights approach, including religious doctrines and natural rights ideas, it goes on to describe the rise of the first modern-style human rights statements, associated with the Enlightenment and contemporary anti-slavery and revolutionary fervor. Along the way, it explores ongoing contrasts in the liberal approach, between sincere commitments to human rights and a recurrent sense that certain types of people had to be denied common rights because of their perceived backwardness and need to be "civilized." These contrasts find clear echo in later years with the contradictions between the pursuit of human rights goals and the spread of Western imperialism.

By the second half of the 20th century, human rights frameworks had become absorbed into key global institutions and conventions, and their arguments had expanded to embrace multiple new causes. In today's postcolonial world, and with the rise of more powerful regional governments, the tension between universal human rights arguments and local opposition or backlash is more clearly delineated than ever but no closer to satisfactory resolution.

Peter N. Stearns is Provost and Professor of History at George Mason University, Virginia. He is Series Editor for Routledge's Themes in World History and founder and editor of the *Journal of Social History*. He is co-author of *Premodern Travel in World History* (2008) and author of *Childhood in World History* (2nd edition, 2010), *Globalization in World History* (2009), *Sexuality in World History* (2009), *Gender in World History* (2nd edition, 2006), and *Western Civilization in World History* (2003)—all in this series.

Themes in World History
Series editor: Peter N. Stearns

The Themes in World History series offers focused treatment of a range of human experiences and institutions in the world history context. The purpose is to provide serious, if brief, discussions of important topics as additions to textbook coverage and document collections. The treatments will allow students to probe particular facets of the human story in greater depth than textbook coverage allows, and to gain a fuller sense of historians' analytical methods and debates in the process. Each topic is handled over time—allowing discussions of changes and continuities. Each topic is assessed in terms of a range of different societies and religions—allowing comparisons of relevant similarities and differences. Each book in the series helps readers deal with world history in action, evaluating global contexts as they work through some of the key components of human society and human life.

Human Rights in World History

Peter N. Stearns

Routledge
Taylor & Francis Group

LONDON AND NEW YORK

First published 2012
by Routledge
2 Park Square, Milton Park, Abingdon, Oxon OX14 4RN

Simultaneously published in the USA and Canada
by Routledge
711 Third Avenue, New York, NY 10017

Routledge is an imprint of the Taylor & Francis Group, an informa business

© 2012 Peter N. Stearns

The right of Peter N. Stearns to be identified as author of this work has
been asserted by him in accordance with sections 77 and 78 of the
Copyright, Designs and Patents Act 1988.

British Library Cataloguing in Publication Data
A catalogue record for this book is available from the British Library

Library of Congress Cataloging in Publication Data
Stearns, Peter N.
Human rights in world history / Peter N. Stearns. – 1st ed.
p. cm. – (Themes in world history)
ISBN: 978-0-415-50795-0 (hbk) -- ISBN: 978-0-415-50796-7 (pbk) -- ISBN:
978-0-203-11995-2 (ebk) 1. Category. 2. Category. 3. Category.
LVVPD number

ISBN: 978-0-415-50795-0 (hbk)
ISBN: 978-0-415-50796-7 (pbk)
ISBN: 978-0-203-11995-2 (ebk)

Typeset in Times New Roman
by Taylor & Francis Books

For Brian Kingsolver, with respect and affection

Contents

Acknowledgments

A number of people encouraged me in this topic and provided valuable guidance; particular thanks to Carol Gould. Christiane M. Abu Sarah offered exceptionally creative assistance with the research. Laura Bell performed her usual wonders in manuscript preparation. My wife, Donna Kidd, suffered my enthusiasms and distractions with her usual good cheer. My thanks to the editorial group at Routledge, which has been exceptionally supportive. And I thank, as well, my world history students at George Mason, drawn from many countries, who offer valuable perspectives on a complex topic.

Preface

One of the most important challenges in globalization today involves the recognition that each major society has its own distinctive values and culture. These cultural values, in turn, have usually formed over many centuries and offer deep meaning and identity to most members of that society. The values will differ from one society to the next, and a key goal of contemporary global understanding involves appreciation and acceptance of these differences. Gone are the old imperialist assumptions when one society—the West—could presume that its standards should be imposed worldwide, because all other regions were inferior. As imperialism is cast aside, and more nations rise to significant claims to economic and political power, it's essential that we learn how to tolerate and accommodate differences. One size does not fit all, and peace in an interconnected world requires that contemporary publics—particularly in the societies with a strong imperialist past—come to terms with that fact. Reasonable coexistence and simple justice both demand flexibility.

One of the most important challenges in our globalized world involves the successful promotion of human rights across political and cultural boundaries. Every person, regardless of race, or religion, or gender, or social class, should enjoy those standards and protections we increasingly realize are vital to a meaningful life. Human rights involve freedom from compulsory labor and the opportunity to enjoy whatever religious faith one chooses—or none at all. They involve legal and political equality for women, as well as safeguards against abuse or sexual violence. They involve freedom to criticize or dissent, and the related freedom to express oneself openly and to assemble in pursuit of one's views. Obviously, enjoyment of basic human rights is not yet uniform around the world, but it is a sign of progress that virtually everywhere key individuals and organizations share a commitment to extend human rights. Never before have there been so many groups, from agencies in the United Nations to grassroots associations defending political prisoners or labor leaders, devoted to spreading knowledge about human rights and calling attention to violations wherever they may occur.

Both these statements—about the need for tolerance and the need for more vigorous pursuit of basic rights—are persuasive and defendable. Both might easily win approval from individuals proud of their cosmopolitan and enlightened views. Both arguably express powerful currents in contemporary world history.

But the obvious point is: they are not readily compatible. We will see that there are human rights advocates, particularly outside the West, eager to reconcile elements of the two approaches, and especially to make sure that human rights definitions are not dominated by the West alone. But, on the surface, reconciliation is not easy. Sincere, zealous, often moralistically self-righteous advocates of human rights—for example, for the full legal equality of women—find it understandably difficult to accept the argument that any distinctive culture is so valuable that it deserves a pass: human rights should apply to all. Sincere and zealous defenders of particular national values and needs find it understandably difficult to accept human rights advocacy as anything but unwarranted outside interference, dangerous to social order and cultural identity alike: human rights organizations, as a result, should be kept away.

The resultant clash between two quite reasonable positions may not be the greatest problem in the globalized world today: the deep poverty of at least a sixth of the world's population and the threat of mounting environmental degradation could compete for the prize here. But the clash is both interesting and significant, promoting recurrent misunderstandings among different parts of the world. This book, assessing the origins and evolution of human rights approaches but also their diverse receptions, seeks to promote a greater understanding of the fundamental dilemmas involved, and how they might best be addressed.

Human rights as a factor in world history focus attention on the last two centuries or so: the basic story is a modern one. A full conception of human rights emerged anywhere only from the later 18th century onward—it was at this point, after all, that revolutionary documents began talking about "self-evident" truths that "all men" were created equal, or began adopting titles like "Declaration of the Rights of Man." It was only at this point, as well, or just a few decades later, that societies essentially around the world began interacting regularly and deeply enough for human rights messages and judgments—or effort to resist such messages and judgments—to become global. Both aspects of modern world history—the human rights component and the new levels of interconnection—underpin this important and difficult feature of contemporary society. There is a premodern backdrop, which helps situate this aspect of world history, but the core exploration targets the recent past, when human rights arguments became important enough, but also pervasive enough, for societies to quarrel over them.

This book explores the historical origins and development of human rights in various manifestations: philosophy, law, organizational support, reactions, and impacts. The exploration is global, with consistent attention to how international exchanges have affected the course of human rights and how, in turn, human rights have colored international interactions. The global perspective also requires discussion of regional differences and patterns of resistance or adjustment where human rights are concerned. The global canvas is essential, but it does not allow a single portrait alone.

Indeed the book's first chapter, focusing on current issues, lays out a number of the complexities in the human rights story, including regional concerns about some of the implications of standard human rights agendas. We then move back to the historical record, talking about major societies before explicit attention to human rights emerged. That emergence, in the 18th century, needs to be described and explained—the subject of Chapter 3. Chapter 4 turns to the first global consequences of human rights, stretching through the 19th century and into the troubled decades after World War I. This was the first period of what can be called the globalization of human rights, but it also surfaced great variety and many obstacles and retreats. We turn then, in Chapters 5 and 6, to the successive bursts of human rights activity after World War II, up to the present, but also to the impediments that continue to dog the field. Chapter 6, as well as the Conclusion, thus return to recent problems, including a more systematic consideration of the regional variants and also renewed effort to craft a definition that will have fuller global appeal.

There is a substantial literature on human rights. Most of it stems from legal scholars, but contributions from philosophers also loom large. Sociology and anthropology have contributed studies, particularly on the actual impact of human rights in specific regions. Important historical work also exists, though the range is not vast. And philosophers and legal scholars often offer brief historical considerations as preface to their own work.

Through all this, several related historiographical tensions emerge, and this book will explore them at various points. The big issue has already been briefly evoked: the relationship between Western values and other cultures in the human rights field. How do universalist approaches to human rights encounter the fact of cultural variety and cultural relativism?

A second issue involves modern human rights as rupture or continuity: as more specific human rights arguments emerged, to what extent did they build upon previous legal, philosophical, and religious structures, and to what extent did they have to break new ground? This links directly to the West/non-West issue. If human rights approaches were largely new and initially primarily Western, what relationship did they have to other political traditions, and how would this condition react to human rights innovations?

A third issue involves what kind of focus to take in studying human rights history. Many approaches emphasize intellectual developments, the way leading thinkers have considered humanity and society. Others focus more on actual political arrangements, in trying to figure out, among other things, how particular human rights ideas or innovations actually worked out in practice. Surely some combination is essential here, but the balance is not easy to strike.

Finally—and among other things, this is why a purely intellectual history approach will not work—there is the question of evaluating human rights in terms of contributions to progress. Most modern human rights advocates believe, often passionately, that they know how to make things better for people in many societies. Has their work in fact improved things? If progress has not occurred, is this because human rights efforts have been thwarted (as they often have), or because the dominant human rights approach itself is off the mark? Or a bit of both? This returns us also to the question of change and historical background: If human rights were not badly served before modern times, even amid different cultural and political contexts, then maybe recent progress cannot be as great as progressive advocates themselves claim. How bad were things before the modern human rights movement, and how much less bad have they become?

There is much to consider, interesting in terms of historical issues and of obvious significance in evaluating the world around us today.

"Human rights violation": the term has an ominous ring, and in many cases it should have. In the contemporary world, various United Nations agencies and associated courts spend a great deal of time monitoring human rights behavior, encouraging compliance with international standards, and sometimes arresting and prosecuting violators for "crimes against humanity" (an even more ominous term). The United States government regularly produces reports on other countries' human rights record, in an effort to encourage improvement and to engage in some global moral one-upsmanship. A host of private groups diligently record abuses and seek to generate expressions of outrage in world opinion. Human rights form an important part of the contemporary international climate.

The modern evolution of human rights offers an important story of efforts to further human progress, ultimately on a global scale. It embraces many exciting and passionate visions. It also serves as a source of discord within and among key nations. It has prompted and continues to prompt lively discussions about alternatives. From all these standpoints, it serves as a dynamic part of the larger unfolding of world history for the past 250 years.

Further Reading

The following books and articles help launch interdisciplinary inquiry on human rights: Samuel Moyn, *The Last Utopia: Human Rights in History* (Cambridge, MA: Harvard University Press, 2010); and "The First Historian of Human Rights," *American Historical Review*, 116(1) (February, 2011), pp. 58–79; Costas Douzinas, *The End of Human Rights: Critical Legal Thought at the Turn of the Century* (Portland, OR: Hart Publishing, 2000); Jack Donnelly, *Universal Human Rights in Theory and Practice* (Ithaca, NY: Cornell University Press, 2003); Lynda Schaefer Bell, Andrew James Nathan, and Ilan Peleg (eds.), *Negotiating Culture and Human Rights* (New York, NY: Columbia University Press, 2001); John M. Headley, *The Europeanization of the World: On the Origins of Human Rights and Democracy* (Princeton, NJ: Princeton University Press, 2007); Amartya Sen, "Human Rights and Asian Values," *New Republic*, July 14–21, 1997. Online at: http://www.mtholyoke. edu/acad/intrel/sen.htm; Kenneth Cmiel, "The Recent History of Human Rights," *American Historical Review*, 109(1) (February, 2004), pp. 117–135;

R. Panikkar, "Is the Notion of Human Rights a Western Concept?" *Diogenes*, 30(120) (1982), pp. 75–102; Jack Donnelly, "Human Rights and Human Dignity: An Analytic Critique of Non-Western Conceptions of Human Rights," *American Political Science Review*, 76(2) (June, 1982), pp. 303–316; Jack Donnelly, "Cultural Relativism and Universal Human Rights," *Human Rights Quarterly*, 6(4) (November, 1984), pp. 400–419; Michael J. Perry, "Are Human Rights Universal? The Relativist Challenge and Related Matters," *Human Rights Quarterly*, 19(3) (August, 1997), pp. 461–509; Talal Asad, "What do Human Rights Do? An Anthropological Enquiry," *Theory and Event*, 4(4) (2000), pp. 1–28; Richard Bauman, *Human Rights in Ancient Rome* (New York, NY: Taylor & Francis, 2000); Brian Tierney, *The Idea of Natural Rights: Studies on Natural Rights, Natural Law, and Church Law, 1150–1625* (Grand Rapids, MI: Wm. B. Eerdmans Publishing/Emory University Press, 2001); Richard Tuck, *Natural Rights Theories: Their Origin and Development* (Cambridge, UK: Cambridge University Press, 1998); Francis Oakley, *Natural Law, Laws of Nature, Natural Rights: Continuity and Discontinuity in the History of Ideas* (New York, NY: Continuum, 2005); Micheline Ishay, *The History of Human Rights: From Ancient Times to the Globalization Era* (Berkeley, CA: University of California Press, 2004); Surya P. Subedi, "Are the Principles of Human Rights 'Western' Ideas? An Analysis of the Claim of the 'Asian' Concept of Human Rights from the Perspectives of Hinduism," *Californian Western International Law Journal*, 30 (Fall, 1999), pp. 45–70; John M. Peek, "Buddism, Human Rights, and the Japanese State," *Human Rights Quarterly*, 17(3) (August, 1995), pp. 527–540; Susan Ford Wiltshire, *Greece, Rome and the Bill of Rights* (Norman, OK: University of Oklahoma Press, 1992).

1 The contemporary dilemmas

The idea that there are some universal human rights, though building on earlier cultural developments including religious prescriptions, began to emerge clearly for the first time in the later 18th century. This was when groups like the framers of the American revolutionary bill of rights began to argue that all men had a right to "life, liberty and the pursuit of happiness." The first concrete movement that captured this new thinking was the abolitionist campaign against slavery, specifically on grounds that holding people as property contradicted their obvious rights as human beings. But various revolutionary movements also began to project ideas that there should be protection of other rights, such as freedom of the press or religious choice. Here was a major addition to those factors shaping, or potentially shaping, the development of societies around the world.

Obviously, human rights have not gained ground as rapidly or uniformly as their proclamations might suggest. Western nations themselves, though supporting human rights notions in some respects—gradually, for example, turning against slavery systems—often contradicted these same notions in their reach for imperial power. Other interests, including local power elites, often ignored or actively opposed human rights that might challenge their own position. And masses of people were—and some still are—unaware of human rights arguments in any event. At the same time, however, human rights advocacy continued to expand, in two ways. First, new parts of the world picked up the message. By the later 19th century, for example, human rights thinking on slavery spread rapidly in Brazil and other parts of Latin America. New policies on women's rights surfaced in Turkey by the 1920s. New international organizations, such as the League of Nations after World War I, picked up the language as well. Specific groups formed to promote awareness of human rights and to report on abuses, with particular vigor from 1961 (the formation of Amnesty International) onward. The second aspect of rights expansion was almost as important as the first: the range of rights discussions itself widened steadily—depending, of course, on the advocate involved—to include gender issues, labor issues, age group issues (children or the elderly), homosexual issues, as in the gay rights movements that fanned out from the American civil rights decade of the 1960s, and other areas as well.

By the 20th century, human rights ideas and advocacies had become a significant aspect of international diplomacy. In many cases, even countries and groups that had no intention of living up to human rights obligations had learned that it was prudent at least to vow agreement in principle.

Chapters that follow in this book will amplify this evolution. Relevant developments prior to the explicit exploration of human rights arguments form an obvious backdrop, helping to explain why rights arguments could ultimately emerge but also some of the barriers in earlier social and cultural traditions. The effective birth of the human rights idea must be explained, and then its various expansions traced from the 19th century onward. This is an important part of the global experience of the past two centuries, though it is not usually adequately captured in world history approaches that take a primarily regional approach.

But the human rights story must also include failures and barriers. Lots of groups have maintained an interest in sidestepping or blocking human rights. Authoritarian governments resist political freedoms that might promote their downfall. Some profit-seeking employers resist even basic rights for their workers. At an extreme, while slavery has been officially abolished almost everywhere—a meaningful human rights triumph during the 19th and 20th centuries—de facto slavery continues to exist in many places, including women and children sold into sexual bondage, but also foreign workers whose passports are held by manufacturers so that they can expel anyone who makes the slightest bit of trouble. And while human rights may be most widely ignored amid deep poverty or civil strife, abuses surface almost everywhere—including the United States, where illegal sex slavery claims thousands of hapless victims. Western countries often lead in human rights advocacy, but they continue to violate their own principles on occasion—as in the notorious abuses of Iraqi prisoners by United States authorities after the invasion of 2003.

Human rights and inherent tensions

Outright resistance and abuse are not the only complication to a story of progressive triumphs. Human rights arguments themselves generate problems and limitations. Here too, following chapters will explore the complexities human rights campaigns have fostered—including, but not confined to, purely exploitative resistance. In this chapter we offer a foretaste, so that the subsequent history can be clearly connected to contemporary concerns.

Three basic categories emerge: first, and most important, the increasingly obvious rift between the idea of universal rights and the deep-seated regional cultures that some human rights approaches clearly threaten. This is the most interesting and fundamental tension in the current climate of globalization: where the universal clashes with regional claims to voice and identity. Two other categories, however, also warrant attention in helping to explain gaps between human rights fervor and achievement. By the later 20th century, at least, a legitimate question was arising simply about the length of the human rights list. Additions could be hailed as new triumphs of human enlight-enment, but they would also rouse new resistances and, potentially, some new internal contradictions in the human rights approach. Finally, the tension between human rights needs and efforts to solve other identifiable problems raised issues as well, again quite apart from clashes with tradition or self-interested privilege. Human rights history is not simply a record of the contest between the forces of progress and a backward combination of ignorance and abuse.

None of the complexities should obscure the importance and potential validity of human rights concerns. One of the key reasons to venture a new brief history of the human rights movement is to assess how and why it became such a moral and political force to be reckoned with. As we will see, even most opponents hesitate to oppose human rights arguments without some bow to their power. But the inherent tensions need their history as well. Laying out the contemporary state of play helps motivate and organize the historical analysis that will follow. We begin with the most obvious dilemma that can pit human rights as a good thing against another good thing, to wit greater regional equality and self-expression.

Universal rights and regional cultures

It's become something of an annual dance for the past decade or so. Human rights organizations and some individual governments, headed by the United States, routinely criticize the People's Republic of China for a variety of offenses against human rights. Official reproval varies a bit, depending on other agenda items where Chinese cooperation may be sought, but the human rights groups themselves are consistently fierce. And the American State Department, issuing a "Human Rights Report" annually, itself routinely castigates the Chinese record. The complaints are echoed strongly by human rights advocates and groups within China itself, like Chinese Human Rights Defenders (CHRD), though their activities are sometimes curtailed by government repression. In response, the Chinese may acknowledge a few problems—the Chinese president publicly admitted in 2011 that there are some human rights issues that warrant attention, though he said this with only a few months remaining in office—and occasionally, to placate foreign critics, will release a prominent political prisoner. Rarely is anything structurally done, however, and the government also has its own line of defense against the whole chorus: human rights must be defined differently, conventional formulations don't take Chinese needs for political order into adequate account, critics should look at the problems caused by excessive individualism before they presume to comment on China. In other words, lay off.

The list of human rights claims is fairly long. The State Department's 2010 report signaled, for example, "increased attempts to limit freedom of speech and to control the press," basic human rights categories. Newspapers may be forced to close down, offices shut, the movements of suspected dissidents monitored or restricted; and outright arrest for speaking out is not uncommon, even though the 1982 constitution officially guarantees freedom of speech. Recent efforts also include blocking key Internet sites to limit access to differences in views. Advocacy of greater independence for ethnic minorities—a particular concern in Tibet but also for the Muslim Uighurs in the northwest—is routinely punished. Religious issues parallel the problems of political expression. The Chinese government is frequently accused of repressing Buddhist activity in Tibet, including the influence of the Dalai Lama, Christian worship, and Muslim practices in its northwestern territories; harsh repression of the religious Falun Gong movement, including arrest and possibly the torture of many practitioners, has drawn particular attention. Massive propaganda is directed against certain groups, again especially the Falun Gong. Labor rights form a third category, with independent union activity banned and controls placed over the movement of rural workers. Sheer harshness is a problem: China executes more people than all the other countries in the world combined, and accusations of torture are widespread, though in 2010 new regulations emerged nullifying evidence gathered through violence or intimidation. Finally, official policies designed to limit population growth, instituted in 1979 and banning more than one child per couple in many cases, is often cited by foreign critics as a human rights abuse, particularly when, critics contend, it leads to forced abortions or female infanticide.

Criticism varies, of course, and there are some outright factual disputes. Many American observers are particularly incensed about limitations on religious activity. Some commentators assume that the Chinese record is so awful that it should condition diplomatic relations with the giant nation; others lament more moderately while conducting business as usual in other respects. The American State Department dropped China from a list of top ten violators in 2008, in part because of some reforms—like a 2003 constitutional amendment assuring that "the State respects and preserves human rights"—in part from a desire for better economic and military relations despite rights concerns. But no one concerned with human rights in the usual sense would give China a free pass.

Against this recurrent storm, official Chinese response is varied, but never largely acquiescent. It is vital to realize that, despite their rejection of many conventional human rights arguments, key Chinese officials seek to conciliate at times—as in the 2003 constitutional amendment. They sometimes want to woo Western colleagues for other purposes, making concessions in the process, or they may sincerely resonate to a need to measure up to some human rights standards as a matter of international prestige. Thus, when the Chinese won the opportunity to organize the 2008 Olympic Games they promised freedom of public assembly, partly as a matter of calculation, partly from a real desire to seem progressive in international eyes—even though, in the end, human rights observers felt the actual performance fell well short of what had been pledged. And of course, for whatever reason, Chinese authorities frequently dispute the accuracy of critics' claims, for example, about instances of torture. Finally—a matter to which we will return—Chinese defenders also point to

Western violations of human rights principles, as in United States actions in Iraq, arguing that accusers should put their own house in order before nagging China.

The core position, however, rests neither on conciliation nor factual debate. Rather, Chinese authorities argue with some passion that their values, which they sometimes phrase as "Asian values," place the welfare of the whole society over the rights of any individual. The basic human right, in this argument, is to participate in a "harmonious society," and individual interests may have to be sacrificed to this end. Public order and a strong, stable authority come first. In this view, of course, Western societies, consumed with human rights claims, have gone much too far in surrendering a larger public good: high rates of crime and family breakdown follow from excessive individualism and the impossibility of curbing individual appetites. "Too much freedom is dangerous," and in fact, in undermining social stability and cohesion, it is the West that violates actual human rights. Additionally, the Chinese point to their promotion of economic growth and prosperity, again on an overall, collective basis, as evidence of living up to human rights goals more broadly construed. An interesting combination of Confucian attachment to the primacy of social order and a residual communist commitment to greater economic justice generates a distinctive path. Emphasis varies: at times Chinese advocates push for a different, more embracing international definition of human rights; at times they stress the need to acknowledge regional cultural differences. Either way, the Western list of individual rights is simply not seen to fit the Asian giant.

The debate is not simply an official preserve, with different government representatives posturing against each other. Chats with two Chinese exchange students, informally so that they do not feel singled out, yield a surprising example of differentiation. Both, seemingly quite comfortable with an American classroom atmosphere with fairly open discussion and disagreement, immediately protest the notion that China could or should adopt an American approach to human rights (however flawed in practice). The reason? Chinese society would collapse without strong collective controls, there are too many diverse interests and too much potential selfishness. Here too, the need for order, but also a sense of its precariousness, come first, and human rights concerns must fit around the margins. Are the students simply parroting an official line, despite a willingness to criticize Chinese conditions in other respects? Or do they reflect a deep cultural conditioning about the tensions between the individual and the social and the imperative to place the social first?

China offers only one example of regional differentiation over human rights, of course. Several other East Asian cases have similar story lines. In 1994, for example, an American teenager was arrested in Singapore for vandalizing cars, mainly by scratching their paint. He was sentenced to a short jail term and four strokes by caning. Many Western observers were appalled, and even the American president tried to intervene: by Western human rights standards, this seemed a harsh, even brutal type of punishment, contradictory to human rights. Defenders in Singapore argued, of course, that their law was their law, but also that their standards helped prevent the kind of individualistic excess that create massive vandalism in cities like New York. Again, on a small stage, the tension between valuation of social order and individual rights proved difficult to reconcile.

East Asia is not alone. Human rights criticism not only of the Soviet Union but of Russia since the end of the cold war often mirrors that directed against China. From the later 1990s onward, increasing government control over mass media, disruption of opposition political meetings, arrests and murders of political dissidents were suggesting important limits on freedom of expression. Regulations against outside missionary activity, particularly by American evangelicals, raise another set of concerns in some quarters. Not surprisingly, the Russian government has responded, among other things, by severely limiting activities by outside human rights organizations. Many Russians themselves, aware of repressive policies, seem acquiescent, sometimes openly claiming that the need to protect an orderly state comes first, that only after this is assured can a proper version of democracy function.

Human rights confrontations in the Middle East have sometimes simply repeated the tensions that surface whenever authoritarian regimes try to stifle political dissent and individual expression. In the so-called "Arab spring" of 2011, clashes between repressive political police and various dissidents were common, and in places like Syria the forces of repression used military force, arrests, and beatings to try to win out. Growing religious intolerance in some societies also threatened new attacks on religious groups—like Christians in Iraq or Egypt, or Shi'ite Muslims in Sunni-ruled Bahrain—that roused extensive human rights concerns. In many societies efforts to limit new (usually Christian) missionary activity raised complex issues. Turkey, for example, claimed ready tolerance of established Christian groups, but hostility to aggressive proselytizing by foreign evangelicals.

On the whole, however, it was gender and family issues that suggested the most pervasive tensions between cultural tradition in this region and the interests of contemporary human rights advocates. Extremes most readily catch the eye. A religious court in Iran or Afghanistan sentences a woman to be stoned to death for adultery. Human rights groups rise in outrage, sometimes successfully, against the brutality of the punishment and the unfairness of attempting to regulate women's sexuality so closely. Gay foreigners are subject to arrest in Dubai, where officially simply being gay earns a prison term of ten years; gay websites are blocked at least as carefully as political dissent is in China; a gay French teenager is badly beaten by some fundamentalists and then arrested for his sexual preference in addition. The extremes, however, may be less revealing than more subtle tensions. Islamic law, for example, makes it far more difficult for women than for men to obtain divorce, and commonly deprives a divorced woman of custody over her children. This was once true of Christianity as well—traditional Islam was clearer that women did at least have the possibility of divorce—but equality under the law has come to prevail in most Christian regions, creating a potential rights gap between the two great religious traditions. Do women have the right to choose what kind of costume they wear? Most Islamic countries do not have fixed requirements here, but Iran and (under the Taliban) Afghanistan were exceptions, and many Muslim families in the Middle East set definite rules. Many women themselves believe that costume constraints must be accepted, even praised, as part of defending regional identity. Even some Muslim feminists, while hostile to fundamentalist extremes, urge a distinctive approach, building on the protections in the *Quran* rather than primarily on Western values, or even claiming that the Western approach is too individualistic, that a proper defense of women needs greater emphasis on community and family rather than enhancement of individual capacity. In these and many other cases, the question is where human rights begin, particularly for women, and where appropriate family and social authority end—and the answers are no easier to determine than they are amid Chinese arguments about political harmony. The point is clear: as against many regional traditions, key human rights claims seem disruptive and foreign, attempting to enforce a questionable set of priorities. The issues run far deeper than the maneuverings of any particular authoritarian political regime, into fiercely held social and familial values.

Many of the clashes between human rights advocacies and regional traditions may seem one-sided, particularly of course to a Western audience where the validity of many rights may simply be taken for granted. Even regional defenders often show a bit of hesitation, defending their values but also suggesting that they might perhaps improve on the human rights front as well. After all, human rights may come across as a global gold standard, a measure of the state of the civilization, and the moral fervor of many proponents enhances this vigor. It would be a mistake, however, to dismiss regional concerns as backward or outdated. Who can be sure, for example, whether China's deep commitment to social harmony will really yield much in favor of a more individualistic rights approach? The uncertainty means, in turn, that both sides need attention and understanding—and possibly, as many rights proponents increasingly recognize, some innovative compromises as well. It's not merely a matter of waiting for the inevitable triumph of universal rights.

Even seemingly easy calls, where the human rights arguments seem almost unassailable, raise unexpected complexities. A final initial example restates the regional problem in a case where the human rights arguments would seem to be particularly compelling.

The subject is female circumcision, sometimes also known as genital mutilation. In a number of countries in Africa, mainly between the Sahara and the equator, 43% to 97% of all women are circumcised, with all or part of their clitoris removed (precise procedures vary a bit), usually before adolescence. This is a rite of passage, performed usually by an elder village woman, and highly traditional in the societies involved. Women of various religions—Muslim, Christian, animist, even one Jewish sect—participate, and, while the ritual is seen as having religious overtones, it is not attached to any particular faith. Critical observers assume that the ritual developed as part of a male effort to control women's sexuality and assure that husbands are the fathers of the children their wives bear, in this extreme case by removing the possibility of female sexual pleasure, though at this point the custom is maintained by women at least as much as men, and assumed to be a vital step in assuring a woman's respectability, including her virginity upon marriage. While most girls in the societies involved have little choice, many are eager to undergo the procedure as a means of measuring up to social norms; in many cases, uncircumcised girls simply cannot marry, and in some instances resistance is overcome by force.

Outside awareness of female circumcision developed slowly, but certainly many European administrators became aware of the practice during the imperialist conquests of the later 19th and early 20th centuries. Some of them openly deplored this treatment of women, but they hesitated to intervene for several reasons. The level of concern was not necessarily very high—few administrators were deeply affected by any feminist awareness—and in some cases the whole matter might be dismissed as part of "native" inferiority. More important was a desire to get along with existing village authorities: rocking the boat might rouse resistance and make colonial rule less acceptable, more difficult to maintain. So nothing much was done during the bulk of the colonial period, until after World War II, when some governments did move to ban the practice in principle (rarely with any real effort at enforcement). Many African nationalists, in contrast, actually defended the practice as part of traditional identity and family unity; the great Kenyan leader Jomo Kenyatta contended that, as "mere body mutilation," there was no reason for action. United Nations officials began to take notice by the 1950s, but a proposal for condemnation by the World Health Organization in 1958 was rejected on ground that "the ritual operations in question arose from a social and cultural context." Growing information about the adverse health consequences of circumcision, including frequent infection, plus greater awareness of human rights arguments applicable to women, began to prompt greater activism. African women's leaders spoke out in 1959, and the World Health Organization finally condemned the practice in 1962, though there was no formal recommendation of government action until 1979. Action committees fanned out in twenty countries during the 1980s. Treaties on rights of children and a Convention to Eliminate All Forms of Discrimination Against Women embraced clauses relevant to female circumcision. A United Nations conference on women in 1995, in Beijing, finally generated direct language condemning the practice as a "human rights violation."

Even then, change was slow and uneven. The same hesitations that had caused delays in action now affected implementation. Local leaders feared popular resistance. While individual women sought sanctuary—one famous case brought asylum for a young woman from Togo in the United States—there was no groundswell of sentiment against the practice—polls suggested slightly more female support than male in the regions involved. There is no indication that rates have significantly declined in the relevant countries, though there are some signs of a change of heart among younger women. (In Sudan, as a result, one study suggested a decline from 96% down to 89%—hardly a revolutionary change—between the late 1970s and the late 1980s.) Even emigrants to Europe, where stringent laws have been enacted to ban the practice, often evade detection, most commonly by sending young women back to Africa, where the operation will be performed. Ideas that uncircumcised women are unclean and sexually unreliable persist strongly, along with other notions about the relevance of circumcision to fertility, infant health or male sexual pleasure. In this context, human rights arguments, often coming from Western organizations, either fall on deaf ears or provoke outright resistance. One circumcised Somali woman thus bridled against the human rights pressure: "When they order us to stop, tell us what we must do, it is offensive to the black person or the Muslim person who believes in circumcision." Even some women opposed to the practice participate in defense arguments, believing that independent identity is more important than international rights standards. Governments are similarly constrained. The president of Gambia spoke out against "such harmful practices" in 1997, but then backtracked amid political opposition. In 1999 he argued that circumcision "is part of our culture and we should not allow anyone to dictate to us how we should conduct ourselves." More ominously, he warned Gambians who spoke out against the practice that "there is no guarantee that after they deliver their speeches they will return to their homes."

The whole example is, again, both extreme and revealing. Virtually any Western or East Asian observer finds female circumcision appalling, whatever their reaction to the full set of feminist demands. The violation of decent norms should be obvious. To be sure, a few critics have noted that Western women accept some unsafe practices, too, like cosmetic surgery, amid considerable social pressures, but while the distraction is interesting it hardly seems comparable, much less conclusive. Yet, to many Africans involved—both as leaders and as ordinary participants—the notion of human rights pushes more toward rejection of outside interference than toward compliance with the standards that seem so straightforward to outsiders. Here again, as in the arguments about rights versus political stability or larger family relations, it's clear that, at least in the short run, the rights movement involves trying to make some groups behave against their conscience—in a field where conscience is supposed to be the dominant guide. Small wonder that many concerned leaders have backed off confrontational campaigns in favor of quieter educational efforts, aware that the results, if any, will be more gradual than any advocate wishes. In the meantime, of course, tens of thousands of young women continue to be circumcised every year.

As we will see, historically, very few major human rights planks have fully won out around the world over various forms of regional resistance—and this includes some efforts going back over two hundred years. The future may still be with the rights campaigns—there are also few cases in which some inroads cannot be recorded, which is another reason human rights must be taken seriously as a modern world-historical force. But the conflicts are painful and complex, and they often generate bitter misunderstandings, some with serious diplomatic consequences, in the process. Passionate conviction does not line up on one side of most human rights arguments.

Human rights vs. reforms

A second dilemma in the contemporary human rights scene, again with important historical precedent, involves often unexpected clashes between human rights principles and equally sincere advocacy of other types of reform designed to improve people's conditions. Obviously, in some cases human rights advocates encounter no reformist alternatives—they guide the progressive agenda without much contest. In other instances, however, certain kinds of reformers identify problems that in their judgment simply cry out for other remedies, even at the expense of denying people certain rights at least in the short term. The result can certainly complicate the rights agenda and at times generates real opposition.

We have already touched, if briefly, on one key dilemma. China began to introduce its population control policy in the late 1970s, involving for many families the prohibition, against rather severe penalty, on having more than one child. Many progressives outside of China welcomed this move. A society that embraced about a sixth of the world's population had been growing very rapidly, under a previous communist regime that believed that a large population would be a source of national economic and military strength. The results arguably drained resources away from more fundamental economic growth— the race to feed new mouths alone took vast amounts of labor and capital. More broadly, population growth at traditional levels threatened the availability of necessary resources—for example, in water supply—and burdened environmental quality among other things with growing amounts of unprocessed human waste. Global environmental needs and a more stable pattern of development in China itself both pushed for new forms of population control, and if the government could be part of the solution, given the nation's strong political tradition, so much the better. The results would contribute to greater wellbeing. Chinese decisiveness in this area was often contrasted with the weaker results in India, where the government was unable to guide popular behavior to the same extent, and where population growth continued at a more alarming pace. This was the context in which a population agency of the United Nations provided some funding to support the ambitious Chinese project.

From a human rights standpoint, at least in a narrow sense, the policy was, however, wrongheaded. It forced families, and particularly women, to decisions they might regard as against their own self-interest. For traditional or other reasons, families might want more children. Prevention unquestionably involved compelling many people against their will. Specific results added to the critique. Some women were forced into abortions or other measures that threatened their health, as well as contradicting their plans and wishes. Many families turned out to maintain such a preference for boys that the population control policy led to many abortions simply for gender preference, as well as an overabundance of girls committed to orphanages. Growing population imbalance, with far more men than women, was a further result, with its own potential for discontent in the future as many men realized that they lacked opportunities for marriage simply because of supply shortfalls. It was not hard to mount a vigorous human rights argument against the Chinese policy, embellished by some of the more specific problems involved. The United States, for example, contended under President George W. Bush that the right "to found a family" was one of the rights assured by the United Nations and that Chinese policy was therefore wrong.

This was a different type of dilemma from the regional one, though there was some overlap, in that reformers from the same culture might simply disagree about what constituted progress and what programs most conduced to progress. Demographic experts, deeply concerned about potential overpopulation with adverse environmental results and potentially violent clashes over resources, simply defined a different set of priorities from those who sought to avoid compulsion at all costs. As with the regional clashes, this type of disagreement allowed no easy solution in the short run: one simply had to choose.

Several other contexts have generated important disputes between certain types of reformers and the human rights community. From the 19th century onward, in various societies including Latin America, the United States and Australia, many liberal reformers have argued that the backwardness or distinctiveness of a native population was so great that compulsion was essential to draw them into the opportunities of a modern, civilized society. At various points, for example, both the American and the Australian governments seized some Indian or aboriginal children from their families, forcing them into residential schools where, presumably, they would be taught the modern values and skills that would allow them to function as part of the citizenry in general. That some indigenous people would resist the measures was acknowledged— this was a forcibly imposed policy—but the argument was that compulsion was essential for a longer-term, progressive goal.

Many of these sweeping efforts have been discredited, as involving too much disruption and too much scorn for valid local traditions. Seizing native children now seems inhumane. Human rights criteria have in this sense advanced. But there are still important pockets of skirmish. Australia, for example, long maintained policies designed to forbid service of alcohol to aboriginals. Whole communities were declared "dry," with no consultation of the aboriginal residents involved. The argument was that aboriginals showed a disproportionate tendency to alcohol abuse, which in the long run damaged them and their families alike. They simply could not be granted the same rights as white people, because their behaviors were distinctively destructive. This was not an approach congenial to principled human rights advocates. From the 1960s onward, reformers attacked the earlier reform impulse, arguing that aboriginals should have the same rights to drink as anyone else. Aboriginal leaders themselves often joined in, contending that their people should not be singled out and, in fact, contesting the notion that aboriginal alcohol abuse was any more extensive than that of whites—both groups, arguably, had severe problems affecting a minority of their total. From the 1970s onward, alcohol sales became more widespread, and many aboriginal councils actually came to depend heavily on the revenues that resulted. The outcome, according to some reports, was a catastrophic increase in drinking, with some aboriginal communities consuming more than three times the level regarded as safe, and with alcohol-linked violence and health problems impinging not just on drinkers but on the community as a whole. Some aboriginal councils have negotiated restrictions on alcohol purchase as a result, but some government attempts at constraint were actually brought to the United Nations human rights agency as violations of rights. Many see restrictions as continuations of the denial of basic human equality and citizenship rights. As one commentator notes:

> The challenge for developing and implementing alcohol policies for Aboriginal people is to decide whether their exceptionally disadvantaged position and the particularly devastating effects that alcohol has on this group of people justifies policies that are distinct from those serving the general Australian population, or whether it is policy isolation itself that constitutes part of the problem.

In other words: do uniform human rights apply, or is reform better served by a more distinctive and explicitly compulsory approach?

Reformers' concern for particular categories of people relate to another, and even larger, target, where rights often war against other progressive visions. Children are almost inherently a challenge, for they surely deserve active inclusion in any rights argument but they are not fully formed; not always aware of their own best interests; and are dependent, at least for many years, in crucial respects. Where do their rights end, and the need for guidance and even compulsion begin?

Children have been a human rights issue for two centuries, even in the societies where human rights arguments seemed most congenial. Here, too, reform and rights can easily collide. An initial clash focused on education. By the late 18th and early 19th centuries many progressives were arguing for the importance of spreading education and even imposing on certain age groups. Otherwise, the argument went, children would be deprived of mobility opportunities or even simply good jobs later on, in a modern economy, and society as a whole would lose out in terms of its ability to rely on an informed, up-to-date citizenry. Even girls, many contended, should be subjected to these requirements, though (as most thought at the time) their duties would remain largely within the family. But were school requirements compatible with human rights? First, as many traditionalists reckoned, it was really up to the parents, particularly the fathers, to determine what their children should do, and not society at large. At an extreme, some urged that families should have the right to place their children in exploitative workshops, if that's what it took to prepare them for the labor force and support the family. Gradually, the parents' rights arguments weakened—particularly because more and more adults moved to a realization that education was in the family's best interest—and school attendance requirements moved forward. But should they really be enforced against reluctant children and parents alike? Should some children who simply hated school or fared badly not have the ability to opt out? Here was a classic case of social goals confronting potential individual resistance, and it was not always easy to see where the progressive argument lay.

By the 20th century, not only in Western society but in many others, school attendance requirements won out, with serious enforcement attached, and of course they have tended to expand in scope, with teenagers as well as primary-school ages involved. By this point most human rights advocates were eager to list opportunities for education as one of the rights that should be assured to children—whatever their own impulses or their parents' demands. With this, some of the most basic tensions between progressives in general, and human rights arguments specifically, have been alleviated.

Tension remains, however, and contemporary problems generate important new debates. Do parents have the right to determine family discipline, or should up-to-date understandings of abuse force constraints? In some places, as in Scandinavia, spanking has been outlawed; but in other parts of the West, including most American states, many parents defend it as their inherent right. Where do rights apply to children as individuals, as against appropriate adult authority, whether parental or other? Many court cases have been brought to defend children's rights to express unpopular or rebellious views in school, or to resist school dress codes. In most cases children have lost, on grounds that familial or social wisdom should win out over the views of people who have not yet reached an adult age of reason and whose decisions might harm themselves or others. But the contest between larger definitions of wellbeing and progress, and a focused human rights agenda, is always inter-esting and shows no sign of disappearance.

Childhood obesity represents one of the most recent cases in which socially determined progress butts against some versions of human rights. Children's obesity levels tripled in the United States between the 1980s and 2010, and similar patterns cropped up in many other societies. Most experts agreed that personal and social wellbeing would be best served by new kinds of controls. Trying to educate children and their parents, attempting to limit advertisements or other food inducements, were steps in the right direction that did not imperil human rights, but they measurably fell short of curbing this new epidemic. Enter new forms of compulsion or near-compulsion: in some American states, and in places like Australia and the United Kingdom, many school programs began requiring body mass measurements and publicizing the results, so that children and their parents might be shamed into remedial action. Rights to privacy, in this argument, did not apply, because the problem's severity called for more extreme measures. Even this might not be enough. In many places social service authorities began seizing children from parents who, themselves obese, showed no ability to introduce proper eating habits, placing them with foster parents or social agencies as a preferred alternative. Many human rights advocates, along with the parents themselves, were outraged: in a happy family, which simply happened to be collectively overweight, what right did anyone have to interfere so radically with parental authority and children's own wishes? Against this classic stance, other reformers urged, first, that the problem was too great to dwell on legal niceties—only more radical solutions showed any promise—and second, that human rights themselves, properly construed, should cover a child's right to grow up with maximum chances for good health and successful functioning, and obesity's damage would inevitably limit this right. Here was a fascinating contemporary version of the classic quarrel between individual rights and sincere championship of a higher reform goal—and there was no easy resolution.

Indeed, health hazards more generally, and not just concerns for children, illustrate the capacity of modern societies to continue to toss up dilemmas that inevitably lead to contest over human rights. Like children, or native populations, people suffering from certain kinds of ailments may be seen as requiring a level of social control or guidance that clashes with basic rights concerns. Key issues arise for groups like the mentally ill or behavioral categories like smokers, but again obesity has generated some of the most interesting recent tensions.

For in the eyes of some experts, including many doctors, the dangers of rising obesity, among adults as well as children, call for new forms of social pressure and even compulsion. Many employers, concerned about their own health costs, struggled for the ability to use obesity as an employment criterion—after all, if an obese person on average predictably jacks up insurance costs or time lost to disability, should management not be able to make judgments on this basis? And would society more generally be better served if people knew there were measurable costs to obesity, and so take the matter in hand more successfully? But human rights standards seemed firmly opposed to countermeasures of this sort. The Canadian Human Rights Act, for example, specifically banned "harassing or treating a person differently in a way that is harmful," along with "refus[ing] to employ or continue to employ a person." And American law, under the civil rights umbrella, began to defend the rights of the obese from the 1980s onward; as a New York Court of Appeals in 1985 found with a woman 100 pounds overweight, whom the Xerox Corporation had refused to hire. In Britain, as in the United States, defense groups sprang up specifically to protect the obese from legal or social discrimination, with their rights as individuals front and center—thus the International Size Acceptance Association of the United Kingdom.

Smokers admittedly fared much worse, because their habits more clearly affected the health of others as concerns about second-hand smoke expanded. Their increasing loss of rights, as smoking bans extended steadily, simply illustrated the larger dilemma. Societies continue to find groups whose behaviors seem to warrant special intervention, for their own good and that of society at large. Reform, including the ability to expand human rights definitions to cover poverty, health, and other issues, and a narrower interest in protecting freedom of individual choice and determination, will not necessarily go hand in hand. Some older tensions, for example concerning compulsory education, have yielded to time and compromise, but other issues emerge quite steadily. Here, even in some of the strongest regional havens for human rights, is a second area of complexity and confusion. Human rights sometimes capture the vision of a better future and wider welfare, but not always.

The growing list: no end in sight

A final dilemma—though related to disputes about reform and regional dissent alike—involves the clear impulse to expand human rights categories to include more and more aspects of human and social behavior. On the one hand, this expansion is impressive testimony to the basic power of the human rights argument, and the need, as some abuses begin to yield, to ferret out additional areas. Expanding definitions of justice, a willingness to tackle more and more historic wrongs, testify to the power of the basic vision. But expansion also brings costs, at least in the short term. Groups wary of basic rights definitions may balk further when they realize the list may prove inexhaustible: why make any concessions, when the rights groups will simply come back with additional demands? Societies favorable to a basic rights list, at least after some period of habituation, will inevitably splinter anew when additional rights are claimed. The process assures continued complexity and dispute. Yet expansion also seems unavoidable. Certainly the zeal of human rights advocates seems to feed on opportunities to identify yet another vital cause, with the same fresh outrage that accompanied the last one. The process is invigorating, but it can also be challenging to the wider enterprise.

The fundamental human rights vision has remained fairly consistent, despite changes in terminology, since the 18th century. As Amnesty International puts it, human rights are "basic rights and freedoms that all people are entitled to regardless of nationality, sex, national or ethnic origin, race, religion, language, or other status." The universality of human rights, the entitlement to them simply by virtue of being human, is a core commitment. What's less self-evident in the equation, and what has proved particularly open to redefinition and expansion, is the determination of what one means by "basic rights and freedoms," and what kinds of abuses or group deprivations can be identified when they are not fully actualized. A 1993 declaration in Vienna, from a World Conference on Human Rights, emphasized that "all human rights are universal, indivisible, and interdependent and related"—in other words, if there's an agreed list of human rights, it should be all or nothing. "The international community must treat human rights globally in a fair and equal manner, on the same footing, and with the same emphasis." Accordingly, many rights advocates urge that any defined violation, whether of long-established rights or newer ones, deserves high priority attention. In fact, of course, most societies end up emphasizing some rights more than others—some Western countries, for example, including the United States, are firmer on civil and political rights than on economic rights such as free access to health care, whereas some other societies are more comfortable with social rights than with political. Still, the notion of interconnectedness, along with the steady factual expansion of rights claims, helps explain why a long list can cause some discomfort.

Expanding concepts show up in many ways. Simply within three decades of the 20th century, thanks to a combination of additional thinking and bitter experience, human rights moved, in international diplomacy, from cautious hedging to elaborate definition. The League of Nations Covenant, adopted in 1919, referred to "fair and humane treatment of labour," to "just treatment" of "natives" in colonial territories, and to efforts to prevent traffic in women and children. But there was no elaborate rights statement—despite the fact that many countries individually had moved far along this path—and specific recommendations, like a Japanese effort against racism, were rejected (in the Japanese case, because of American and British opposition). Rights discussions advanced during the League's brief existence, particularly with more endorsement of women's rights as well as attention to international labor standards, but the range remained both limited and hesitant.

In contrast, the basic Charter of the United Nations, adopted in 1945, explicitly "reaffirms faith in fundamental human rights, in the dignity and worth of the human person, in the equal rights of men and women." And quickly, in 1948, the body adopted its "Universal Declaration of Human Rights," far and away the most elaborate global statement to that point. The preamble made the sweeping vision clear: "recognition of the inherent dignity and of the equal and inalienable rights of all members of the human family" was essential to peace and justice; it also clarified one of the key reasons for an expanded statement, in the "barbarous acts" of the 1930s and World War II that explicitly demonstrated the results of disregard for basic rights. Rights were to apply regardless of race, class, gender, or religion. But it was the list of rights itself that most impressively affirmed how widely the concept was moving. Rights now included: equality before the law and freedom from inhuman punishments; personal and family privacy; freedom of movement; freedom of choice in marriage; equal pay for equal work and fair conditions of work (here picking up on a League theme but extending it); education and an adequate standard of living (a huge move); the right to vote (another big step); and, of course, basic staples including freedom of thought, religion, conscience, and expression, as well as freedom of association. And, in case something was left out, "In the exercise of his rights and freedoms, everyone shall be subject only to such limitations as are determined by law solely for securing due recognition and respect for the rights and freedoms of others."

And the process of expansion had only begun. The United Nations established an agency specifically to monitor human rights and, in subsequent
decades, moved to define further rights for women and, even more creatively,
rights for children as well. The international umbrella, at least in principle,
was becoming very large. The process was exciting, but we have already seen
that it could also draw fire. Nations and groups that might be willing to sign
on to a briefer endorsement of human rights might see more troubling issues,
for example, in documents that moved more clearly to the terrain of gender
with discussions of consensual rights in marriage or equal pay, or to stipulations about a child's right to education implicitly regardless of parental
wishes. And, if resistance to one of the newer categories seemed necessary,
might this also affect commitments to some of the earlier staples of the rights
platform?

There are other ways briefly to illustrate the growth potential of the human
rights agenda, but also its complicating qualities. Human rights arguments
began to be transferred to the terrain of warfare in the 1860s. A Swiss-Italian
banker, Henri Dumont, was appalled by the suffering he saw among troops and
prisoners during the French-Austrian war over Italy, and in 1862 published a
book urging international redress. His concerns led to the foundation of the
Red Cross, as an agency for humanitarian relief during wartime, but also to the
initial Geneva Convention, which sought to regulate the behavior of belligerent
nations in the interests of protecting legitimate rights of soldiers. The goal was
centrally in line with human rights thinking: people, even as soldiers, deserved
attention to their dignity and wellbeing. Initial provisions of the Convention
provided for medical assistance to wounded soldiers even from a hostile army,
and the treatment of prisoners of war must be humane as well—with good
material conditions and protection from torture. From its inception in 1864,
the Geneva Convention was recurrently expanded, in a standard pattern in
which more generous ideas were combined with the hard realities of modern
warfare to produce more ambitious goals. Later provisions, for example, tried to
establish human rights assurances for civilians in militarily occupied territories.
Already a 1949 revision referred more explicitly to the rights of non-combatants,
including protection of women against rape or "any form of indecent
assault"—an important extension of rights language. Bitter experience in later
20th-century warfare led to further additions in 1977: against the use of
weapons that "cause superfluous injury or unnecessary suffering," as well as
still greater safeguards for civilians during civil wars. The 1977 additions
provided elaborate language about the importance of protecting civilians to
the maximum extent possible, no matter what the type of conflict.

The idea of rights even in war zones, and the steady elaboration of categories
and definitions, in one sense represents a triumph of human values: even in
the worst of manmade situations, there should be some clear rules of behavior. Not surprisingly, almost all recognized nations have signed onto the
conventions at one point or another: no one wants to seem to be planning to
be uncivilized. But the expansion of provisions raises some risks, which

returns us to the complexities of this aspect of human rights. Most obviously, the more rights established in principle, the greater the chance of violation, particularly again in the extreme situations of human combat. Geneva Conventions gain great credit for their role in improving the treatment of many prisoners of war. But they have not measurably changed the ways civilians have been handled by belligerents overall, and they have had little or no impact on the horrors involved in contemporary civil wars. Yet when they misfire—for all their desirably good intentions—does their hollowness jeopardize human rights more generally, creating a situation in which defiance or neglect become standard operating procedures? The question goes beyond the conduct of outright war criminals, whose behaviors in war combine with a fairly general scorn for human rights. Treatment of some wartime prisoners by the United States, for example, in the Iraq conflict of 2003, raised jarring questions about whether even this rights-conscious nation was abiding by the Geneva codes, which in turned provoked widespread American defensiveness and efforts to excuse or ignore a number of arguable violations. Might this generate a larger pattern of national evasiveness toward difficult rights obligations in future? Would it have been better to have a shorter, more manageable list of rights in wartime, which a larger number belligerents would have been willing to aspire to more fully?

Still more straightforward is the extent to which definitions of new rights may divide nations or groups that previously had been largely aligned on rights issues, where former allies find themselves on opposite sides of an innovation. The death penalty is an intriguing contemporary case in point.

From the outset of human rights thinking, new questions were raised about a variety of traditional punishments, very much including the administration of death as a response to conviction for crime. After all, a right to "life" readily accompanied rights to liberty. New concerns, by the later 18th and 19th centuries, prompted considerable soul searching about the number of crimes sanctioned by the death penalty, and usually a substantial scaling back resulted. New questions were also raised about the tradition of dealing the death penalty in public, which increasingly seemed barbarous to the new sensibilities. But no large group of human rights advocates at this point turned against the death penalty entirely. Certain crimes still seemed to require this kind of punishment, though it should be meted out privately, and as painlessly as possible. By the 1930s, however, a variety of individuals, in places like Britain and the United States, began to attack the brutality and unfairness of the death penalty, though there was no widespread movement. Particularly after World War II, and amid widespread knowledge of the dreadful death experiences of the Holocaust, a good bit of human rights attention began to revisit the topic more systematically. The Labour government in Britain, for example, suspended capital punishment as an experiment in 1948. Several European countries moved against the death penalty entirely by the 1950s, and the growing movement for European unity picked up the sentiment explicitly. Leaders began seeing the death penalty as a "denial of human dignity"—an affront, in other words, to human rights. By 2003, the European Union required abolition of the death penalty as a condition for membership, and well before this time majority European opinion had reached the same conclusion: the death penalty was barbaric, unworthy of a civilized nation. Rights arguments were front and center in this movement: Switzerland, for example, in abolishing the death penalty, referred explicitly to its "flagrant violation of the right to life and dignity" (the same words were used in South Africa in 1995, for a similar abolition). Many Latin American countries signed on to the cause as well. References to the incompatibility of the penalty with adherence to the United Nations rights documents, with their own commitment to the sanctity of life, attached the cause firmly to the human rights agenda.

But other societies, arguably at least as favorable toward a more limited list of human rights, did not make the same move, and the United States was—and largely still is—prominent among them. Some individual states did abolish the death penalty, but as late as the 1970s, 66% of the American people continued to profess belief in capital punishment (by the 1990s, the figure had risen to 80%), while American courts also normally ruled that the death penalty, properly administered, did not violate constitutional rights. For a time, the United States was one of only two nations supporting the death penalty even for children guilty of capital crimes. Many Americans believed that the death penalty was a vital measure in the prevention of crime, and simply did not see a human rights issue involved. Not surprisingly, the split of human rights opinion led to vigorous denunciations of American policy and of many particular executions. Individual Europeans, formal government bodies, even the Pope, periodically protested American behavior. Major death penalty cases routinely drew European outrage at this American defiance of human rights. While other countries—China, Japan, India, most Muslim countries—were at least as attached to the death penalty (the government of Singapore in the 1990s explicitly stated that the death penalty was not a human rights issue), American actions drew particular anger precisely because the country was expected to live up to the most advanced human rights standards.

Here was a clear case, in sum, where opinion vigorously divided over one of the more recent additions to the human rights cause. And the expanding definition simply passed some regions by, at least for the moment, potentially generating larger cracks in any global effort to unite behind human rights agendas.

Similar fissures resulted from the human rights revisions that resulted from the civil rights ferment of the 1960s. It was in 1969, for example, that resistance to a police raid on a gay bar in New York generated a widespread gay rights movement (an extension previously identified with only a handful of activists). Just as African Americans and women were demanding equal treatment under the law, so homosexuals now picked up the same mantle. Initial focus on legal discrimination against gays, including anti-sodomy laws, then steadily amplified into demands for equal rights to marriage and adoption.

Similar movements began to develop in other countries, particularly in the West, again following the larger logic of applying human rights criteria to previously exempted groups and behaviors. Needless to say, important groups in these same societies, at least somewhat comfortable with more conventional human rights targets, strongly resisted the new inclusions: homosexuals might still be seen as outside the pale, their demands not part of a common humanity, and the steady intensification of demands to include traditional categories like marriage simply compounded the problem. Again to use the gay rights example: for people taught that homosexuality is a sin, efforts to force tolerance of gay behaviors can seem to be a rights violation on its own account. Here again, expanding definitions created new divisions and, for some now cast into opposition to the latest cause, might limit acceptance of human rights arguments more generally.

The three main sources of division and complexity over human rights causes all burn bright in the contemporary world. A host of causes—like the current furor over obesity—prompt deep arguments over priorities, with key groups convinced that simple human rights claims must be overruled in favor of more important goals. The expansion trend, the growing profusion of rights causes, continues to create its own confusion. The sheer volume of contemporary human rights claims limits the ability to identify priorities, and risks tiring relevant audiences with the whole process. When so many groups shout about their injustices, new sources of opposition surface, and really catastrophic suffering may be drowned out in a sea of more superficial claims.

In some cases, time itself may provide some remedy. The history of human rights, over more than two centuries, is dotted with cases where a new claim initially roused resistance, but gained acceptance over decades, as more and more people identified with the arguments and as earlier arguments eroded. There are signs, already, that this process is occurring, at least in some important cases, for both the death penalty and gay rights. By 2005, for example, only 64% of the American people still supported the death penalty, and federal courts had completely outlawed capital punishment both for the mentally retarded and for children, in an explicit attempt to adhere to international human rights standards. Japanese public opinion was also increasingly turning against the death penalty, which had been stripped back to apply only to particularly horrible crimes. Gay rights, though still a hot-button item, won increasing support in places like the United States, and it was particularly revealing that younger people had become largely favorable. Even countries like India began to introduce gay rights legislation. It would be premature to argue that all initially contentious gay rights advocacy ultimately wins out, but there are some interesting trends over time.

Regional resistance, however, is another matter. We have seen that most regions that resist key human rights arguments show some sensitivity to the cause; outright rejection of all human rights claims is unusual. And, without question, some human rights advocates believe that here, too, time will work further miracles. As China becomes more deeply involved in the world economy, and steadily more engaged with global communication mechanisms like the Internet, so the argument runs, it will inevitably loosen its opposition to dissident opinions. And perhaps so. But it is equally possible that growing economic success and global influence will deepen Chinese commitment to a separate political path and intensify insistence that human rights campaigns back off from challenging core values and identities. Historically, similarly, while it is true that some regions, initially remote from human rights concerns, increasingly entered the orbit—Latin America is a case in point—others show no signs of yielding on key disputes. There is no reason to assume that complexity and disagreement, so obviously attached to global human rights issues today, will magically diminish in the future. The need for nuanced understanding remains.

The history of human rights is, often, a history of great passion. Emotions generated against slavery, 200 years ago, can be found again in contemporary defenses of gay rights or the importance of protecting women against rape or domestic abuse or the imperative to end the death penalty. At any point, many human rights advocates gain core strength from a belief that they are absolutely right, defending a clear moral truth, and that they must prevail in the future.

But the history of human rights, and its contemporary context, also present scenes of great passion in opposition. Defenders of alternative views of regional values can be absolutely sure of the validity of their cause, convinced that rights organizations represent nothing more than dangerous foreign interference. In some cases, flexibility may actually decrease as regional partisans seek to defend their truth against outside attack. On a second front, reformers convinced that, for a greater good, some rights must be denied—for example, the rights of parents to keep overfeeding an obese child—are quite willing to clash with other advocates on a terrain of moral certainty. And, on the third front, the sheer growth of human rights causes, with no end yet in sight, creates new lists of division and new sources of opposition, even in places where the initial human rights arguments initially took root.

Amid this complexity, human rights causes have always involved difficult choices—more difficult in that many advocates claim there should be no choice involved, just the one moral path—and sometimes painful compromise. Obviously, when new rights are identified it often takes time to gain any real hearing at all, and even then acceptance may come slowly—clearly the case today, on a global basis, with gay rights, for example.

Some of the most intractable debates in the contemporary world thus involve different takes on human rights, where no easy middle ways can be identified. This is precisely why a historical understanding of the whole phenomenon is timely as well as fascinating—a history including, of course, current efforts to define human rights with greater sensitivities to global diversities. Exploring how the idea of human rights emerged, how it became a global force but also how it provoked various resistances, directly contributes to an active grasp of major issues in the global community today.

Further reading

Major interdisciplinary treatments of human rights include: Carol Gould, *Globalizing Democracy and Human Rights* (Cambridge, UK: Cambridge University Press, 2004); Charles Beitz, *The Idea of Human Rights* (London and New York, NY: Oxford University Press, 2009); Lynn Hunt, *Inventing Human Rights: A History* (New York, NY: W. W. Norton & Company, 2008); Jack Donnelly, *International Human Rights*, 3rd edition (Boulder, CO: Westview Press, 2006); Patrick Hayden (ed.), *Philosophy of Human Rights* (Paragon, 2001); Michael Goodhart, (ed.), *Human Rights: Politics and Practice* (Bath: Oxford, UK: Oxford University Press, 2009); Micheline Ishay, *The History of Human Rights: From Ancient Times to the Globalization Era*, 2nd edition (Berkeley and Los Angeles: University of California Press, 2004); and Samuel Moyn, *The Last Utopia: Human Rights in History* (Cambridge, MA: Harvard University Press, 2010).

For general but diverse comments on regional cultures and human rights, see Amartya Sen, *The Idea of Justice* (Cambridge, MA: Harvard University Press, 2009); Mark Goodale, *Surrendering to Utopia: An Anthropology of Human Rights* (Stanford, CA: Stanford University Press, 2009); and Harri Englund, *Prisoners of Freedom: Human Rights and the African Poor* (Berkeley: University of California Press, 2006).

On East Asian issues more particularly, see Lucie Cheng, Arthur Rosett, and Margaret Woo, *East Asian Law: Universal Norms and Local Cultures* (New York, NY: RoutledgeCurzon, 2003); Rosemary Foot, *Rights beyond Borders: The Global Community and the Struggle over Human Rights in China* (London and New York, NY: Oxford University Press, 2000); and James Seymour, "Human Rights in Chinese Foreign Relations," in Samuel S. Kim's *China and the World: Chinese Foreign Policy Faces the New Millennium* (Boulder, CO: Westview Press, 1984). Also see Lynda Bell, Andrew Nathan, and Ilan Peleg (eds.), *Negotiating Culture and Human Rights* (New York, NY: Columbia University Press, 2001); and Peter Van Ness (ed.), *Debating Human Rights: Critical Essays from the United States and Asia* (New York, NY: Routledge, 1999).

Concerning more specific human rights issues: on female circumcision, Frances A. Althaus, "Female Circumcision: Rite of Passage or Violation of Rights," *International Family Planning Perspectives*, 23(3) (September 1997); Myres McDougal, Harold Lasswell, and Lung-chu Chen, "Human Rights for Woman and World Public Order: The Outlawing of Sex-Based Discrimination," *American Journal of International Law*, 69 (1975), pp. 511—516; Bolanle Awe et al. (eds.), *Women, Family, State and Economy in Africa* (Chicago: University of Chicago Press, 1991); Donald R. Wright, *The World and a Very Small Place in Africa: A History of Globalization in Niumi, the Gambia* (Armonk, NY: M. E. Sharpe, 2004). On aboriginal issues, David Martin, "Human Rights, Drinking Rights? Alcohol Policy and Indigenous Australians," *The Lancet*, 364(9441) (October, 2004), pp. 1282–1283. On obesity, see Naeomi Priest et al., "A Human Rights Approach to Childhood Obesity Prevention," in Elizabeth

Waters et al. (eds.), *Preventing Childhood Obesity: Evidence, Policy, and Practice* (West Sussex, UK: Blackwell Publishing, 2010), pp.40–48; Sander Gilman, *Fat: A Cultural History of Obesity* (Cambridge, UK: Polity Press, 2008); and Heather Keating, "Protecting or Punishing Children: Physical Punishment, Human Rights and English Law Reform," *Legal Studies*, 26(3) (September, 2006), pp. 394–413.

On the death penalty, refer to Amnesty International, *The Death Penalty in America: Study Guide* (2006); Michael Radelet and Marian Borg, "The Changing Nature of Death Penalty Debates," *Annual Review of Sociology* 26 (2000), pp. 43–61; John Peck, "Japan, the United Nations, and Human Rights," *Asian Survey* 32 (1992), pp. 217–229. See also EU Memorandum on the Death Penalty, http://www.eurunion.org/legislat/deathpenalty/eumemorandum. htm, accessed August 3, 2011.

2 Human rights in premodern world history

A full concept of human rights did not emerge until the 18th century (though not as yet under that label explicitly), but important precedents were set in the many centuries that came before. Scholars have debated, and continue to debate, the claim of modernity, seeing significant rights statements in some of the major world religions and also in ideas of natural law that emerged in Roman society and elsewhere. The debate is not merely an academic exercise. Contemporaries who argue, for example, that the Quran stipulates important rights for women are actively contending that the more recent versions of human rights, derived from Western thinking, are not the only game in town; a wider perspective is essential both for historical accuracy and for contemporary inclusiveness.

For the whole question of human rights origins relates directly to the crucial debate about Western values versus global response. Understandably, some scholars eager to generalize the human rights initiative make some excited claims about the larger historical trajectory. One, for example, argued in 1988 that "the concept of human rights can be traced to the origin of the human race itself." He goes on to claim that all major philosophies and religions embrace the human rights idea. This probably overstates the case, and in claiming a more recent origin for human rights this book obviously takes a different position—while sympathizing with the effort to claim a more universal birthright. What is true is that *elements* of human rights thinking show up in many different times and places, and it's important to lay these dimensions out clearly enough, not only to provide accurate historical background but to allow some test of the more comprehensive claims.

This chapter focuses on key developments in the prehistory of human rights, with enough detail to allow readers, should they so decide, to make the case for wider and earlier origins. Key topics here include the implications of the emergence of formal ideas of law, plus the relevant contributions of the major religions, plus some interesting beliefs about natural law, or prescriptions in principle applicable to the whole of humanity, that emerged well before modern times. Unquestionably, well in advance of the 18th century, ample foundations had been laid for human rights thinking, though we will also contend that some measurable gaps remained between these foundations and an explicit human rights superstructure.

But the chapter also must deal with various traditional barriers to human rights realizations—a tough topic because it involves using modern criteria to judge very different societies in the past. Core features of most premodern societies—for example, the predominant thinking about gender relations—simply did not measure up to what most human rights advocates routinely put forward today. Further, some societies began developing signature approaches that sit at the origin of some of the contemporary tensions with human rights groups—as in the heavy emphasis that emerged in China on the importance of political and social harmony. A focus on patterns before the 18th century, then, reveals both crucial steps, in law, in philosophy, and in religion, that provided clear foundations for human rights, if not early statements outright; and significant barriers and counterthrusts that explain why most scholars do not see a full human rights agenda established before the 18th century *and* why some regions and particular issues raise measurable issues even in the present day.

Needs of the species

By definition, and quite obviously, human beings are the only species capable of formally defining rights for other members of the species—and some have even gone further, during the same centuries that modern rights interests have taken shape, to attempt to posit some animal rights as well. It can also be suggested, however, that compared to many, perhaps most, species, humans also have particular needs for rights to be defined. The species is capable of remarkably violent and wide-ranging aggressions against its own number—and not just the weakest members (several species attack some newborns or aging individuals) but normal adults as well. At an extreme, humans are one of the only species at all likely to murder or formally war with others in the species. Many species will see fights or efforts to intimidate, in sexual rivalry or in gender relations. But few kill. Chimpanzees alone rival humans here, among higher mammals, and some observers believe that humans are a bit more restrained than their ape cousins. One theorist has speculated that, about 70,000 years ago, humans underwent some genetic modification toward somewhat greater mutual civility, a change that chimpanzees have not experienced. Conceivably, human rights interests build on this establishment of some innate attachment to social civility. Still, the human propensity for abuse of fellow humans can run quite high, and we see this all around us still today.

And certainly, in contrast to other species, as they organized their unique talents and also formed societies, humans have steadily added ways in which abuse can be expressed, and not through murderous violence alone. At various points in human history, for example, humans introduced new weapons, and weapons training, that gave advantages to some groups, including soldiers and other government officials, over civilians in general. Humans alone gained the capacity to imprison some of their fellows, for widely recognized crimes, of course, but also for behaviors like religious or political disputation. Torture was also introduced into the human arsenal early on.

Some measures of repression have grown worse in recent centuries. Weapons differentiation, between armed professionals and ordinary citizens, has almost certainly widened with the more sophisticated guns developed over the past century. While even early societies had some prison cells, extensive prison systems required funding and organizational capacity that have emerged fully only over the past few hundred years. In Western Europe, for example, elaborate uses of prisons for punishing criminals and others took shape only from the late 16th century onward. An important point to keep in mind, then, in considering modern human rights movements is the extent to which they have to counter a new range of repressions—premodern societies may have needed less in this area, because opportunities for abuse were not as great.

But some forms of human cruelty, again apart from outright murder, developed very early; torture, for example, does not depend on highly advanced technology or political organization. Human societies also, again early on, showed an interest in establishing clear differentiations among certain social groups, based on gender or property control. Laws and other rules, in this situation, would not apply evenly across the board—another human rights challenge with which societies still grapple.

As we turn, then, to early movements toward defining some elements of human rights, it is vital to keep this broader species background in mind. Humans do not automatically respect each other, and many rights efforts, both in premodern societies and more recently, are clearly designed to restrain some deep impulses within the species.

Laws

For several thousand years, even after the advent of agriculture, human beings lived in societies without formal states, and some of these "stateless" societies would persist into recent times. And of course hunting and gathering peoples, both before and after the arrival of agriculture, lived in small bands without institutional political structures.

We know, of course, that individuals in many of these societies were subject to violence and other abuses. Forensic anthropologists, among others, have documented many cases in which people were beaten or killed, as evidenced by surviving skeletons.

On the other hand, smaller societies offered many protections for individual people. Many even provided a fair degree of equality among many members. Hunting and gathering societies, for example, typically provided significant opportunities for women, whose economic contributions as gatherers of seeds and nuts often outstripped those of male hunters. Women might be regarded as separate, but they had opportunities for expression and sometimes participated in informal councils.

The fact is that we know very little about the extent to which really early human societies offered much thinking that even vaguely resembles human rights ideas. But it is also possible, given small-group interactions and some limits on inequality, that abuses were uncommon, at least within a particular band of people, or that even rudimentary ideas about rights would have been relevant or necessary.

In this context, the clearest first step toward some notion of rights occurred when increased numbers of larger and more organized societies developed and began to generate formal, written laws. Chronologically, the first legal system that left clear records was that established in the Middle East, by the Babylonian king Hammurabi, around 1800 BCE. Provisions of Hammurabi's Code illustrate clearly why virtually any effort at formal law also produced some formal notion of protective rules—but also why this initial approach differs from human rights principles as currently understood.

The Code offered a variety of protections against violence, mainly by stipulating comparable injury to any perpetrator on the principle, literally, of an eye for an eye. Thus: "If a man put out the eye of a free man, they shall put out his eye." Similar punishments applied to broken bones or knocked out teeth. Simple blows were more complex: "If a man strikes the cheek of a free man equal to himself in rank, he shall pay 1 maneh of silver." But "If a man strikes the cheek of a free man who is superior in rank, he shall be beaten with 60 stripes with a whip of ox-hide in the assembly." And if a slave struck a free man, his ear would be cut off. Lesser people—ordinary folk, for "free men," were clearly an elite—were protected from violence but not as fiercely, for they only received payment, not equivalent violence to the perpetrator. Violence to slaves would also be punished, but through payments to slave owners to compensate for damage to the property. There were some other interesting limitations to the protections. If a free man was struck in a fight but the perpetrator swore it was an accident, that he did not mean to, he got by through a payment to the doctor who took care of the wound, and even if the person died, and again the perpetrator swore it was unwitting, he owed only a payment in silver to the victim's family.

Still, despite complexities and related varieties in punishment, the Hammurabic Code clearly intended that people should be shielded from violence to the extent that a system of penalties would allow. In modern terms, they had a "right" to social protection against violence, though the precise nature of the right depended on social rank.

The Code also provided a variety of protections for property, often here with punishments that exceeded the eye-for-an-eye approach. Thus theft from the royal palace was punishable by death, and even receiving such stolen property was a capital crime. Similarly, breaking into a home warranted death by hanging, in front of the house where the offense occurred. A more prosaic theft from a servant—of an animal or a boat, for example—earned a fine ten times the value of the item stolen, and "if a thief has not the means of payment he shall be put to death." If a house caught fire and someone entered to put it out, but took an item in the process, "that man shall be cast into the fire." Other provisions of the Code sought to protect landowners from property damage by renters, through heavy fines, and even sought to assure doctors of a certain level of payment for life-saving operations performed. Interestingly, if a robbery occurred without subsequent arrest, the local government was supposed to compensate the victim—a social right that is not consistently established in contemporary societies. Finally, law codes usually spent a considerable amount of time specifying rules for inheritance on the death of spouse or parents.

The Hammurabic Code thus protected what can reasonably be termed rights to property, as well as rights to life, even though the term "rights" was not used in either instance. Extreme punishments showed the fierce protective intent, as well as the absence of regular policing or prisons: harsh retaliation in most early societies seemed essential to provide deterrent examples to potential offenders.

Other protections arguably went beyond these basics. The Code put a great deal of effort into trying to assure people against false accusations, again in a society that could not afford lawyers or police investigators to check on accuracy. Thus if someone accused another of murder, but could not sub-stantiate the charge, the accuser would be put to death. The same applied to accusations of felony when it was a capital crime. Even testifying falsely about a claim for damages could yield an equivalent fine if the case was dismissed. Women were also protected against false accusation, in a society where sexual respectability was extremely important. "If a man causes a finger to be pointed at ... a married lady and does not substantiate his slanderous comments, they shall flog that man before the judges and shave half his head." In other words, again in modern terms, people had a right to guard against inaccurate or malevolent actions that might involve legal jeopardy or simply damage to reputation.

On a somewhat similar basis, the Code tried to assure against corrupt or inept judges. A judge who changed or varied his ruling would thus be subject to fines and removal from office. This was the closest the Code came to offering protections against the state itself—a fundamental feature of more modern human rights definitions—but it was an interesting extension.

Finally, the Hammurabic Code sought to provide protections in family life. Women guilty of adultery could thus be punished—men should be able to expect sexual fidelity. (Men, however, were not subject to equivalent rules, in a society that clearly accepted a sexual double standard.) Wives received some assurances as well, though. If a husband abandoned his wife or failed to provide for her materially, she was free to leave the household. Again in modern terms, a wife had the "right" to expect support, or the marriage bargain was broken.

The establishment of written law codes did not necessarily provide more protections than simpler societies offered through widely understood rules that communities supported and enforced, but they certainly codified an approach that offered various assurances. Of course, these assurances hardly constituted guarantees: thefts and violence and bad family behavior might still occur when the threatened punishments failed to deter. But at least in principle there was an effort to make it clear that human behavior required some constraints against damage to people or property or even unfair actions by courts of law or other family members.

And of course this same basic approach could be found in comparable law codes in other organized societies, as formal states emerged in other parts of the world. Thus key provisions of the Jewish Ten Commandments—against killing or stealing—might add up, in modern terms, to a comparable effort to establish "rights" to life and property. Texts in classical India sought, like the Hammurabic Code, to protect against arbitrary behavior by state officials. A political tract around 300 BCE thus insisted that judges should not impose penalties that were not formally stipulated by law. Reflecting early Hindu religious values, Indian laws also sought to protect some people against torture. The death penalty, with or without torture, was widely applicable, as in Babylonia, not only for crimes of violence but also many thefts. Torture was an acceptable means of inducing confessions; no sweeping rights were even implied here. But priests, holy men, and also children, pregnant women, and invalids were protected against the use of torture, suggesting a slight concern about this kind of treatment that, obviously, modern human rights arguments greatly expand.

Not surprisingly, specific rules varied with the society, as in this partial concern about torture in early India or the relatively detailed Hammurabic concern about false testimony. Quite widely, however, the establishment of law codes covered much of the territory that had been sketched in Babylonia; protections against violence and theft reflected widespread human concerns and, again without using a rights vocabulary, an implicit agreement that people should be able to avoid violence or loss at the hands of others. Early codes from Egypt to China to Russia offered similar approaches, along with widespread use or threat of extreme punishments in their enforcement.

The same early codes, however, normally contained a number of features that clearly differed from a more contemporary approach—not surprisingly— even aside from the absence of any explicit rights vocabulary. All sorts of issues that a contemporary advocate might expect as routine inclusions are simply absent. And the protections that were established, while important, varied by social rank and gender, as opposed to envisaging a common humanity even within a single society—and at least one group, the slaves, was normally excluded altogether.

The huge disparities between any early law code, like the Hammurabic, and even a run-of-the-mill contemporary rights declaration, are glaring. The codes do not talk about freedoms of expression, religion, or assembly. Except for the admirable concern about honesty and consistency in judges, they do relatively little to offer protections against government abuse, though the Indian attention to torture is an interesting if modest addition. They do nothing with rights to education or social welfare. They reflect, in sum, a very different (as well as much narrower) sense of purpose. Though a few rights historians have probed and criticized these early statements in great detail, it's likely that the huge distinctions in scope, once noted, are hardly worth belaboring.

The distinctions do generate, however, one set of additional questions that must at least be invoked. Where do the more restricted definitions in the codes arguably reflect deficiencies, and where do they represent simply an absence of problem? The arguable deficiencies, of course, depend on contemporary criteria which are by definition anachronistic, unfair to the earlier societies involved, but they do not describe the whole universe of differentiations.

An initial example makes this obvious. Law codes until fairly recently did not include freedom of the press, because there was no press. There was, of course, writing, though often only a small number of people possessed the capacity, and issues of expression did arise. But it might have been hard, absent a more coherent set of opportunities, to identify a coherent force of the sort that a modern "press" or media provide, to conceive of a relevant category. On another front: the agricultural societies in which early law codes took form lacked the vision, but also the resources, that would have made any legal provisions for educational access meaningful. With rare exceptions, China being the most notable, education was not seen as a social issue; rather a matter for families and religions in economies where, for most people, the need for child labor easily trumped any opportunity for significant schooling. As with press freedoms, the lack of reference is real, but not particularly meaningful. Even the absence of provisions for religious freedoms may not be as telling as might be imagined. These early societies had religions, of course, and often linked the state closely to religious practice. The Hammurabic Code itself begins with invocations of a god's support for the ruler. Relatively few early societies, however, tried to enforce religious uniformity; many groups often coexisted. Even the Roman Empire, which periodically attacked early Christians because of concerns about their political loyalty, was normally quite tolerant. The point is that the lack of reference to religious freedom in any of the classic law codes certainly reflects a real conceptual difference from more modern human rights thinking, but also in many cases the absence of a systematic problem. In these instances and others, the codes must be interpreted less through formal categories than in terms of the ways these very different societies actually functioned.

On the other hand, some distinctions really mattered. The normal lack of protection against torture, for people accused of crime, is a case in point. Premodern leaders and jurists clearly thought differently about this subject than modern human rights advocates do, and this could have real impact on human experience. Failure to recognize rights to assemble might have had real effects also, though it is unclear, given the common lack of police forces, whether this constrained people—particularly, those rural majorities living far from the centers of authority—quite as much as might be expected.

The organizers of early law codes had, in sum, a distinctive conception of what society was all about and what deserved particular attention, compared to many contemporary formulations. They also, however, faced a distinctive set of needs. Differences in inclusion reflect both points, complicating the interpretation of how much some apparent deficiencies mattered in the actual quality of human life.

Just as the codes offered their own lists of topics, so they commonly qualified the protections they did specify through insistence on social inequalities. It was quite clear in Babylonia, for example, that, while people's lives and property were to be protected against violence and theft, the level of deterrence varied greatly with social class. Striking a "free man" rained down far more punishment than hitting an ordinary peasant or craftsman, and slaves counted for even less. There was no uniform definition, because there was no vision of a common humanity sharing and meriting some core rights. The same disjuncture applied to gender. It was really important that early codes offered some protections for women—they were not left out entirely; in principle at least, a male-dominated family could not entirely determine their fate—but their security and obligations were quite different from those for men. Contemporary human rights approaches still struggle with the legacies of class and gender differentiation—hence the need to identify explicit programs of women's rights—but the effort is in principle egalitarian, and most premodern codes were not.

There were differences, to be sure, from one society to the next. India's caste system offered even more legal variance than Babylonia did. A number of Mediterranean societies would also feature a slave class, with far fewer legal protections than the bulk of the population enjoyed. Jewish law, in contrast, specified more obligations and protections across class lines. China also tailored laws less widely to social class. In contrast, however, both Chinese and Jewish law offered women even less formal protection than the Hammurabic Code did. The idea that social groups required separate legal stipulations was widespread in the premodern world, in obvious and important contrast to the universalist rhetoric of contemporary human rights, even though the specifics varied from case to case.

Finally, there were some outright omissions in terms of group coverage, in most of the traditional law codes. Sexual preferences were not identified as a category, though this does not mean that various groups did not exist or, necessarily, that minority groups encountered abuse. Even more obvious, however, from a contemporary standpoint, was the absence of reference to children—even beyond the lack of any conception of educational rights. In most traditional societies, children were the province of the family, not to be singled out in legal statements by society at large. In Jewish law, to take an extreme, parents in principle could even punish a disobedient child by death. Even more widely, the notion of trying to define protections for children against their parents or other adults, save perhaps in cases of extreme violence, was simply not in the cards. This does not mean that children were unprotected in fact; again, it's vital to look beneath legal formalities at the ways lives were lived. Many historians have argued that traditional societies often used community oversight, particularly in rural villages, not only to monitor children's behaviors but also to make as sure as possible that parents did not defy group norms in disciplining their offspring. There may, as a result, have been less outright physical abuse of children than occurs in some contemporary settings. But all of this was a matter of informal arrangement, not the kind of thinking that went into formulating legal policy. Here, clearly, was another area where the traditional law codes were noticeably less comprehensive than would be the case later on.

Law codes were not the only contribution of premodern societies to the context in which human rights concepts would ultimately emerge. The basic protections the codes offered did represent a recognizable step in what would become, in very different social settings, human rights arguments—beginning with the effort to protect life itself. Well before modern times the growing experience with law codes fed two other changes that generated further strides toward a more formal idea of rights. Both in the major religions and in some philosophical traditions, theorizing about human nature and natural law picked up on some of the implications of the codes but moved beyond their level. In both cases, the changes involved helped prepare the human rights approach—without yet completing the effort. In the case of the major religions, particularly, the changes also raise additional questions about whether pre-modern societies did not offer realistic alternatives to what, more recently, more explicit human rights efforts have sought to achieve.

Contributions from philosophy: natural law

The process of developing and refining basic law codes continued in world history for many centuries. Russian kings, for example, began codifying laws on more than a regional basis only in the 10th century. As we will see, when human rights ideas began to solidify in the 18th century, one early impact was an effort to revise characteristic traditional law codes, for example, in reducing the number of crimes subject to dire penalties and more generally cutting back on physical punishments in favor of imprisonment. At the same time, however, rights ideas continued to build on the achievements of the basic codes, in seeking to protect human life and assure impartial behavior by judges. The long history of premodern law codes, in other words, did provide building blocks for rights efforts, even though they differed from these efforts in important ways.

Beginning in the 6th and 5th centuries BCE, in a number of major civilizations, a variety of philosophers began taking up ideas about justice and law, reflecting the experience of the early law codes but often thinking more generally and abstractly. In several cases—most obviously, in classical Greece and Rome—political philosophy contributed additional ingredients to the process of developing relationships between individuals and social/political institutions. This in turn added components to the foundations of what ultimately became a human rights approach. It is not always easy to determine the initial impact of the philosophical efforts—they generated fewer immediate actual contacts between states and individuals than the law codes did—but there were some connections. And there is no question that, at least in principle, many philosophers went beyond the law codes in generalizing about the nature of equity and considering the nature of humanity itself.

Philosophers in many classical societies worked hard on ideas about justice and moral behavior, often apart from any specific legal formulations. In classical China, for example, Confucius (551–479 BCE) urged leaders to be compassionate to the people and develop their moral capacity through education and altruistic devotion. He also saw common, and basically good, qualities in "the human race" more generally. Writing in a period of political confusion in China, with frequent regional warfare, Confucius emphasized the importance of building solid social relationships and durable political order. Individuals should combine education and self-awareness to contribute to the larger social good. When a person is "reverent and does nothing amiss, is respectful towards others and observant of ritual," then he is at peace with his fellows throughout the society. More specifically, Confucius wrote of the need for privileged people—the "gentlemen"—to pay attention to the general good and the needs of ordinary folk; in return for fair treatment and attention to their welfare, ordinary people should be deferential toward their social superiors and devoted to productive work. Human dignity should be respected on both sides of the relationship. Confucius saw society as an analogue of a well-organized, hierarchical family, with mutual obligations between members but also different specific obligations depending on rank. The result could certainly be seen as imposing limitations on the behavior of rulers, while urging compassion. At various points in Chinese history, popular risings pointed to selfishness and corruption among ruling groups as reasons leadership should be replaced. Confucian standards could even be construed as suggesting a "right" to rebel against bad leaders or to make claims against an unresponsive elite—but, while the standards were present, there was no phrasing in terms of rights, and much greater weight was given to deference and order. Some contemporary Chinese theorists see in Confucianism, and in the Chinese political tradition more broadly, a more direct contribution to a human rights endeavor, particularly in pointing to the desirability of a sympathetic approach to humankind in general. At the same time, the Confucian approach led more obviously to emphasis on social good, and the need for personal restraint of passions and self-interests, than to definitions of explicit individual rights. There is no question that Confucianism formed a vital part of the Chinese political approach and greatly contributed to a long history of political success. Debates over the relationship to the more contemporary human rights approach, not surprisingly, mirror larger discussions about Chinese values and international standards.

A specific aspect of early Chinese law, shaped by Confucianism, shows the tension between accepted standards and any idea of rights. Prisoners sentenced to a death penalty could appeal, and this might be taken to suggest that they had a right. But the appeal was not phrased in terms of rights, but rather as a share (*wen*) in a social or community good—the prisoner was asking society to grant him a boon. The matter was entirely up to what society chose to assign—there was no inalienable birthright involved, or any inherent protection from arbitrary punishment. Nothing in this approach specifically constrained a ruler from administering death penalties—recognizing that this was the pattern in classical civilizations more generally.

Political philosophy in the Mediterranean took a slightly different approach from the Chinese tradition—though there was a shared interest in personal ethical behavior as part of an orderly political system—amid considerable variety. The actual political history of classical Greece was less successful than that of China, with more frequent periods of disorder and bitter quarrels over the best form of state organization. At the philosophical level, however, Greeks and, in their wake, Romans introduced important innovations in their thinking about law and humanity.

Beginning tentatively with the philosopher Plato, in 5th-century Athens, Greek thinkers pioneered the concept of natural law—that is, in principle, legal provisions that would be applicable in any proper human society. Greeks readily understood, of course, that actual laws varied widely, but they were interested in certain legal provisions that should transcend purely local formulation. For Plato and Aristotle, the universe in which people live was basically orderly, operating on a rational basis that should therefore be comprehensible to human reason. Part of the orderliness of nature, in turn, was the possibility of identifying certain laws that could be generally applicable. As Plato put it, the ideal society would be "established in accordance with nature." Aristotle carried this thinking further, becoming the clearest originator of the idea of natural law and, with it, potentially, natural rights. An ideal political community would reflect this "common" law of nature, though he was rather vague on what this law would contain and at points even suggested that law was not the best basis for a political system.

The group of thinkers called Stoics, who ultimately took root in both Greece and Rome, pressed further. Stoic philosophers extended the belief in a rational and purposeful order to the universe, expressed in a generally applicable, unchanging law by which a rational being could live in harmony. Far more than with Aristotle, Roman Stoic thinkers like Cicero turned the idea of natural law into a statement of the basic commonality of all human nature, regardless both of local political arrangements and social hierarchies. Cicero saw the purpose of law as providing "the safety of citizens, the preservation of states, and the tranquility and happiness of human life." There were two implications in this view, beyond the principle that natural law applied to humanity in general. First, as with the Confucian school in China, natural law obliged individuals to contribute to the good of the larger society; virtue consisted of living in "union and charity" with one's fellow man. But second, natural law should be a standard against which actual, local laws should be measured. It should be possible to use natural law to determine what statutes were "wicked and unjust," "anything but laws" in fact, because of their lack of harmony with natural, universal principles.

This kind of thinking could obviously feed into concepts of human rights. The ideas that laws might apply to the whole of humanity, and that certain laws inhered in nature and provided standards of justice by which actual human law could be measured (and, where found wanting, condemned), were huge changes in principle. Greek and Roman thinkers amplified natural law arguments by wider discussions of common humanity. Greeks, for example, frequently explored the term *philanthropia*, referring both to people in general and to common values of benevolence; Roman thinkers referred to *humanitas*. Like natural law, both terms could be used as a criterion for assessing political actions. Thus a Greek thinker praised several city-states for their equality and freedom of speech, consistent with philanthropia, but then noted that some of the states participated in massacres of innocent envoys which was contrary to the "common laws of nations," a "violation of the rights common to all men." Small wonder that Greek, and particularly Roman, ideas, including the works of Cicero, were widely known and cited by Western thinkers in the 18th century, unquestionably helping to shape the emerging notion of human rights. The connection, across time, was real and significant.

The problem, for the premodern experience itself, comes in figuring out whether much of this thinking actually affected Greek and Roman societies, in ways that would be suggestive of a move toward human rights at the time. The answer, inevitably, is complex and debatable, but arguably boils down to "yes, but not much." Aristotle's thinking about natural law was important, but it did not stop him from praising the institution of slavery as essential for the operation of society. As with most classical leaders, extensive social and legal inequalities were taken for granted as part of freeing resources for a ruling elite. Massive gender differences were also assumed, particularly in Greece. Natural law thinking, in other words, did not generate any active sense that there were certain rights that would cut across social levels. The spread of slavery in Rome suggested a somewhat similar disjuncture between what we can see as a human rights potential in natural law ideas and the actual structures of the time, which, broadly speaking, reflected differences in legal status common in agricultural societies more generally.

As in China, of course, the idea of established laws and principles did provide some ability to measure and define improper political arrangements or leaders who were behaving arbitrarily and unjustly. Confucian ideas could be directed this way, and so could the Greco-Roman interest in law. Roman historians, for example, speaking of the origin of laws in their own early republic, contrasted the results with the "despotism" that had prevailed earlier, when rulers were unrestrained by any legal codes. The result fell short of any specific concept of rights, but it did move in the direction of holding leaders accountable and providing bases for condemnations of arbitrary actions or cruelties.

Links to relevant philosophy moved further in Rome, under both the republic and the subsequent empire. Roman leaders spent a great deal of time developing, and thinking about, the law. Roman jurists were not in the main interested in abstractions. They prided themselves on very practical responses to legal situations, where laws could be defined that promoted economic life and settled disputes. But, as Rome expanded, the idea that laws needed to be crafted that would apply to a variety of people obviously gained force. In particular, Romans developed a category called *lex gentium*, or "law of the people," which applied to the many foreigners in their midst; and they also extended Roman citizenship to a minority of individuals throughout their holdings, in order to cement loyalty, and here too common laws and privileges were attached. No specific concept of rights emerged. But there was an effort to think about laws that were both just and widely relevant, limiting arbitrary behaviors and helping to generate some shared sense of fairness. These developments, and the fame of Roman law itself, would—like natural law philosophy—form part of the classical heritage that helped shape later European thinking.

Overall, the advent and evolution of more formal political philosophies clearly supplemented the operation of legal codes in generating notions of what kinds of protections a proper society owed its people and even adding some ideas—beyond any particular state or government—of a common humanity. The results could contribute to evaluations of actual leaders and actual regions, helping among other things to define and measure unacceptable treatment. Natural law ideas call particular attention to philosophical develop-ments in Greece and Rome, but philosophical efforts in several societies could be connected, later on, to more formal thinking about human rights. At the same time, limitations in the relationship between the most generous theories, and actual legal and social arrangements, caution against pushing the links to human rights too far or, historically, too fast. The most interesting theories were not always widely applied.

The great religions

At widely varied points in world history, between the last millennium BCE and the 7th century CE, important new religions arose in many societies in Afro-Eurasia, replacing or challenging more traditional polytheistic systems. Many of these religions—headed here by Buddhism, Christianity, and Islam—showed a capacity to spread widely, fostering active missionary efforts that significantly altered the religious map.

The religions varied widely, and so too did their implications for human rights endeavors—in premodern history, and still today. In general, however, the key religions added two major components to the ultimate foundations of human rights thinking, and they implied a third—in a combination that was inherently complex.

1. First, though to different degrees, the religions emphasized the primacy of spiritual concerns and, often, the quest for spiritual rewards, in ways that

could supplant or at least compete with political goals. Both Jesus and Mohammed thus urged their followers to accept even unjust states, because worrying about political remedies would distract them from their basic, religious obligations. Deep religious commitments could, and still can, constrain any urgency about human rights issues. In practice also, the religious faithful might judge a ruler more through what he did to support religion and display piety than in terms of anything like a human rights standard.

2. Second, and this pointed in a different direction: most of the major religions saw people as sharing some spiritual qualities across political and social boundaries. We have already noted the impact of Judaism in the Middle East, in contrast to Babylonia, where shared religion reduced the importance of social inequalities (though not in gender) in the application of laws and punishments. Many Jewish scholars extended the Torah precept of "loving thy neighbor" to a commitment to the equal worth of each human being. More universalistic religions might extend the same idea of shared humanity on a wider scale. The three great missionary religions certainly looked to a common humanity as potentially capable of receiving religious truth and participating in a shared religious endeavor. Islam and Christianity stipulated that all people—women and men, slave and free— had souls. Buddhism insisted that all people, again women as well as men, shared in the divine essence. All people, in this vision, could or at least should share in a common religious purpose. The idea of treating others as you would be treated—"doing unto others"—stemmed from the same vision of spiritual sharing and could be potentially transposed into political relationships as well. This kind of thinking did not, in fact, wipe away social inequality, and we will see that important issues resulted. But there was in principle a new sense of a common humanity or at least a common religious universe, which could in turn contribute to a belief that the same humanity should deserve some common, minimal standards in this world. Religious thinkers could, and did, contribute directly to human rights concepts, from the 18th century onward and, while the development was new, the connection was not accidental.

   Even before the modern period, most of the major religions had promoted one key change in culture: a strong commitment against infanticide, based on the belief that children, too, had souls. Though even here not framed in terms of rights, the approach had some of the same uniformly protective flavor, and, compared to previous practices in places like classical Greece, the result could be truly significant in protecting interests of a vulnerable human category.

3. Third, the rise and gradual spread of newer and often larger religions created new communities, again often across conventional political boundaries—but also new barriers and tensions. Muslims could, and did, share an active sense of religious kinship, by the 15th century CE, from Morocco to Indonesia. Experiences like the pilgrimage to Mecca, where coreligionists

from various places could swap stories and concerns, gave this large community genuine reality. Christians in one region, similarly, could get upset about problems Christians in another region were facing. These large communities could generate some shared sense of purpose and religious rights. At the same time, however, many of the major religions were fiercely committed to their own version of religious truth. New questions inevitably emerged about religious minorities in the new Afro-Eurasian map, and also about relationships of the major religions on their own mutual frontiers. Issues of religious coexistence were not new in human history, but they took on far greater importance. This, too, would ultimately feed, and complicate, the human rights agenda.

Furthermore, many religions repeated some of the common provisions of law codes, adding religious endorsement, and often religious punishments, to the protections sought against murder, theft, and other depredations. Belief that human beings shared in an element of the divine or had been created in God's image lent new fervor to the protection of human life. The general impulse to extend religious sanctions—the possibility of divine punishment—to the standard basics of the law codes was a prominent feature of early Judaism, from the Ten Commandments onward. Zoroastrianism, in Persia, offered comparable provisions. Religions characteristically generated additional rules, about God's rights—the honor and duties owed to the divinity—but since these stipulations varied, they could add to the problems of coexistence among different religions.

4. Finally, many religions, again including Judaism, gave people rights of asylum in certain holy cities or places. Slaves might seek sanctuary, but so could people in trouble with state authorities. The approach clearly suggested a notion that divine sanction superseded mere human authority. It could be meaningful to individuals in certain situations. At the same time, obviously, no generalizable rights were involved.

None of the religious changes transformed the human rights scene overnight, though Islam had perhaps the clearest claims. Over time, however, and well before the 18th century, religions significantly affected the domain. Along with key law codes and the contributions of political philosophy, the result rounded out the foundation for what would become a human rights approach, while also adding some durable complications.

Hinduism and Buddhism

As Hinduism developed in India, it increasingly incorporated legal principles, though without any generalization about rights. Specific protections were extended on a group by group basis. Thus: children could not be given away or sold; slaves had a right to daily food (though husbands could withhold food from wives and children); more widely, sons born into a particular social caste had the right to pursue occupations appropriate to the caste and to inherit property if they had not "sinned" against their parents. The Laws of Manu, crafted between 200 BCE and 200 CE, assured rights to property; rulers would protect the property of orphaned children, and grant them full ownership when they became adults. A "righteous king" would severely punish thieves. Freedom from violence was another important Hindu emphasis. Hindu thinking, in other words, confirmed many of the protections provided by law codes in most complex societies. The same Laws of Manu, however, made it abundantly clear that few social provisions applied to everyone: divisions by caste, and the huge gap between men and women—with women never to be independent, but always subject to father, husband, or (if widowed) to sons— predominated over any consideration of people in general. Even dharma—the moral duties incumbent on every individual—stressed the duties specific to each caste. As many contemporary Indian thinkers have suggested, Hinduism can be seen as compatible with many human rights provisions, from freedom from want to tolerance, but until modern times the religion did not specifically add to any incipient human rights agenda.

Buddhism's implications were more complex. The Buddha's objections to early Hinduism included an attack on the caste system, and Buddhists unquestionably found it possible to identify a common humanity. Beliefs in human participation in the divine essence included often vigorous defense of the spiritual capacities of women, though commitments here varied and may have declined over time. As a minority religion in India, Buddhism also opposed discriminations based on religion, and was normally widely tolerant of other religions—even when it gained majority status in some Southeast or East Asian societies. No proclamation of a right to religious freedom emerged—Buddhist leaders did not have this kind of legalistic orientation— but, unlike many religions, Buddhism was certainly compatible with the principle. Buddhist aversion to violence went further than with most religions as well, and could be invoked not only in protection of human life but in opposition to cruel physical punishments. These categories help explain why some contemporaries see in Buddhism an "embryonic concept" of human rights.

Two aspects of Buddhism, however, limited the connection without contra- dicting it. First, the principal obligations of a Buddhist focused on self-denial and a submersion of self and worldly pleasures to contemplation and ascetic discipline. Definitions of anything like rights in this world, including opposition to political injustice, could easily seem secondary to these spiritual goals. Even important features such as the frequent commitment to provide spiritual opportunities for women did not yield any equivalent political gesture, for this would not have been religiously relevant.

Second, where Buddhism did stipulate protections in ordinary life in the world—often reflecting at least a partial sense of equality across classes and genders—it normally talked in terms of duties (the Buddhist version of dharma), rather than rights. Here, Buddhism shared features with many early legal and religious systems, including Confucianism and Judaism. Thus Buddhist dharma stipulated that "a husband should support his wife," rather than saying that wives have the "right" to be maintained by their husbands. Some contemporary scholars have argued that a duty clearly implies a right; others, however, urge that there is a real difference, among other things because, without a right, it may be difficult to gain redress just because someone else—like a husband—is not doing his duty.

It was striking, certainly, that even a rudimentary idea of rights was missing in many Buddhist societies. No word for the concept of rights existed in Japanese, for instance, until 1870, when Western example created the need for a vocabulary change.

Christianity

Like Buddhism, Christianity was born as a minority religion, separate from the state and, periodically, in its early centuries, facing state persecution. This did not lead traditional Christianity to a consistent embrace of religious freedom. When the emperor Constantine granted tolerance to the new religion, in 313 CE, he stipulated that "every man may worship according to his own wish"; and some Christian thinkers themselves defended religious freedom—it was Lactantius who stated, "Liberty has chosen to dwell in religion. For nothing is so much a matter of free will as religion, and no one can be required to worship what he does not will to worship." Generally, however, Christian leaders became comfortable with, even insistent upon, religious dominance—as in requesting later Roman emperors to execute religious heretics. As a religion of the book, fiercely attached to correct beliefs, Christians could be vigorous in attacking other religions or perceived deviance or heresy in their own religion. Christianity did have a stake, however, derived from its minority origins, in defining religious principles as distinct from and superior to mere political issues. A state or ruler could be condemned on this basis for actions against proper religious values and rules. The result was no quick conception of measurable rights, but there were grounds for seeing some need to protect individuals, in certain circumstances, from the state. Christian leaders normally urged obedience to the state, however since there should be no distraction from religious goals. And over time, many states, adopting Christianity, assumed an active role in promoting the religion rather than preserving its separation. The whole strand of Orthodox Christianity, in the Byzantine Empire and elsewhere in Eastern Europe, linked church and state in ways that measurably inhibited the opportunity to define rights against political authority.

Early Christian texts had little to say that bore on the human rights domain. Christian insistence that all humans are created in the image of God clearly suggested a basic equality, as against the social hierarchies that affected Greek and Roman legal thinking. Certainly believers were equal before God: thus the New Testament urged, "there is neither Jew nor Greek, there is neither slave nor free, there is neither male nor female: for ye are all one in Christ Jesus." This commitment did not translate into relationships in this world: slaves were expected to remain slaves, and wives were still expected to obey their husband. But it was possible, later on, for Christian ideas to be translated into more direct claims for equality as a right.

And Christian thinkers did worry about extreme inequalities, like slavery, without attacking the institution systematically. Slaveholding, particularly of Christians by Christians, seemed uncomfortable, given comparable spiritual worth. It is generally believed that slavery declined in Christian regions because of this discomfort, in the centuries after the fall of the Roman Empire. It did not disappear, however, and other forms of inequality, like serfdom, were accepted readily—and, of course, Christian Europeans would take a lead in extending slavery later on, as they carved out estates in the Americas and organized massive traffic from Africa. Even before the rise of the Atlantic slave trade, Christian thinkers spent considerable time explaining why, though natural law stipulated that men were free, there was no right to claim freedom from hereditary slavery. Indeed, as Christian law largely confirmed protection of property, it could be invoked toward preservation of rights to own slaves. Still, there was a relevant hesitation that would reemerge as part of early human rights arguments in the 18th century.

Somewhat similar tensions emerged over the Christian commitment to individual souls, as Christian law evolved, particularly in Western Europe, from the 11th century onward. On the one hand, Christian individuals were defined by the rite of baptism, which gave people entry into the Christian community with whatever rights might attach to this. On the other hand, people who were not baptized—people of other religions, or Christians excommunicated from the church for whatever reason—had no protections whatsoever, and might be subject to outright punishment. And, even if baptized, children had no rights in evolving Christianity. Parents had duties to provide Christian instruction to their children, and to introduce them to other relevant sacraments, but children had no independent rights against parental authority— again, as was characteristic throughout most of the premodern world.

Christian thinkers by the 10th and 11th centuries did discuss a "right" to resist political tyrants. This reflected some appropriation of ideas of natural law but also rights to self-defense, and it also related to the earlier Christian possibility of defining higher principles in evaluating the state. As we have seen, several cultural systems, including Confucianism, also provided a basis for attack on unjust rulers, but the Christian acceptance of the idea of a right was unusual.

Christian legalists also began to discuss a "right" of subsistence. Parents and masters had the duty of providing material sustenance to children and servants, as part of common humanity. This common conception slid, however, toward some thinking in terms of rights. Thus, in times of severe hardship, the legal authorities argued, the poor and needy could take enough to sustain themselves from the property of others without committing theft. Though there was no indication this idea was accepted in fact, the notion was interesting. More practically, slaves or children, if left without support, had the right to think of themselves as free from obligations.

Christian thinkers took up the question of self-incrimination in courts of law, arguing in general that people had a right not to betray themselves—though they could be punished anyway if they had done wrong. They also defended, in principle, the notion that people should be free to decide whom to marry. In fact, many people, particularly women, were pushed into marriage by parents, but in Christian law active consent should be present—otherwise, an arrangement was going against legal propriety. But, while this reflected a belief that Christian individuals, male or female, deserved protection in this kind of choice, the argument was not framed in terms of rights. Rather, officials urged more practically that "forced marriages have unhappy outcomes." More important still, the lack of a firm legal statement of rights meant that any ability to appeal to a court against a forcibly arranged marriage was normally extremely limited.

Christianity, in sum, generated no wide new commitments to human rights. This was simply not the purpose of a vibrant religion devoted to converting people to religious truth and preparing them for salvation. Attacks on the life and property of people who were not Christian, and particularly people suspected of heresy, added new categories to the history of persecution. Many discussions that seemed to suggest some idea of human rights remained abstract. In a society in which many marriages were arranged in terms of property gains, few people gained new opportunities for active consent. Many slaves remained slaves, and in general the typical premodern notion that society was composed of unequal layers was not seriously disputed. In the 16th century, when Spaniards began seizing lands in the Americas, some Christian observers protested on grounds of the property rights of the natives—but even this traditional category was cast aside in the interests of gain and in the belief that the natives were both different from, and inferior to, European Christians.

Still, there were suggestions of some change, at least in principle, particularly when Christian thinking combined with earlier Roman notions of natural law. Christians were urged to see at least fellow Christians as individuals of equal spiritual worth, and given some protections in consequence. They did perceive some separation of religious life from the hand of the state, and could advance some new thinking—again, at least in principle—about rights against abusive tyrants. Deep interest in Christian law, and the revival of study of Roman law, helped form some notion of rights—in the emerging French language, "law" and "right" turned out to be the same word (*droit*).

A suggestion of modest change, but also the importance of more traditional categories, emerged in England in the 13th century. In 1215, a bitter quarrel between leading English nobles and the king led to a document, the Magna Carta, restricting the king's powers in various ways. The document had little effect at the time, though its implications would later be revived and reinterpreted as part of a more modern constitutional monarchy. But the thinking was interesting for the 13th century, and not only for England. Most of the document sought to specify rights the nobles had against arbitrary royal seizures of property or other measures. No general rights were intended; simply the specific interests of the upper class in a stratified society. The freedom of the church was assured—again, an interesting aspect of Christian tradition at least in principle. Children could be assigned in marriage, though only to someone of equal social status—so much for the theorizing about consent (but, interestingly, widows could not be compelled to marry). In case of murder, a woman's testimony should not lead to any arrest, unless it was her husband who had been killed—a revealing sign of gender inequality. Property rights of Jewish moneylenders were restricted. But, somewhat more broadly, "free men" could not be punished disproportionately—possibly implying a right (but the nobles were still treated separately; they could only be fined by judgment of their peers). Judges were to know the law and be "minded to keep it well." Mostly, the Magna Carta affirmed protections that traditional societies had widely developed. It carefully reflected class and gender hierarchies, and defended the customs attached, along with the safeguarding of Christian church from state. But in framing all this, the Magna Carta's language could imply just a bit more, both in terms of suggesting a somewhat wider right to protection from acts like arbitrary arrest, or in the specific reference to words like "liberties, rights, and concessions" granted to "men in our kingdom" "in their fullness and entirety for them and their heirs ... in all things and all places for ever." The Magna Carta was not a modern declaration of rights but, reflecting changing political patterns in Western Europe and some of the implications of Christianity, it was not entirely a traditional document, either.

Islam

Like Christianity, Islam, as it took shape from 600 CE onward, was first and foremost a religion bent on conveying religious truth, assuring appropriate worship, and guiding believers to their primary goal of salvation. As it developed, however, and particularly as Muhammad and his successors gained political roles, Islam also established important codes and an elaborate legal tradition. In the process, the religion staked out some new precision in defining the protections due to various kinds of people. It is important to note that a number of different sects and legal codes developed within Islam, which complicates generalization, but some main lines are clear particularly for the majority Sunni faith.

Islam emphasized the dignity of all people—the Quran stipulated that "we have conferred dignity on the children of Adam"—and the sanctity of human life. Provisions against infanticide were unusually explicit. Believers and leaders alike were urged to pursue justice. Again, from the Quran: "Stand out firmly for justice, as witnesses to Allah ... whether it be against rich or poor."

The Quran also urged religious freedom: "Let there be no compulsion in religion." Those who renounced Islam and attacked the faith were to be treated as enemies, but there were no set punishments for people who simply did not believe. While a number of complications surrounded this approach in practice, as we will see, Islam was noticeably more tolerant of nonbelievers than Christianity, at least until the 17th century.

Islam's extension of protective rules applied particularly to women, where Muhammad explicitly introduced important reforms into previous Arab practice. Many provisions in the Quran and in subsequent laws insisted on women's right to own property, including inheritance from parents, and rights to divorce and remarry and, in some instances, to custody of young children. On the property point, where Islam went well beyond standard Christian prescriptions: "Men shall have the benefit of what they earn and women shall have the benefits of what they earn." Two caveats are vital: first, no explicit rights language was employed, though some provisions moved in a comparable direction. Second, men and women were not treated equally in law. It was much harder for women to divorce than for men, and men's share in inheritance was larger—"the male shall have the equal of two females." Some debates within Islam over gender issues mirrored those in Christianity, for example, as to whether women's consent was needed for marriage.

Slavery was another arena in which Islam sought some clear protections, displaying real discomfort over the tensions with beliefs in the dignity of all people, while ultimately endorsing the institution and the treatment of slaves as property. In principle, Islam stood against holding fellow Muslims as slaves. In practice—partly because, for many reasons, imported slaves often converted to Islam—a prohibition did not seem practical. Instead, common conventions sought at least to make sure that Muslim slave families were not split up if slaves were sold. Freeing slaves when an owner died was encouraged. Special legal protection extended to slave women who bore their owners' children. Such women could not legally be sold at all, nor could her children, and all were granted freedom when an owner died. These provisions were almost certainly not always observed, but they did have some impact. Islam, in sum, accepted legal inequality, but at the same time offered some subsidiary rights to certain kinds of slaves. It was an interesting combination, somewhat different from the patterns that developed within Christianity.

Many contemporary scholars urge that basic features of Islam are fully compatible with human rights provisions, around principles such as a commitment to human dignity but also through the experience gained in using law to protect against unfairness or abuse. The principles were not merely abstract: studies of Islamic states like the Ottoman Empire have shown widespread interest in providing fair trials (with the accused seen as innocent until proven guilty), protecting property, and assuring specific rights for women, following key provisions of Islamic law. Traditional Islam also, however, accepted various kinds of social differentiations and did not move to explicit commitments to a thoroughgoing rights agenda. The Ottoman Empire itself placed much greater emphasis on communities and community justice than on subjects seen as individuals.

Between the establishment of basic law codes, and the end of the period of the great classical empires by 600 CE, it is hard to point to any kinds of systematic gains for human rights in world history. In places like China, where Confucian principles guided important political changes, other kinds of protections emerged, but not clearly along human rights lines. The further impact of world religions, and particularly the approaches taken in Christianity and Islam, opened the way to some new policies, in various ways affecting groups like women and slaves, in the centuries after 600, though there was no dramatic overturning of prior approaches. Suggestions of change might be amplified when the religious impulse was combined with earlier ideas about natural law.

Natural law revisited

Both Islamic and Christian scholars helped revive interest in natural law arguments, extending them in some respects partly by adding a greater certitude that divine authority ultimately lay behind "nature."

As Islam took hold in the Middle East and beyond, where Greek learning, particularly, had already influenced scholarship, a variety of philosophers and scientists began to consider natural law issues. Some argued that natural law was brutal and oppressive, the law of the jungle, which could only be overcome by divine law. Others, however, commenting on Greek thinking, picked up the idea that people in all societies agreed on certain natural principles including the unlawfulness of killing and stealing. Natural law was compatible in this sense with Islamic law, though less complete, and could be judged to condemn certain harmful acts. Reason alone, in other words, could evaluate some behaviors and find them good or evil.

This kind of philosophical work in Islam gained a new audience in Europe by the 12th century, when scholars began to take a growing interest in complex issues, using both Islamic example and a revival of Greek and Roman principles. One early Christian commentator in this vein argued simply that natural law and God's law were the same thing, which simplified the relationship but pulled away from what the Greeks and Romans had intended. It was not until the 13th century that the master Christian theologian Thomas Aquinas made it clear that natural law was a function of human reason, different from divine law though compatible with it. Aquinas went on to clarify that human laws should be measured by their relationship to natural law—and of course they could be found wanting. But where they differed, human law was at fault: an unjust law is not, in a full sense, law at all—it is a "perversion of law." Aquinas implicitly suggested situations in which the law proposed by a state—for example, by a tyrant—might differ from natural law and be rejected on this basis. There was more than a hint of human rights thinking in this approach: "A tyrannical law, through not being according to reason, is not a law, absolutely speaking." To be sure, Aquinas did not go on to spell out what might be done about such a law, and he placed great emphasis on the importance for citizens to be obedient. But the tension was clear: true laws should be natural and should promote the common good. But

> laws may be unjust ... by being contrary to human good ... as when an authority imposes on his subjects burdensome laws, conducive not to the common good but rather to his own cupidity or vainglory ... Such are acts of violence rather than laws ... Therefore, such laws do not find in conscience. Laws of this kind must in no ways be observed, and in such cases a man is not obliged to obey, if without scandal or greater damage he can resist.

During the same period, in the 13th to 15th centuries, natural law thinking deeply affected the development of the legal tradition in England. Henry de Bracton, for example, argued in the 13th century that the king is under the law—in contrast to imperial Roman ideas that the ruler's will is law. Bracton went on to quote an Italian jurist: "Justice is the constant and unfailing will to give to each his right." Not surprisingly, 18th-century thinkers, later on, like Thomas Jefferson, revived attention to Bracton and this earlier English tradition. Various English legal thinkers continued to argue that there was a law of nature that took precedence over any actual law, though some of them placed greater emphasis simultaneously on their belief that the law of nature also insisted on obedience to the king.

Still, it would not be an unreasonable leap to suggest that European thinking, relying on the revival and extension of natural law beliefs but in a context further enhanced by the Christian separation of church from state and some of the aristocratic efforts to define limits on monarchs, had moved close to a point at which an idea of human rights was emerging, at least in principle. After all, the American Declaration of Independence in 1776 itself based one of the arguments on the need for separation from the British crown on "the separate and equal station to which the Laws of Nature and of Nature's God" entitled the revolutionaries. Here was a clear appeal to natural law as a basis for judging the legitimacy of a government and for determining rights on the same basis.

But before this connection, though quite real, was fully made, this Western pattern was itself interrupted. Some scholarship on natural law continued in the 14th to 16th centuries, for example in a few centers in Italy, but the bulk of attention shifted elsewhere. Politics in the Italian Renaissance tended to emphasize the power of princes, and of course the great political writer Machiavelli specifically discussed the legitimacy of any measure a prince might take in order to seize and maintain power. As monarchs sought to extend their claims in countries like France or in England under Henry VIII, they too tended to discourage natural law thinking. New claims about a king's "divine right" to rule as he saw fit gained ground, in a tendency that moved still further under the so-called "absolute monarchs" in France and elsewhere during the 17th century. Louis XIV's famous boast that "the state is myself" hardly reflected natural law humility. Natural law notions did not die—indeed, they would revive in the very same 17th century. But they were on hold for 200 to 300 years, which means in turn that a jump from Aquinas to human rights would be decidedly premature.

For it was only in the 17th century, in various parts of Europe but particularly England and the Netherlands, that natural law thinking fully revived, blending classical and Christian contributions but pushing as well into newer territory, particularly concerning the relationship between individuals and the state. The Dutch lawyer Hugo Grotius, for example, early in the 17th century, returned to the claim that a universal natural law reflected human reason and was common to all peoples, anywhere in the world. Customary law in any actual country must be constrained by natural law principles, beginning with a right to self-preservation which any individual possessed. Grotius re-echoed earlier thinking, in arguing that "anything is unjust, which is repugnant to the nature of society, established among rational creatures." But he went further, expounding at length on the notion of rights, seeing rights as part of the justice defined by the laws of nature. Grotius talked about different kinds of rights— to property, or to authority over others (like parents over children, or masters over servants), but he was interested in the rights people had among equals and could come up with strikingly modern-sounding phrases like "a state is a perfect body of free men, united together in order to enjoy common rights and advantages" and to argue that natural-law definitions of this sort applied in principle to everyone, everywhere even though in fact actual laws varied greatly.

Grotius even talked about protections people should enjoy during wars. Many earlier thinkers, in places like classical China, had urged restraint during combat, for example in treating prisoners decently, but mainly as a matter of sensible tactics, not rights. Grotius however talked about rights that must not be subject to violations by mere force, and about limits that must be observed to prevent needless slaughter. He specifically attacked practices like wartime rape, where both the injury to the victim and the "unrestrained lust" of the act required attention; "consequently" rape should "not go unpunished in war any more than in peace." In these areas, Grotius was advancing claims that formal human rights efforts would not pick up again until the later 19th century.

To be sure, 17th-century thinkers engaged in active controversy over the proper dimensions of natural law or whether indeed the argument applied at all, compared for example to the divine right of kings or the belief, held by Thomas Hobbes, that human beings are naturally unrestrained, warring for personal survival, and that any government that kept them in line was justified in whatever it needed to do to keep order. In this exchange, a few thinkers pressed further on natural law lines: Richard Cumberland, for example, taking exception to Hobbes, urged that "the pursuit of our own Happiness" leads directly to desiring the wellbeing of our fellow humans, for happiness consists in "the most extensive Benevolence." Here was another seed, along with the use of natural rights as a hedge against unjust rule that would more fully flower in the 18th century, where a new kind of humanitarianism linked directly with more straightforward definitions of human rights. And then, at the end of the 17th century, John Locke pushed further still, seeing rulers as obligated to observe natural law and so protect "life, liberty and property" and arguing that, if they failed, people could justifiably overthrow the existing state and create a new one. Natural law thinking, leading toward a clearer corresponding sense of natural rights, was now heading clearly into a human rights domain. But it's vital to remember that all of this was part of an active debate, with no clear predominance until the 18th century. There were opponents aplenty, eager to justify the actions of any ruler regardless of natural law, and there were even interesting skeptics, like Pierre Charron in 1601, who quite simply observed that, whereas natural law assumed some universal respect based in human reason:

> instead there is nothing in the world that is not subject to contradiction and dispute, nothing that is not rejected (by many nations), nothing that is strange and (in the opinion of many) unnatural that is not approved in many countries, and authorized by their customs.

Natural rights ideas were gaining ground in the most prominent political thinking of the 17th century, but it was still an uphill climb in an age still dominated, in fact, by limitless royal claims and strong doses of religious intolerance.

Most important: it was only at the end of the 17th century that what had been vigorous but largely abstract thinking about natural rights translated into some measurable innovations in actual policy—beginning with the so-called Glorious Revolution in England in 1688–1689. But this translation, along with the further delineation of natural rights implications by John Locke, takes us effectively, if not quite chronologically, into the 18th century and into what, at least for human rights history, more clearly becomes modern times.

The premodern legacy

Evaluations of the long stretch of premodern world history—that is, world history before the emergence of explicit human rights thinking—is obviously complicated to the extent that any history of something that doesn't fully exist is always challenging. Is it reasonable, for example, to talk about the causes of a lack of completely articulated thinking about human rights? Candidates would be: the pronounced tendency of most premodern agricultural societies to think in terms of major social and gender inequalities, rather than shared rights; the tendencies of most monarchs (and monarchy was the most characteristic form of government) to claim extensive powers at least in principle; the extent to which major religions prompted people to think more about supernatural goals than about definitions of this-worldly rights; and the tendency of most philosophies and religions to urge loyalty to the state at least in most circumstances. But obviously it's impossible to be very precise about the causes of an absence, so the claims should not be pressed too far.

Historical evaluations of premodern history, in terms of an ultimate interest in human rights, often opt for one of two extremes—neither, arguably, terribly useful in relevant judgments. On the one hand, some analysts delight in pointing out how no premodern agenda even began to measure up to current human rights subtleties, as if this condemns premodern history to harsh irrelevance. On the other, some are so eager to embrace all major traditions in a hopeful glow that they find human rights evidence everywhere, leaving it unclear whether differences mattered or whether any major further change would be needed to generate human rights campaigns.

The first approach, mindlessly presentist, can be illustrated through the litmus of gay rights. Gay rights have legitimately become one of the most sensitive contemporary measures of a broader human rights commitment, and we must discuss this further in due course. But it's a quite new addition, still not firmly established anywhere and hotly disputed in many cultures. In this context, to belabor premodern societies for not recognizing gays is simply not terribly revealing. It is true that they did not. Islam, for example, clearly took note of explicit protections for women, but offered nothing similar for different sexual orientations. A few societies did recognize certain gender identity groups, like the berdaches common in the Americas, but this is not the same thing as gay rights or individual rights at all. So if gay rights are one's measurement of a society's readiness for human rights, premodern history fails pretty much across the board. But it is not clear that this tells us very much, particularly if the list goes on to include the omission of other contemporary categories like children (infanticide protection aside).

It is also worth noting that, while premodern societies did not single gays out for specific legal protection, many were fairly tolerant of homosexual behaviors in fact. Christianity was not in the main, but Islam was, and so were several East Asian societies.

And this leads in a way to the second extreme: the temptation to find friendliness to human rights in all the major regional historical traditions. Our brief look at systems like Hinduism or Confucianism shows clearly that all traditions developed some definition of justice and all sought some recognition of human dignity, though sometimes amid extensive differentiations according to one's place in the social hierarchy. All complex societies had systems of courts of law, with some protections in principle for those accused of crime. What this means in turn is that all major traditions offered at least in theory some features that are still part of any human rights program and that all major traditions may prove compatible with human rights standards, at least after some adjustment. It is certainly possible to find elements that can be blended with human rights criteria in either Confucianism or Buddhism. But the operative term here is "blended": they were not human rights cultures in and of themselves; they have to be modified or added to. And this means that too much generosity in finding seeds of human rights everywhere probably obscures the historical record.

The challenge here is a balance between recognizing that many traditional societies were not only quite successful but even tolerant in many ways—while seeing some of the differences that remained from any clear human rights commitment. Confucianism is clearly responsible, over the centuries, for much of the basic durability of Chinese government forms and political principles. Its emphasis on mutuality and protection for the masses could, at best, keep governments and upper classes under some restraint, and as we have seen the principles could be invoked in protest when conditions deteriorated too badly. But individuals were not singled out for human rights defenses. Community interests predominated, and individuals helped themselves mainly by appealing to community protection—not by invoking an individual rights language that in any case was not available. There is a difference between success and flexibility, which many premodern societies had, and a modern level of devotion to human rights. Very few traditional societies had firm protections in place for what we would call rights, despite the influence of cultural principles in their legal codes; there was great dependence on the personal inclinations and ethics of a ruling group, for example, in the treatment of political prisoners. This whimsical element has hardly disappeared in contemporary societies, but it is arguably less prominent in many cases given the greater specificities that human rights principles introduce.

It is also true that many traditional societies did not offer some of the threats to human rights that modern societies do. This is a point too often neglected, but it helps explain why traditional societies could function without too much grinding injustice even without a human rights agenda. In the days before large police forces and sophisticated communications technology, the reach of even the strongest governments was limited. Rulers could certainly act arbitrarily even so—against people suspected of active disloyalty, for example—but the vast majority of ordinary people were not normally affected. We have seen also that many traditional governments did not too vigorously seek to enforce religious uniformity. Here, too, there were exceptions, but minority religions flourished in many places even though no society enshrined formal protections for freedom of conscience. We will see in the next chapter that the surge of interest in human rights, while it had many sources, was in part a response to new problems that had not been characteristic of premodern world history.

Another complication to any effort to equate the various traditional political cultures with current definitions of human rights is the frequent gap between professions of principle and actuality. This is a problem that will persist in our evaluations of contemporary human rights: many societies, even some of the original homes to human rights campaigns, do not fully live up to their professions or even dilute their responses through competing ideas.

The complication could be front and center, however, in premodern societies. We have seen, for example, that the elaborate discussions of natural law in the

West, in the 13th to 15th centuries, did not prevent a strong contrary tide with the rise of Renaissance states and then the so-called absolute monarchies. Natural law thinking was not irrelevant, but it often remained more theoretical than practical and it certainly did not prevent rival systems from gaining ascendancy. Similar examples dot other societies. Greek and Roman natural law interests did not inhibit frequent tyrannies or the effort to make state and emperor predominant in the later Roman Empire. Confucianism in China was quickly rivaled by the competing system of Legalism, which tended to argue that powerful states must run roughshod over many subjects, whose interests were selfish by nature, for the sake of establishing and maintaining political order. Legalists and Confucianists agreed, to be sure, on the primacy of a stable, strong state, but Legalists were unconcerned with Confucian interests in mutuality and respect for human dignity. The competition between the two political approaches not only weakened Confucianism at key points, but also gave the Chinese state, in practice, the chance to combine the two impulses, emphasizing Confucian restraints when possible but ready with a more forceful Legalist undercurrent when popular loyalty wavered. On another front: many Islamic leaders sincerely proclaimed the importance of free religious choice, and in fact it was much rarer for Islam to attempt to impose itself by force than was the case for Christianity in Europe. But Islam commonly combined some tolerance for religious minorities, like Christians and Jews in the Middle East, with a clear principle of legal inequality, requiring the communities to pay much higher taxes in return for their existence. Religious freedom technically persisted, but not in the form any human rights advocate would accept.

But this returns to the main point. Human rights advocacy was prepared by many developments in premodern world history, but it was not really present in that history. Major cultural systems looked to other mechanisms to provide suitable protections, often amid recognized inequalities, and there were often countervailing forces,—like Chinese Legalism or the idea of divine right monarchy—that widened the gap from any human rights agenda. Some of the most striking overlap between premodern developments and later human rights efforts, as with natural law, often had more theoretical than practical implications, resting more in the sphere of intellectual history than actual political arrangements, despite some spillover into operating principles in Roman or English law.

It was also true, and important, that key societies generated different emphases in their political culture. Islam and Christianity, for example, as religions of the book, both influenced by Greek and Roman political thinking, generated more interest in legal principles than did Buddhism. This was relevant at the time—for example, in Islamic assurance of certain legal protections for women, as opposed to Buddhism's more holistic approach. It could also be relevant to human rights reactions later on. The strong Chinese interest in political order, and on social relationships that would support this order, shines through clearly. Christianity offered different implications for ultimate human rights agendas depending on whether it became closely associated with the state, and state supervision, as in the Eastern Orthodox tradition, or maintained a greater separation between religion and the state, at least in principle, as was true in Western Europe. Societies with slaves—recognizing that slavery in traditional societies was quite varied and not always severely repressive—obviously offered social organizations different from other settings. Extensive serfdom, as in Western Europe, also had implications for human rights; while serfs were technically protected, for example, in their share of property, they also had special legal liabilities. Here, as with slavery, some changes would be absolutely essential to convert from customary hierarchies to frameworks open to a human rights approach. The variations among premodern political and social systems set up differing challenges in the dimensions of change that a human rights agenda would suggest, and prepared varying reactions to particular portions of any new agenda as well. As a global movement, contemporary human rights inevitably mirror the complexities of global/regional interactions, and established traditions play a key role in this process.

Finally, of course, there is the question of change over time before the 18th century and the advent of a definable commitment to human rights directly. We have already seen that, during most of the long stretches of premodern history, from the organization of complex agricultural societies and the early law codes onward, it would be hard to identify any clear transformations relevant to human rights. Changes occurred, for example, with the advent of Confucianism and then Legalism in China, but in no particularly consistent overall trajectory. After 600 CE, with the spread of world religions (including the emergence of Islam), some shift might possibly be identified. A somewhat more general commitment to the idea that human beings share some fundamental spiritual equality did potentially alter outlook, at least in principle, though new tensions among religions and the continued acceptance of inequality in this world modified the implications of change. Specific shifts, like the religiously inspired decline of infanticide (outside of China) and the implications of the more uniform effort to protect newborns, pointed in the same direction. But, even with developments like the identification of new (if still unequal) legal claims for women in Islam, it remains hard to point to an overall trajectory. For example, during precisely this same period, after 600, foot-binding requirements began to apply to many Chinese women, with no real right to dissent to this socially imposed standard. There was no global trend relevant to protections for women.

At most, this mixed premodern picture might have begun to clarify a bit further when Islamic and Christian scholars began to combine religious interests in a common spiritual humanity with renewed attention to natural law. Here was a combination that could generate new thinking about how to evaluate injustice emanating from the state and to extend an understanding of what protections human beings should be able to expect in a just society. The gains remained more a matter of philosophical speculation than practical reform. By the 17th century in Western Europe, however, many leading political theorists were shifting the terms of debate, pushing natural law, and natural rights, beyond previous levels. Premodern societies had already generated law codes and a variety of efforts to assure mutual relationships within a state. These foundations were now on the verge of more substantial redefinition, when the accelerating explorations of natural law combined with other key developments in early modern Europe. The first phase of a real human rights era in world history, with its drawbacks as well as its obvious advantages, was about to emerge.

Further reading

For background on pre-18th-century religious and philosophical ideas that provided precedent for human rights arguments, see Richard Bauman, *Human Rights in Ancient Rome* (New York, NY: Taylor & Francis, 2000); Brian Tierney, *The Idea of Natural Rights: Studies on Natural Rights, Natural Law, and Church Law, 1150–1625* (Grand Rapids, MI: Wm. B. Eerdmans Publishing/Emory University Press, 2001); Richard Tuck, *Natural Rights Theories: Their Origin and Development* (Cambridge, UK: Cambridge University Press, 1998); Francis Oakley, *Natural Law, Laws of Nature, Natural Rights: Continuity and Discontinuity in the History of Ideas* (New York, NY: Continuum, 2005); Micheline Ishay, *The History of Human Rights: From Ancient Times to the Globalization Era* (Berkeley, CA: University of California Press, 2004); and John M. Peek, "Buddhism, Human Rights, and the Japanese State," *Human Rights Quarterly*, 17(3) (August, 1995), pp. 527–540. Other good texts and readers include: Micheline Ishay (ed.), *The Human Rights Reader: Major Political Essays, Speeches, and Documents from Ancient Times to the Present* (New York, NY: Taylor & Francis, 2007); Jon E. Lewis ed., *A Documentary History of Human Rights* (New York, NY: Carroll & Graf Publishers, 2003); Patrick Hayden, *The Philosophy of Human Rights* (St. Paul, MN: Paragon House, 2001); Paul Gordon Lauren, *The Evolution of International Human Rights: Visions Seen* (Philadelphia, PA: University of Pennsylvania Press, 2003). See also Berdal Aral, "The Idea of Human Rights as Perceived in the Ottoman Empire," *Human Rights Quarterly*, 26(2) (May, 2004), pp. 454–482.

For information on religious human rights, see John Witte, Jr. and John D. van der Vyver (eds.), *Religious Human Rights in Global Perspective: Religious Perspectives* (The Hague, Netherlands: Kluwer Law International, 1996); Liam Gearon (ed.), *Human Rights and Religion* (Brighton, UK: Sussex Academic Press, 2002); Arvind Sharma, *Hinduism and Human Rights: A Conceptual Approach* (New York, NY: Oxford University Press, 2003); Damien V. Keown, Charles Prebish, and Wayne Husted (eds.), *Buddhism and Human Rights* (Surrey, UK: Curzon, 1998); and Carmen Meinhert and Hans-Bernd Zollner (eds.), *Buddhist Approaches to Human Rights: Dissonances and Resonances* (Bielefeld, Germany: Transcript, 2010). Also see Michael J. Broyde and John Witte, Jr. (eds.), *Human Rights in Judaism: Cultural, Religious, and Political Perspectives* (Northvale, NJ: Jason Aronson, 1998); and John Witte, Jr. and Frank S. Alexander (eds.), *Christianity and Human Rights: An Introduction* (New York, NY: Cambridge University Press, 2010).

3 The new push for human rights

This chapter deals with the origins of explicit attention to human rights issues, as part of cultural and political changes in the West during the 18th century. The goal is to establish what changed—always in relationship to the previous patterns discussed in Chapter 2—and also to explore the causes of change. This was a vital moment in human rights history, and we need to locate the reasons as well as the content. Various new philosophical commitments emerged, but also new declarations and political efforts and, as a first global extension of the movement, an unprecedented surge of outrage against the enslavement of other human beings.

Two preliminaries are essential. The first is easy enough. Many historical comments on human rights, particularly by non-historians, locate the origins of the whole movement in the post-World War II decades. It is certainly true that a vast expansion of human rights efforts accompanied the end of the war—resulting in a vital new sub-period in the longer history of the whole endeavor. And we will deal with this in due course, allowing readers to make their own judgments about the timing of the most crucial innovations in this field. But the 18th-century origins of modern human rights seem pretty clear, so we will not be lingering on this issue too lovingly. Again, there will be ample chance to weigh subsequent developments in later chapters.

The only real complication was the fact that people in the century in which modern human rights ideas were born did not use the term "human rights"—this did come into vogue only from the 1940s onward. And the terminological distinction has some significance, as we will see. But the basic ideas were there, even without the contemporary words, so there is no reason to register a huge distraction. What the 18th century meant by "rights of man"—the huge issue of gender aside—overlaps so fully with human rights ideas that to quibble about terminology is simply distracting.

The second preliminary concerns locating the innovations in Western Europe and the Americas. There is no question, first of all, that some discussions of human rights history ridiculously, indeed offensively, exaggerate the virtues of the West. A sample: While there are things wrong in the West, "the modern West is unique because it alone in the history of the world has the means—economic, political and moral—to set right wrongs." This is hugely inflated and simply untrue, for many societies and many traditions offer reformist potential. It should be taken as a given that locating initial human rights work in the West in no sense so grossly misstates the relationship between the West and the rest of the world.

Even with this, there are issues, particularly with the tenor of the world history field as it has gained importance in teaching and research alike. Most world historians, over the past several decades, have spent a great deal of time trying to take a genuine global view of their subject, as against the overemphasis on Europe and European initiatives that characterized so much historical work in the first half of the 20th century. Collectively they make it clear that the West was not nearly as important as some other societies, in the long period between the fall of Rome and the early modern centuries. Even in the 18th century, where a few human rights historians have associated Western origins with the rising world importance of the West more generally, we now know that many other societies, particularly in Asia, retained great strength and independent validity; the "rise of the West" theme must not be overdone even as new human rights arguments took shape. Finally, world historians have contributed to rebalancing the West-in-the-world story by correctly noting the many dubious initiatives associated with the West, beginning with the Atlantic slave trade and continuing through an unusual propensity for war or the injustices associated with imperialism. In this context, identifying the first wave of human rights with the West may seem provocative, sure to draw attack.

In response, several points. First, locating initial human rights initiatives with the West feeds some of the key debates we have already noted, and to which we will return. Western origins for part of the human rights agenda are precisely what make some human rights demands seem partially foreign to countries like China or Russia—they do come, at least at first, from another political culture. Western origins also require careful consideration against the various premodern cultural traditions discussed in the previous chapter: how much was really new, with the initiative now at first in Western hands, and what kinds of factors—unflattering as well as flattering—explain new Western positions?

Then: there is no need to simplify the relationship between the West and new human rights efforts. By no means was the West united behind the efforts. Many things that Western leaders did, and still do, blatantly contradicted human rights, in the West itself and certainly in the world at large. We will deal explicitly with some of these vital tensions in subsequent chapters. One of the reasons human rights sometimes face tough going is not only because they emanated from the West but also because the West so often fails to live up to its own prescriptions. Also: locating initial human rights in the West does not mean that the West somehow gains moral superiority over other societies (though some advocates have clearly believed this). We need more assessment of the whole movement, and its complex relationship with other societies over time, before even implying this kind of conclusion. Further: origins in the West do not mean that the West retained monopoly over the effort or its definition. We're dealing here only with a first step in a new aspect of world history, not its permanent characteristics. Human rights advocacy has moved well beyond purely Western origins, with important input and redefinition from ardent groups in virtually every part of the world.

Finally: the idea of locating the initiation of an important innovation in world history in one particular society, because of its particular circumstances, is hardly novel. World historians delight in pointing out that, for many centuries, China led the world in manufacturing technology, for reasons peculiar to Chinese strengths and needs, with the rest of the world gradually copying but long at a disadvantage. It is hardly a jolt to note that India deserves disproportionate attention as a source of peace initiatives, from the emperor Ashoka to Gandhi—recurrent leadership here relates to some specific features of Indian culture and politics. The Middle East was long the initiator of new types of commercial practices and outreach. And so the list goes. Particular societies are the source of innovations that ultimately have wider impact, and over time they often lose control of a process that becomes more genuinely global. This is arguably the case with human rights: for specific reasons we must explore, the movement began in one place, and it is no denigration of other parts of the world to note this fact. The ultimate question is what the rest of the world chooses to do with the initiative—in other words, what's the history after the 18th century?

Ultimately, of course, it's a question of fact. Can we measurably define what relevant new developments occurred in the West? We must in the process prove, without belaboring the points, that the developments were new—we've noted already a real debate here—and that they were at first Western, and what the reasons for this linkage were. It's time to turn to the data.

Symptoms of change

Between the very end of the 17th century and 1800, several related changes occurred that add up to the dawn of the human rights era, first in the West and ultimately more widely. Some of the key changes had been anticipated by individual thinkers or policies and laws in other societies earlier—by no means was everything brand new. But the accumulation of changes, the extension of human rights thinking into new areas, and the sheer pace of human rights developments, had no precedent in world history previously.

First, from John Locke onward a procession of thinkers adopted rights discussions as a central part of their political philosophy. Human rights arguments served as a vital part of the 18th-century Enlightenment, with contributions from scholars and publicists in Britain, the Low Countries, France, Italy, Germany, and ultimately beyond. Never before had such successive efforts occurred in such a relatively short span of time. Many of the new statements, further, were not confined to the realm of formal philosophy: many

Enlightenment figures were also active publicists, urging their audience to join in accepting human rights arguments and actively attacking sources of abuse, particularly in the monarchies and churches of the day.

Second, core rights arguments themselves began to move into new areas, including but going beyond more familiar territories like rights to life or property. Freedom of religion now became a central platform. Slavery—though not a new topic—now came in for explicit condemnation as a violation of rights, and not just a source of religious anxiety. Freedom of the press and rights to dissent against government moved front and center. Torture and excessive punishment became another human rights staple, as discussions expanded. A host of topics came up for review as the conception of basic human rights firmed up.

Third, at the intellectual level but also among some of the audiences for the new theories, some broader innovations began to emerge. Greater precision about human rights linked to a growing sense of individualism in Western culture. A new sense of humanitarianism also emerged, an interest in applying some minimal standards of justice to the whole of humankind.

Fourth, human rights arguments began to motivate active campaigns against injustice. The emerging anti-slavery movement was in a real sense the first globally relevant human rights effort, and while further developments would occur after 1800 the 18th century itself was clearly the seedbed.

Fifth, human rights platforms moved directly into political life. There were hints of this new connection in the Glorious Revolution in Britain, in 1688–1689, but they became much clearer in the wave of revolutions on both sides of the Atlantic from the 1770s onward. Attention to human rights now justified revolutions directly, and served as targets for many of the first moves by revolutionaries once in power.

All of these related developments had further consequences. They created new levels of resistance: a dividing line between liberals and conservatives, by 1800, formed around positions toward human rights. They brought still further philosophical statements, notably in the emergence of a rights-based feminist argument by the final decades of the 18th century. And—though this is the subject of the following chapters—they clearly created potential for wider global application and agitation. Human rights were on the move.

This chapter focuses on the five linked changes, and then the late 18th/early 19th century aftermath within the West itself. We begin with the new ideas, from Locke onward, with an emphasis on what kinds of basic thinking were involved in this new embrace of human rights. We move next to the new areas, like religious freedom, to which rights arguments began to apply, and then to the larger propositions about a whole new mentality. The vital question of causation comes next. What lay behind the new thinking and the wider openness to human rights arguments? Why the 18th century, and why the West? We then turn to the further initial ramifications of the human rights movement, and particularly the new political and social movements based on what was clearly becoming a significant moral force.

Extending human rights arguments

The bridge between earlier natural rights discussions and a new precision about individual rights took shape at the end of the 17th century. John Locke published *Two Treatises* on government, anonymously, in 1689. The first volume of the book attacked the idea of some divine authority for royal power; the second, more positively, laid out a theory of society based on natural rights and an implicit contract between the government and the governed. The context for this work rested on English politics during the previous two decades. Reigning monarchs, with their Stuart house restored after the earlier English Civil Wars, claimed considerable authority and also seemed to veer toward Catholicism in a country that was now largely Protestant. Locke was in a group that hoped to prevent the second of the Stuart kings, James II, from taking power in the first place, and government responded by forcing Locke into exile. In 1688, an essentially peaceful "revolution" forced James from power and replaced him with a new monarch, William, and his Stuart wife Mary, and a clearer recognition of the rights of Parliament to a share in governing authority. Locke's work—still anonymous, because of the volatile political situation—was designed to provide theoretical legitimacy to the new regime, basically on grounds that legitimate governments must have the consent of the governed, rather than ruling arbitrarily.

While Locke's political philosophy most clearly pointed to the issue of rights, he also worked, more generally, on questions of human knowledge. Firmly opposed to beliefs in original sin, Locke argued that people were basically rational and capable of acquiring new knowledge through education and the experience of their senses. This optimism about human potential, and the implications about individual capacity, had a bearing on human rights thinking as well.

But it was Locke's *Second Treatise* that really launched the new round of discussions about human society that would extend through the 18th-century Enlightenment. Locke posited an initial state of nature, before government was created, in which people were perfectly free and also equal:

> in which all power and jurisdiction are reciprocal and no one has more than another. It is evident that all human beings—as creatures belonging to the same species and rank and born indiscriminately with all the same natural advantages and faculties—are equal amongst themselves.

Government became necessary only because disputes among free people could not easily be resolved. But government operates legitimately only on popular consent, which in turn prevails only when the same government does not infringe on freedoms arbitrarily. No one can legitimately surrender rights to life, liberty, and property, and people have not only a right but an obligation to revolt against any tyrannical governmental authority.

Locke's references to liberty were at once strong and vague. People in the state of nature have "perfect liberty," but they give up some of this in order to form a state. The state, however, is itself intended to provide better protection for the individual, "his liberty, and his property." Rights, for Locke, begin with an absolute right to self-preservation, which no one can surrender. And Locke devoted great attention to the right of property, which he broadly understood as control over the fruits of one's labor. There is no long list of rights beyond this. Locke's contributions lay elsewhere. First, his vision of society was a collection of individuals, and he implied that individuals also had to evaluate any government to see if it was living up to its side of the bargain. "Freedom of men under government is to have a standing rule to live by, common to everyone of that society." Even law, properly construed, should not be seen primarily in terms of restraint: "the end of Law is not to abolish or restrain, but to preserve and enlarge Freedom." The right of revolution obviously follows from this same approach: it is not only possible but essential to be able to define abuses of power and to act on this definition. And, while a social agreement may introduce some inequality, Locke's emphasis on the basic commonality of all men was another key element in his philosophical structure.

Locke's approach also could be read as a refutation of slavery, though the relationship between his statements of principle and any actual evaluation of slavery was complex. If, however, men were naturally free and even in society could "not be under the dominion of any will," then the legitimacy of slavery could not really be established. Here was another seed that, a half-century later, would begin to grow, with many references back to Lockean ideas. Finally, though in separate writings, Locke also defended the importance of religious tolerance, save for outright atheists.

Locke's main ideas, though linked to the new kind of monarchy that was emerging in England after the Glorious Revolution, did not have wide impact immediately. They were, however, revived and widely influential from the middle of the 18th century onward, when a variety of other thinkers, though rarely so systematic, begin to add to the philosophical underpinnings of human rights.

Thus the French philosopher Rousseau, writing in the 1760s, sharpened the language and some of the concepts relevant to defending freedoms against abuse, deliberately echoing Locke's ideas in key respects. "Man is born free," Rousseau proclaimed, "but everywhere he is in chains." Rousseau railed against any idea that states gained legitimacy in ruling by force: "force does not create rights, and ... we are obliged to obey only legitimate powers." Slavery was absolutely unjustified. A person had no right to alienate his own freedom, much less that of his children, who, like all people, were "born free." "Their liberty belongs to them" and even a father's legitimate authority does not extend so far over his children as to be "contrary to nature."

Rousseau did talk about a "general will" in society that might have great power, and historians have legitimately seen in this notion a precedent for the huge rights over individuals that revolutionary leaders have periodically claimed. But Rousseau also made it clear that society should not exercise any unnecessary authority over individuals. Liberty and equality were the great goals of any legitimate society and, while Rousseau did not spell out a precise list of rights, he urged the importance of limiting potential abuses by any state. And on basic equality he was unequivocal: in any just society, individuals equally pledge to observe basic obligations and therefore "all enjoy the same rights." "Equality of rights and the idea of justice which such equality creates originate ... in the very nature of man."

Locke and Rousseau both spun out rather elaborate intellectual concoctions, and it is easy to lose sight of what they added to the foundations of human rights; and, of course, their ideas were hardly identical in any event. Both, however, painted strong pictures of a humanity that, by nature, enjoyed extensive freedoms, from rights of self-preservation on up. States existed by human consent, at least implicitly, and they made sense only insofar as they made basic rights more secure; if they failed in this purpose, they became abusive and illegitimate. And while certain de facto inequalities among people might be tolerated, people were by nature and in principle equal. Huge distortions of equality and freedom, and particularly that constituted by slavery, were simply wrong and indefensible.

These were powerful positions. Further, they began to reach a wide audience that saw both motivation and guidance in these ideas. Lockean thinking was picked up by political leaders in colonial America, such as Thomas Jefferson. Versions of Rousseau's ideas spread among literate middle-class and artisanal sectors in France and, by word of mouth, potentially beyond. Through this, in turn, the concepts spilled over into practical, often literally revolutionary, politics.

Finally, the conversations continued to the end of the 18th century. In 1791–1792, as the French revolution proceeded, the Englishman Thomas Paine issued his pamphlet, "Rights of Man," which in turn translated and further popularized many of the basic Enlightenment ideas about human rights. By this point, conservative theorists, recognizing that the old divine right justifications for government didn't resonate any more, were turning to other appeals, about how the state needed continuity and tradition as against constant individual claims and demands for change. Paine reasserted the now-standard argument that governments could be legitimate only on the basis of recognizing and defending natural rights, which in turn applied to all people (or at least all men) in equal measure. Paine also made it clear—here reflecting virtually a century of recurrent systematic additions to political philosophy— that classical thinkers had simply not made an adequate case; their notions about natural law moved partway to the truth, but left a gap. Insisting on "the illuminating and divine principle of equal rights," Paine repeated Locke and Rousseau on the centrality of freedom in the state of nature and the obligation of government to protect this freedom to the greatest possible extent. And, while the ideas were new, the natural essence was not: "The equality of man, far from being a modern doctrine, is the oldest on record."

But the natural condition of man was only the beginning. People ultimately accepted governments, for their greater protection, but they had no intention of giving up their rights in the process. Natural rights become civil rights. And Paine listed some key components, going beyond some of his predecessors. First came "all the intellectual rights, or the rights of the mind," presumably involving freedoms of expression and religion. Then "those rights of acting as an individual for his own comfort and happiness," presumably including some assurance of property but ranging more broadly. Society merely protects, notably through laws and courts; it does not create separate value. The individual is the measure of society's adequacy, and governments must be judged on that basis.

Paine's work won wide attention and admiration (though ironically Paine himself encountered all sorts of troubles in his later life and died a poor man in upstate New York). American revolutionaries hailed an earlier work, called *Common Sense.* The "Rights of Man" won a substantial audience as well, including in revolutionary France, where Paine was for a time elected to the national legislature. The point was that, by the end of the 18th century, a great deal of human rights thinking had become common currency, at least among literate circles. And, while the ideas did generate criticism and counterattack, as we will see, there were lots of relatively ordinary people who assimilated the basic premises and preferred themselves to think and act as if they had a variety of rights. Both the range of the argument, and the dissemination, were new phenomena.

And, while the most sweeping philosophical discussions about rights trailed off, mainly because they became so widely accepted, important work continued the line of thinking and even pressed further. Immanuel Kant, in Germany, refined some of the natural rights arguments. Various liberal thinkers in Britain, headed ultimately by John Stuart Mill by the mid-19th century, extended the contention that people should have rights to do anything they pleased so long as they did not harm others. We will see that political philosophers in the 20th century have picked up the argument as well, now speaking explicitly in terms of universal human rights, yet also explicitly going back to older sources, like Locke or Rousseau, as part of the basis for their own contentions.

Areas of application

Along with the basic philosophical groundswell, a variety of writers in the later 17th and 18th century picked up particular causes around which they constructed elaborate, often passionate, definitions of individual rights. Their work often drew more attention than the general philosophies, and it was particularly important in developing a sense that traditional societies had generated abuses that cried out for correction. Three examples, each important in its own right, illustrate the wider pattern.

From the 17th century onward a growing number of people began to defend freedoms of speech and expression. To be sure, there had been scattered efforts earlier. Socrates, on trial in Athens in 399 BCE, eloquently defended his right "to speak his mind" rather than say what the government wanted him to.

The Caliph Umar first proclaimed freedom of speech in Islam in the 7th century. The Renaissance Christian writer Erasmus, in 1516, put the case simply: "In a free state, tongues too should be free." But systematic interest awaited the later 17th century. At this point a variety of British writers specifically attacked government policy requiring approval and a license, from the state, before anything could be published. The poet John Milton, who fell afoul of this system, specifically urged that "he who destroys a good book, kills reason itself." Various continental philosophers amplified wider arguments about the importance of freedom of expression and, by extension, of the press. John Locke, interestingly, was not actively in this camp, arguing that groups like atheists deserved no voice at all. But the wider campaign proceeded. The English Bill of Rights, in 1689, rather timidly defended freedom of speech—but just in Parliament; this was, however, itself an indication that the ball was in motion.

By the 18th century, freedom of speech was being discussed by thinkers all over the Western world, and it became a staple topic in the Enlightenment. The widely popular French philosopher Voltaire spoke out passionately for the right to speak and write as one pleased. It was long believed that he summed up his thinking with the famous phrase, "I disapprove of everything you say, but I will defend to the death your right to say it." It turns out that no one has been able to discover these actual words, but they are in fact consistent with Voltaire's thinking, and with his vigorous attacks on governments and churches that tried to punish people for their words. With time, furthermore, arguments about freedom of speech expanded. Always claiming the importance of the right to freedom of expression for individuals, advocates now also argued that the right was vital to society as well. Only through a free competition of ideas could the truth be known, and suppression of any speech, no matter how apparently outlandish or unpopular, actually diminished the social stock.

Small wonder that freedom of speech began to show up in real political life, and not just in argument. A Danish regent issued the first ever edict proclaiming complete freedom of speech, in 1770, though he later imposed a few restrictions. The French revolutionary *Declaration of Rights of Man and the Citizen*, in 1789, explicitly proclaimed freedom of speech as an inalienable right. Its Article 11 stated that "the free communication of ideas and opinions is one of the most precious of the rights of man. Every citizen may, accordingly, speak, write, and print with freedom, but shall be responsible for such abuses of this freedom as shall be defined by law." And the American Bill of Rights, two years later, blessed freedoms of speech and the press. By this point, the category had become a standard component in any practical list of basic human rights.

The idea of religious freedom, obviously linked to freedom of speech, developed strongly during the same period. This too was not a totally new notion, of course. We have seen advocacy of religious freedom, at least in principle, by various religious leaders. Many actual states granted religious freedom historically, some for long stretches of time. What happened in Western Europe in the 17th and 18th centuries was a more consistent effort to seek religious freedom in opposition to the arrangements that predominated at that time, and to associate the whole effort with human rights. Ultimately, this would also yield not only a wider currency to the idea that people should be free in conscience, but also more specific details that could protect people who sought to change religions or adopt no religion at all—going beyond what some societies, where religious toleration had indeed existed, had usually installed.

We have seen that John Locke urged tolerance as part of a just society, though he hedged his bets against outright atheists. Only an individual, Locke argued, can really decide what he believes: "all the life and power of true religion consist in the inward and full persuasion of the mind"; people must be "satisfied in their own mind," and no external force or government can make that happen.

By the 18th century, and with the Enlightenment, louder voices were raised. Voltaire was fierce on the subject, and bitterly opposed to attacks on non-believers by the Catholic Church. He cited all the woes of religious strife in the past, in which so many people had died in the name of one fanaticism or other. In one dramatic dictionary essay, on "Religion," he cited "the bones of the Christians slaughtered by each other for metaphysical disputes. They are divided into several heaps of course for several centuries each, [for] one heap would have mounted right to the sky." For him, this kind of evidence made it clear that full religious freedom was the only antidote to "barbarism and fanaticism." English philosophers like David Hume and Adam Smith mounted similar arguments. For Smith, religious freedom was a vital means of preventing social unrest, for competition among religions would reduce extremism. The "zeal of religious teachers can be dangerous and troublesome only when there is … but one sect tolerated in society." The competition assured by religious freedom, in contrast, would press each religious advocate "to learn candor and moderation." On another front a German dramatist and philosopher, Gotthold Lessing, penned a powerful drama, *Nathan the Wise*, pressing the folly of placing so much faith in one religion that other religions might be attacked: "let each believe his [religion] the true one," but try to demonstrate the value of the beliefs by good works and benevolence, not through force. By this point, clearly, two lines of reasoning had emerged, mutually compatible: religious freedom was a right of the individual, for only through it would conscience be satisfied; and it was also a social good, in protecting societies against the abuses which intolerance so often fostered. As with speech and press, with which religious freedom was closely linked, advocacy of this right became a standard part of the whole agenda. Like these other freedoms, it gained new levels of political expression with the revolutionary constitutions of the late 18th century.

The third extension of specific human rights thinking during the 18th century takes us into a different territory, concerning torture and punishment. Individuals in premodern societies occasionally worried about the appropriateness of punishments, as we have seen—this was a particularly recurrent concern in India, but it could emerge in other settings. And surely actual rulers varied widely, by circumstance and personality, in the types of punishments they were comfortable with. But we have also seen that premodern societies imposed harsh physical punishments rather widely, and that torture was extensively utilized in dealing with various types of prisoners and captives. Despite frequent discussions about the importance of preserving life as part of legal codes or natural law arguments, the whole issue had not, previously, centered any particular discussion along lines of human rights.

This now changed, again beginning in the 17th century, but more clearly still during the Enlightenment. The English philosopher Thomas Hobbes, in 1652, devoted great attention to society's obligation to preserve human life—otherwise, individuals had no reason to turn sovereignty over to a formal government. Not generally interested in rights arguments, Hobbes in this area—asserting the need for assurances for a right to life—was breaking new ground. Other 17th-century writers began to link excessive punishments with other aspects of tyranny.

But it was Italian thinker and law graduate Cesare Beccaria who really fleshed out this new angle on human rights, in his *Treatise on Crimes and Punishments*, published in 1766. Beccaria offered a first ever discussion of criminal justice and the need for fundamental reforms in penology, based on the general idea that human reason should be applied to this highly traditional area and on some direct evocation of wider natural rights thinking about why people established states in the first place. Beccaria systematically condemned the death penalty, on grounds, first, that the state does not have the right to take lives—the individual right to self-preservation has precedence: "who has ever willingly given up to others the authority to kill him?"—and second, because capital punishment serves no useful purpose. Every member of society deserves assurance that social punishments are proportionate to the crime committed—an assurance which also should prevent torture. Any punishment beyond the necessary "is no longer justice, but an abuse." Again, the issue was twofold. First, Beccaria argued, it was easy for desperate criminals to ignore the death penalty, for they might profit from their crime and then suffer only a day of pain; it made far more sense to look to prisons for real deterrent value. But second, and closer to the human rights angle, "the death penalty is not useful because of the example of savagery it gives to man." No one and no institution should have the power of life or death over other human beings.

Arguments against torture, though less widely known in the history books, were actually at least as interesting as those about the death penalty. People have the right to society's protection until they are convicted of crime. But if torture is used to extort confessions, that is, before conviction, then it is simply a violation of rights. Further, Beccaria added the commonsense addendum: torture is a bad way to get at truth, because strong people may withstand it even if they are guilty, whereas the weak but innocent will say anything to have the pain stopped. Torture is nothing more than a useless cruelty and it should be abandoned altogether.

As with the campaigns for freedom of the press or religious freedom, the passion and specificity Enlightenment thinkers provided had quick results. Beccaria's book went through many editions almost immediately, not only in Italy but well beyond in translation. One Italian ruler soon abolished the death penalty, though he was more persuaded by the argument that it was useless in preventing crime than that it violated rights. Even more widely, the importance of revisiting traditional punishments, to scale back the number of crimes open to the death penalty and to limit torture, became part of the agenda of many societies from the late 18th century onward. Not surprisingly, it remains a key element in human rights efforts, now on a global basis, even today.

The emergence of vigorous programs to define particular rights, within a larger human rights agenda, was an important development, raising new issues but also mobilizing new audiences around the need to correct or prevent various kinds of abuse. It was an important step in the emergence of the modern human rights effort more generally. Additional and quite specific targets might direct energies far more clearly than rather traditional invocations of social obligations to protect life and property could do, more also than the important but rather general discussions of human freedoms in a state of nature.

The new programs raised their own complications, of course. They elicited new opposition. For over a century Catholic leadership would rail against modern ideas of religious freedom. Concern for social order might generate attacks on the new move to prevent torture and moderate punishment. In many ways and in many places, debate continues to this day. And even where basic rights were granted, there were all sorts of detailed issues that proved difficult to work out. Freedom of speech might be fine, but when did it impinge on the rights of others? When did a society have a right to intervene to protect security and decorum? Does freedom of speech apply to children, or are the countervailing adults' rights in this category? Is imprisonment, which Beccaria urged as a far more effective alternative to physical punishment, really preferable from the standpoint either of human dignity or crime prevention? What constituted torture, or a cruel punishment? Successive debates in the United States about how to kill convicted murderers while avoiding pain make it clear that it's hard to know how to implement this aspect of human rights even when the principle is accepted.

Developments during the 18th century only opened the door to these kinds of debates, and obviously they continue in full force in many places and many ways. The point is that, initially in Western societies, the changes in thinking began to shift many people from wondering whether there was a right at all—for example, in freedom of the press—to assuming that the right was there and arguing only over its precise dimensions. This was where change was quite real, in redefining this aspect of the political agenda.

The same developments, finally, suggested some wider shifts in popular outlook that various historians have tried to define and that were closely linked to the conversion to a more systematic human rights approach. The larger cultural changes are not easy to pinpoint, and they surely did not apply to everyone in the West. But they did affect a substantial and growing audience, and they merit attention in their own right, beneath the surface of the particular arguments of philosophers and the attempt to define more specific rights categories.

Changes in the broader culture?

Several historians have suggested that, around the Enlightenment and probably connected to it, some broad shifts were taking place in Western popular culture. We know, for example, that science was gaining a new hold, pushing back previous beliefs in magic. This was a fascinating change, but not clearly related to the emergence of human rights thinking (though we will suggest an indirect link later on). Similarly, the 18th century saw the advent of new levels of consumerism and attachments to acquisition, another vital cultural shift that may also be linked to new levels of romantic expectation. Again, the result is really important but probably not part of the human rights domain (save possibly as a distraction from such serious concerns).

Other cultural changes are more relevant, and are worth brief exploration as part of describing the wider context in which attention to human rights could not only emerge but sustain itself, and in helping to explain why, in the 18th century itself, some of the new arguments so quickly generated political changes and new movements for reform. Intellectuals, like the Enlightenment philosophers, helped spell out new human rights arguments, but they were part of a wider set of cultural shifts that motivated them (whether they were aware of this or not) and their wider reception alike.

The late 17th and early 18th centuries were a time of great changes in the ways many Europeans and North Americans thought—what historians have often termed a real transformation in *mentalities*. Of course, not everyone changed. Even many who altered their outlook retained large chunks of older beliefs. But there were important alterations overall, some of which even showed up in daily behaviors like how children were named or what people did when they wanted to find an item they had lost. It is not far-fetched to argue that new approaches to human rights, including the openness of a wider public to ideas spun out by philosophers and publicists, formed part of this shift. As many people thought of themselves more as individuals, or as they began to resonate in new ways to issues involving a larger humanity, they became more prepared to accept elements of a human rights approach. These new trends in popular culture help explain the human rights moves; they also invite a more specific look at what factors were causing the changes in turn. Outside the orbit of purely intellectual history, what was preparing people to innovate in the ways they thought about defining and defending individual rights?

Three developments warrant attention, though each is complex and not easy to pin down. First, by the 18th century, it does seem likely that more people in the Western world were beginning to think of themselves as individuals more than primarily as members of family or community. Obviously, individualism was not brand new at this point. People in many different societies, earlier in history, might try to make themselves stand out as individuals, for whatever combination of psychological and social reasons. Powerful kings, to take an obvious example, worked to make identifiable self-glorifying monuments to themselves. Closer to the 18th-century West, some Renaissance intellectuals, in Italy and elsewhere, had trumpeted what some historians have seen as a new valuation of individual identity and achievement. Thus the Italian writer Petrarch wrote lavishly of his own accomplishments when he climbed a mountain in France, and he and others hailed their individual ability to free themselves from some of the conventional values and styles of the past.

But individualism probably developed further, and reached more widely, by the 18th century, in ways that go beneath the level of vainglorious rulers or Renaissance intellectuals. In a rapidly changing economy, more individual entrepreneurs sought to free themselves from group structures like the guilds, which had long and successfully bent individual activity to more collective norms. On another front: parents began looking for more individualistic names for their children, instead of relying on the names of older relatives or biblical characters. It was revealing that an old practice, reusing the name of a child who had died, now went out of fashion: each child was unique, and a family should not lump individual children together by recycling a name.

Signs of new individualism are not hard to find. Economists began writing about the primacy of individual self-interest as the chief motor for material progress. Other writers, like Rousseau, talked of the importance of cultivating the individual child through new forms of education. The new consumerism had a strong individualistic element, for example, in the quest for more expressive clothing styles. And obviously a strong individualistic element stood out in the new interest in human rights, which sought to protect an individual's thought and expression, for example, from repression by society or the state.

A second current that may have been working its way into Western popular culture was a new estimation of pain. There is an obvious chicken-and-egg issue here. Did the new thinking about torture and physical punishment help cause a wider reassessment of pain, or did some of this reassessment precede the arguments of Beccaria and other reformers? There is some evidence, for example, that, distant from the work of the philosophers, ordinary people were beginning to reevaluate the pain of women in childbirth, to take one example—to extend more sympathy. The spread of popular novels—and the 18th century was effectively the birthplace of the novel in the Western world—gave readers new opportunities to think about other people's pain and suffering (whether physical and emotional), which could lead to new interests at the human rights level. In some circles, a reduction in traditional Christian religious beliefs may have encouraged reconsideration of any idea that pain was somehow meted out by God in response to human sinfulness or that an afterlife should be conceived (for unredeemed sinners) in terms of eternal pains in hell. All of this would go further in the 19th century, when far wider arguments would be devoted to the subject of pain and when practical measures, like the introduction of anesthesia in 1846, allowed new kinds of response; but the process may have begun a bit earlier.

But it's the third innovation in popular culture that most obviously worked in favor of a new openness to human rights concerns: what one historian called a revolution in humanitarian sensibility. People began to feel real emotional distress in learning about certain kinds of suffering of other human beings—simply because of a common humanity, not because of shared religion or nationality or other ties. News of a distant but devastating earthquake, in the 18th century, could cause active sorrow. Certain kinds of problems—and slavery would be the first target, in the 18th century itself—began to elicit a sense of moral responsibility that easily vaulted over geographical and racial boundaries. This was both a cognitive and an emotional change, helping to explain new levels of empathy about other people in pain or about injustice, and helping to motivate passionate crusades for rights that people, as human beings, deserved. The ability to think about a common humanity, to feel deeply about certain kinds of social wrongs not just in one's own neighborhood but around the world, was crucial to the emerging thinking about human rights.

These new dimensions in Western culture were not, of course, uniformly shared, and it is impossible to know exactly how far they extended in the 18th century. We will see evidence that the humanitarian sensibility, applied to slavery, could draw impressively wide attention. But not everyone was involved, and even those affected displayed sporadic, rather than consistent interest. It was also obviously true that the new thinking was highly selective. People might agonize over the wrong of slavery and advocate new rights for individuals held in slavery but ignore sufferings of factory workers or their own domestic servants. On the same basis, human rights advocacy could prove both selective and limited—a problem that has hardly disappeared even today. But the wider cultural changes that helped carry the human rights current in the 18th century were significant even so, helping to anchor the innovations involved in a fuller context.

Causation

New human rights advocacy, bound as it was to several larger cultural realignments, must be approached as an important shift in politics and culture alike, despite its obvious ties to earlier developments in the legal codes, religious approaches, and natural law traditions. Historians who have tried to explain why this occurred, at this point in Western Europe, correctly note how difficult it is to pin down the factors involved. Certainly, any effort at explanation should be carefully assessed and debated.

Several broad factors, many of them involving some of the large overall changes occurring in Europe and Europe's world position, combined to produce the adjustments in segments of popular culture and the new approaches to human rights that resulted. Traditional culture was profoundly altered by the rise of Protestantism and religious wars, and then the advent of new scientific thinking. Capitalism and Europe's new position in world trade set up another set of relevant trends. Finally, and this is an element too frequently ignored, some new problems also spurred change, making the human rights approach more necessary than it might have seemed a couple of centuries before.

The culture shift

The Protestant Reformation took shape in the 16th century, and over the next several decades many parts of Europe were embroiled in bitter battles, sometimes including outright war, over religious affiliation. The reform movement had wide appeal, but Catholics responded vigorously through a combination of internal change and fierce resistance. Germany and the Low Countries ultimately split into Protestant and Catholic regions, but inevitably minorities spilled over messily across state boundaries. France experienced intense religious conflict in the late 16th century, though Protestantism won only minority adherence. Early in the 17th century a major war within Germany, though it had several ingredients, involved renewed religious strife. Britain was the scene of complex but recurrent religious conflict from the 16th century until the later 17th, with an ascendant Protestantism ultimately beating back Catholic opposition. The whole web was exacerbated by divisions within Protestantism, creating additional quarrels in places like Britain, Germany, and Switzerland.

Protestantism itself may have contributed to a new sense of individualism, though initially this was focused on the individual's relation to God. Protestant leaders tried to strip back the role of the institutional church and the clergy in mediating between ordinary people and the divinity. They urged the importance of individual faith. They also encouraged greater literacy and, while mainstream Protestantism tried to discipline the results of individual reading so that they would not endlessly splinter the religious community, the fact was that opportunities for individual interpretations increased. None of this directly applied to human rights at first, but the changes could further the interest in defining and protecting individuals that reached fuller fruition by the 18th century.

But the more obvious result of the splintering of Western Christianity—a splintering that would never be repaired—was that it ultimately forced some new thinking about the necessity, and perhaps even the desirability, of a new level of religious toleration. German leaders realized by the middle of the 16th century that some kinds of compromise were essential given the fact that neither Protestants nor Catholics could fully win out. Initially they thought that each region could be assigned a religion—resulting in a complex internal religious map but no need for internal toleration—but ultimately this broke down in further strife. Small wonder that ultimately many people came to the realization—against the traditions of Western Christianity—that, however intense one's own devotion was to a particular religious truth, not everyone was going to agree. Some admission of pluralism was essential. Again, this happened slowly and grudgingly. The British Glorious Revolution of 1688–1689 granted toleration for many Protestant groups, but not Catholics. France actually turned its back on a toleration measure it had accepted at the end of the 16th century. Over time, however, more and more people came to realize that the past could not be recovered, that somehow many European regions had to come to terms with pluralism. This did not create immediate advocacy of a human right to religious freedom, but it set an obvious context. Precisely because European Christian traditions were so firmly set against flexibility, the actual results of the Reformation forced a bigger change than had been needed in other regions—for example, Buddhist or Islamic regions—when faced with divisive religious sects.

Religious strife also, gradually and along with other factors, turned some Europeans against intense religion altogether. Some parts of Western Europe became increasingly secular, by the late 17th and 18th centuries. And, while secularism was hardly essential for human rights advocacy, it could turn attention to issues in this world and certainly could feed the impatience with old-style religious claims. Here was a further source of support for religious freedom and earthly freedoms more generally.

Into the European cultural mix, by the later 17th century, came of course the unprecedented surge in science. Linking the scientific revolution and its popularization to human rights requires caution, but a few connections deserve consideration. First, of course, belief in science could further the secularization trend, for some people. Second, belief in the particular kind of science that was emerging from the minds of people like Isaac Newton unquestionably extended the sense that physical nature was a rational sphere, operating according to orderly principles accessible to human reason. To the extent that European thinkers were already predisposed to look to rational natural laws, from which some universal rights could be derived, science might further the impulse. In the long run—but probably not yet, fully, in the 18th century— science would also encourage arguments about the importance of freedom of inquiry and expression, to make sure that a competition among ideas would assure the maximum possible gains in knowledge. And science certainly encouraged a belief in human rationality itself. After all, if the human mind could make such gains in understanding, surely people in general must have a rational capacity that should in turn be given free play and opportunities for education. Here, too, connections took time to accumulate, but they were relevant. The most immediate contribution of science to human rights thinking probably lay in the realization that the new research was disproving a great deal of widely accepted traditional thinking—for example, about whether the earth was the center of the universe. If traditional scientific beliefs were often wrong, the same might well apply to other forms of traditional thinking—for example, about the divine right of kings or the necessity of the death penalty. Human rights thinkers like Beccaria made this connection quite directly. Beccaria specifically took note of the potential argument that all societies, everywhere, had relied on the death penalty, claiming that this traditional sanction was totally irrelevant when confronted with the new levels of understanding: customary thinking, as he put it, must "collapse before the truth"—just as outdated scientific ideas had done.

Finally, associated with both Protestantism and science, European literacy was gaining ground substantially, based in part on the development of the European improvements of the Asian printing press from the 15th century onward. Literacy did not guarantee an interest in new arguments about human rights, but it did encourage a sense that new channels of information, and new types of beliefs, were available to ordinary people, and this could again be part of the changing cultural context. Even the new, 18th-century, passion for novels and their encouragement to new kinds of sensibility depended on wider popular literacy and openness to innovation.

World trade and capitalism

It would be tempting to argue that, as Europe began to develop literally global contacts, from the 16th century onward, its inhabitants expanded their horizons to realize the existence of the common humanity. It was certainly true that European traders and travelers began to extend connections steadily, with the Americas, with Africa, and with Asia. Many were quite impressed with the splendor of some of the societies they encountered—the impressive size of the Aztec capital, the wealth and sophistication of Istanbul or the cities of India and China. Some Europeans did gain appreciation for the achievements of other peoples, and this could provide some encouragement to the sense of shared humanity. It was also true that some Enlightenment intellectuals helped invent beliefs about the strength and purity of some peoples—like the "noble savage" ideas applied to Native Americans by some Enlightenment figures, bent on using this fiction as a means of dramatizing the natural virtues of individuals uncorrupted by European customs. It is certainly relevant to note that the idea of common humanity central to human rights innovations took shape at a time and place when global connections were accelerating.

Against this, however, was the fact that most Europeans had yet to learn very much about the rest of the world and the even more important fact that many Europeans proved adept, as they encountered other people, in figuring out reasons to believe that they were both different and inferior. Many of the regions of the world were dismissed as being technologically backward. Actual views of aboriginal peoples were typically harsh, helping to justify European seizure of property and frequent violence. Africans were dubbed inferior to help justify the slave trade. During the 18th century itself, European outlook on the Ottoman Empire worsened, with condemnations of despotism and corruption. Ultimately, of course, Europeans would learn that human rights arguments could be used to further a sense of superiority and to attack other regions for their failure to live up to civilized standards. This, however, was in the future. In the 18th century itself, the European vision of a wider world was at least seriously complicated, if not negated, by a welter of prejudices against other societies.

Europe's global trade was central to the rapid growth of capitalist economic structures and relationships within Europe. This, more than world connections themselves, may have linked to the emergence of human rights thinking in several ways. First, of course, it could feed a sense of individualism, against older, group-oriented economic traditions associated with entities like guilds. Unnecessary state interference with capitalists could, and did, link with broader arguments about the need to protect freedoms of other sorts as well.

Second, as many historians have noted, capitalism quickly created internal economic dislocations that might easily push people to seek human rights issues by way of distraction or escape. The European capitalist economy, by the 17th and 18th centuries, was unquestionably creating new social and economic gaps between people with property and the same laboring poor. By the 18th century, early industrialization, initially in Britain, created a variety of new pressures on the laboring poor, crowding them into dismal urban slums and factories. Here was a situation where many people—including, perhaps, some of the poor themselves—might welcome human rights causes as a means of sidestepping local problems. It was psychologically easier and politically safer to attack slavery elsewhere than to worry about conditions at home. Some of this escapism might be deliberately fostered, by capitalists who welcomed the diversion; some probably emerged more spontaneously. Human rights causes were not simply a result of new domestic problems, but the connection deserves attention.

Third—and here may be the most important claim—capitalism might promote a new interest in certain rights, even the broader humanitarian sensibility, by encouraging a sense that contractual relations were preferable to older forms of human organization and certainly better than relationships founded more directly on violence. As businessmen learned to honor legal contracts with buyers or suppliers, as workers came to accept contractual conditions for their wage labor, they might alter their thinking about relationships more generally. Contracts—in the form of constitutions—might now seem to be the best way to organize the state, complete with provisions about certain rights. Slavery might be rethought in light of the preference for contractual arrangements.

Europe's rapidly changing economy may, in sum, have connected to changes in thinking in several ways, particularly as they operated in tandem with the cultural shifts resulting from religion and science. They opened people to new ideas, and more specifically they encouraged these new ideas in relevant directions.

New problems

Innovations in culture and the economy might be sufficient to explain the changing context in which human rights thinking first took shape, but it is also important to note the role of certain kinds of problems that themselves were new, at least in the European experience of the time.

It was only by the 18th century, for example, that anything like a recognizable press was emerging, with growing sales of books and the creation of small weekly newspapers. These developments built, of course, on printing and literacy, but they began to take on a force of their own. Governments and churches were not sure how to handle the new beast, which certainly could be a source of attack. As many sought to censure certain writings (and the Catholic Church, in response to the Reformation, had created an elaborate process to try to identify and suppress materials of which it disapproved), they unwittingly created a new problem—freedom of the press—that would have been hard to identify earlier on.

In a context in which many Europeans had come to believe, even by the early 17th century, that some measure of religious tolerance was essential, if not as a right at least as a practical matter, continued signs of intolerance could enhance a sense that there was another growing problem to be solved. Thus the French king in 1685 turned against toleration and expelled French Protestants. Puritan New England sought to prevent rival versions of Protestantism. It was not hard for reformers to see these as examples of increasing backwardness, needing new and more sweeping kinds of remedy.

On another front: Atlantic slavery was unprecedented in many ways. The trade itself, taking African captives across an ocean in hideous conditions, was bad enough. The degree of commercial exploitation, family disruption, and sheer physical hardship on many slave plantations in the Americas and the Caribbean might easily rouse concerns that more traditional forms of slavery would have avoided. Many Europeans accepted slavery as remote, or economically essential. But there was a new type of problem that ultimately, as it gained new levels of publicity, helped justify yet another response—the turn against slavery itself in the name of basic human rights.

Probably the most important new problem area, however, resulted from the rise of absolute monarchy, particularly, of course, in France. By world standards absolute monarchs did not wield unprecedented powers or behave with unprecedented cruelty. But in a Europe accustomed to less centralized governments, the potential for arbitrary behavior could seem particularly hard to accept—particularly if, in addition, the kings sought to enforce religious uniformity and restrictions on the press as well. There were all sorts of reasons, by the 18th century, to worry about some of the European monarchies: they taxed a lot, and unfairly, and they engaged in frequent warfare. In no sense did human rights concerns alone spur the kinds of protests that would ultimately lead to revolution. But arbitrary treatment, real or imagined, was definitely part of the list of grievances, and even earlier it helped spur the formulations of the basic human rights arguments themselves.

When the people of Paris stormed the King's Bastille prison, on July 14, 1789, they thought they were attacking a place where a cruel monarchy kept political dissidents; the fact that they only found seven prisoners, mostly in jail for bad debts, in no sense diminished the symbolism of the moment. Absolute monarchs had been abusing decent people to maintain their own power. Scenes of torture were imagined on a scale undoubtedly vaster than existed in fact—but the scenes were enough. A new regime, defining new rights, was an essential response.

The first stirring of human rights thinking, then, reflected a complex but potent mixture of new cultural components, new economic and global frameworks, and new types of problems. Innovative thinking was both enabled and required. But the same sets of causes assured that thinking alone was not the only response. Philosophers and publicists built the arguments, particularly from the 1750s onward, but change did not stop there. New ideas led to new actions, and it was their combination that really made the 18th century the seedtime for human rights.

Rights and revolutions

The 18th century was framed by two revolutionary upheavals. The British Glorious Revolution of 1688–1689 was not a bloody affair—the violence had occurred earlier, in the civil wars. But it did generate not only new monarchs but a new kind of monarchy, qualified by greater power for Parliament and guided as well by a new Bill of Rights. The revolutionary outburst of the late 18th century constituted a more serious affair still, covering as well a much wider geographical area. The American rising of the 1770s, which expelled British control, was followed in 1789 by the great French Revolution, whose influence was felt throughout Western and Central Europe and across the Atlantic, in the Caribbean and Latin America.

Revolution is always significant. People in various societies, at various times, had attacked reigning governments because of economic deprivation, injustice, corruption, unfair property distribution. What was new about the 18th- to early 19th-century "age of revolution" was that explicit demands for human rights figured directly in the revolutionary list of demands. Grievances about government injustice and unfair taxation and, in the French case, deep hostility to the inequitable landholdings of aristocracy and church, certainly counted strongly, linking these risings to other protest movements in world history, like the periodic attacks on corrupt landlords and a waning imperial house in Confucian China. But human rights issues—concerns about religious freedom or freedom of expression—emerged strongly as well, and early revolutionary proclamations reflected this fact. The battles over ideas and the larger factors that spurred new interest in protecting individuals against state or church now paid off in practical politics, as the major revolutions proudly proclaimed their commitment to key human rights not only for the sake of their own nations but in the name of humanity itself.

The Glorious Revolution itself sets a benchmark against which the later 18th-century risings can be measured. The British surge was important, in establishing significant modifications in political structure that could also serve as examples to other nations. The work of John Locke was directly intertwined with the British rising as well. But the Glorious Revolution did not speak in the name of human rights, even if it moved in that direction. A Bill of Rights was issued in 1689—an innovation in itself, constituting something like a set of contractual obligations for government. It focused, however, on firming up the rights of Parliament and attacking past judicial corruption, and defending Protestantism against any possible Catholic takeover. To be sure, the document referred to "illegal and cruel punishments inflicted" by the previous Stuart monarchy; and it defended the "right" of subjects to petition the king, free from any possible prosecution. And it established "freedom of speech and debates"—but within the halls of Parliament. The final paragraphs of the document, insisting that the new king had agreed to the provisions and would therefore preserve the kingdom from any "violation of their rights" moved more visibly in a human rights direction, though of course this was a document for the English alone (and not clearly, even, for non-Protestant English). On the whole, however, the Bill of Rights represented an important new way to implement older thinking about rights, not a set of clear protections for everyone. The protections themselves were framed in terms of defense of older English principles—"the true, ancient and indubitable rights and liberties of the people of this kingdom"—not as propositions applicable across religious, social, and national lines.

In contrast, the proclamations of the great revolutions of the late 18th century spoke a different language—a human rights language. The American Declaration of Independence in 1776 put the case strongly: "We hold these truths to be self-evident, that all men are created equal, that they are endowed by their Creator with certain unalienable Rights, that among these are Life, Liberty and the Pursuit of Happiness." Governments must protect these rights, and if they do not they can and should be replaced. Here was the core of human rights in a nutshell: a set of clear rights applied to everyone, that defined protections that every individual could expect, that operated in a system of legal equality, and that followed from principles relevant to the whole of humanity.

The French Revolution, bursting forth thirteen years later, did the Americans one better. Revolutionary leaders here not only cited grievances against the traditional monarchy in terms of violations of rights, but they also moved quickly to set up a new system, proclaiming the "Rights of Man and the Citizen" within months of the outbreak itself. Insisting that violations of rights were the basic cause of government failure, the document invoked the "natural, inalienable and sacred rights of man," binding on all branches of the new government. The list of specifics was impressive: basic equality of rights; freedom of action whenever the results did not damage the rights of others; careful rules to govern arrests and punishments, with no penalty beyond what was "absolutely and obviously necessary"; no prosecution for opinions, including religious opinions; free communication in speech and writings, as "one of the most precious of the rights of man"; and the right to property. The document ended with a ringing reassertion: "any society in which the guarantee of rights is not assured ... has no constitution at all."

In 1791, the logic of religious freedom was extended with explicit recognition of the equal legal rights of Jews.

The United States, firming up its own new national government, passed its own Bill of Rights in 1791, completing the basic revolutionary documents that so clearly both illustrated and promoted the new thinking about human rights. American leaders had hesitated a bit, with important debates over the appropriate form of government once the revolution was won. The state of Virginia, however, had introduced a powerful bill of rights in its own con-stitution, in 1776. When national leaders assembled in 1787 to set up a more effective federal system, it became clear that a number of powerful figures, including several Virginia leaders, would not accept any document that did not contain explicit definitions and defenses of human liberty. The result, that enabled the overall document to win passage, was a set of ten amendments to the constitution, quickly ratified, that became the baseline American commitment to human rights.

The core freedoms, similar to those just enacted in France, were freedom of religion, speech, the press, and peaceable assembly. Anyone had the right to petition the government. No arrests or punishments could occur unless they followed previously established rules. "Cruel and unusual" punishments must not be inflicted.

Seldom in human history had a set of new ideas so quickly been installed in actual political systems, one in an upstart new nation, the other in one of the most powerful countries in the world at the time. The core documents were clear potential examples for other societies, and the conquests of the French Revolution directly spread some of the new rights to neighboring nations in Western Europe; and they were framed in terms of human universality. They were remarkably congruent, around freedoms of expression, religion, and property, and the obligation of society to avoid harsh punishments.

This was not a fully contemporary list of rights, and the revolutionary era fostered other limitations to which we must return. But no human rights effort since that time has failed to incorporate these 18th-century basics. Clearly, the human rights surge was moving from principle to practice.

The anti-slavery movement

The second real-world application of the new human rights thinking centered on the unprecedented campaign against slavery, one of the world's oldest social institutions. The campaign emanated from several Western nations, directly illustrating the growing belief that all human beings deserved certain minimal rights, and most fundamentally the right not to be regarded or treated as property.

Some concern about slavery was not new, as we have seen. Basic law codes often featured some provisions concerning slaves, though most often to pro-tect the rights of masters rather than slaves themselves. More important was the real discomfort with slavery that several major religions displayed, which could result in some changes in practice and surges in manumissions, though not, usually, outright abolition of the institution. The Catholic Jesuit order had worked against enslavement of Native Americans in the 16th century with some success, but there was no particular Christian resistance to the massive importation of Africans. A systematic effort against slavery showed the power of innovative thinking in the later 18th century and the application of the new humanitarian sensibility. As with the movement toward bills of rights, this was a novel moment, and an important one, in the history of the world.

The anti-slavery push came from two sources. One, of course, was the Enlightenment, and the reassessment of traditional institutions in light of new beliefs in basic human equality and the importance of freedom and natural rights. The second, however, was the emergence of new, minority strands of Protestantism that distinctively applied Christian thinking to the slavery issue. Quakers and Methodists, in Britain and North America, emphasized the universality of their moral code and provided much of the leadership and the fervent passion for anti-slavery efforts. Some other groups, notably Baptists, joined in as well. Both ideological approaches, one secular, the other religious, began to develop the proposition that slavery was a moral wrong.

The ideas were important, but even more impressive were the new forms of action. Organizations proliferated—like the British Abolition Society, founded in 1787—to mobilize public opinion (a new venture in itself) and to put pressure on governments to stop the slave trade and end the institution. The groups combined some central committee structure with a host of local associations, all around the intense belief that slavery was "repugnant to the principles of justice and humanity." Local affiliates sponsored lectures, mounted petition drives, even formed specialty groups for categories like young people—effectively becoming the first grassroots groups ever on behalf of human rights. A vital initiative, much discussed at the time, involved the active inclusion of women.

The movement quickly became multinational, with vigorous links among national associations and frequent travel to help flesh out the linkages. While Britain was a dynamic initial home, groups quickly sprang up in North America, Ireland, and Western Europe. Denmark, for example, responded early, curtailing its participation in the slave trade by 1792. French and British advocates corresponded actively. Early chapters in the United States specifically appealed for British help, because "the literature of Great Britain exercises so vast an influence over the public opinion of America." Anti-slavery, in other words, not only channeled new beliefs about the universality of human rights, it also built wide geographical connections through the same shared beliefs. By the early 19th century, international congresses—populated mainly by people from Europe, Canada, and the United States—were appealing, in many languages, to "friends of the slave of every nation and every clime." An American poet, Whittier, captured the transnational mood: "Yes, let them gather! Summon forth|||The pledged philanthropy of Earth.|||From every land, whose hills have heard |||The bugle blast of Freedom waking."

Along with organizational energy and efficiency, the anti-slavery movement generated tireless pamphleteering, which helped tap into the changing public culture but also built new awareness of human rights issues. Two themes predominated. First were the basic moral principles, focusing on slavery's injustice. But second was a vigorous effort to feature highly personal, dramatic, and often tragic, stories to help give slavery and its evils a human face. This tactic would become characteristic of many human rights crusades right to the present day. Pamphlets and magazines thus highlighted slave auctions, where families might be separated, and harsh discipline, including brutal whippings of disobedient slaves. Branding of slave bodies was another target, while the hardships of family life were designed to appeal particularly to female abolitionists. Novels about slavery, ultimately including Harriet Beecher Stowe's *Uncle Tom's Cabin*, drew wide audiences, and were also utilized in theater productions. Eager reformers easily connected the personal stories to the wider human rights issues:

> Let us remember that they are God's creatures, created by the same power, sustained by the same goodness ... as ourselves; they have a capacity for suffering and enjoyment like our own ... Think of these things, and let your zeal be enkindled and your pity excited, that your exertions may henceforth be commensurate with the miseries of these unhappy beings, and your own responsibility.

The responsibility point was crucial. Human rights thinking, as it was now being translated into action, depended heavily not simply on beliefs about natural law, human rationality, and compassion, but on an active sense that individuals everywhere had a moral responsibility for certain minimal conditions for people around the world.

Along with organizations and literature, finally, came massive recurrent petition campaigns, again unlike anything previously experienced in world history. The goal was to urge one's own government to take action against slavery, but also to apply moral pressure on foreign regimes. Petitions with thousands of signatures became routine. In 1788, 10,000 people in Manchester, England—at that point, a full fifth of the total population—signed on to urge the British government to abolish slavery in its colonies. Drives in the Netherlands and Scandinavia roused wide popular support. Governments, particularly in Britain, came to feel bombarded. As one newspaper put it, "*Vox populi, vox dei*—slavery shall be no more." Slave owners, as well, were targeted, and there were even discussions of boycotts of slave-produced items (like sugar)—another forecast of human rights strategies later on.

What was forming, clearly, was not only an application of new human rights thinking and passion to the slavery question, but also the creation of a sense of public voice on such issues, with potentially worldwide applicability, and a set of tactics to match. Along with the models of constitutions with bills of rights, the result was a durable contribution to global politics.

Anti-slavery crusades had fewer results to show than the political rights campaigns by 1800, although (as we will see) their principles directly helped fuel a revolution in Haiti and helped inspire the French Revolution itself at one point to abolish slavery. But the momentum was inescapable, if somewhat sporadic. Moves against the slave trade—the British abolished its transatlantic trade in 1807—and against slavery itself, that ultimately made the 19th century a century of abolition, resulted directly from the new ideas and the new programs that worked to implement them.

Human rights by 1800

The birth of the human rights movement in the 18th century was just that—a major launch but hardly a full-blown program. All sorts of issues that now seem standard parts of a human rights agenda were absent or at most barely glimpsed. Several limitations were particularly important. But lest the main points be lost, two key conclusions:

- First, what had happened in the 18th century was both new and significant. This was not just a hint of innovation. Political philosophy changed and practical consequences, in revolutionary politics and the anti-slavery campaigns, were profound. While not yet called "human rights," as opposed to "rights of man," a variety of advocates could easily, by 1800, identify some widely shared principles about religion, expression, cruel punishments, and human bondage.
- Second, this substantial beginning would lead directly to further steps. We explore the connections in subsequent chapters, but there's no question of deep relationships between what had happened in the 18th century and the explosion of human rights efforts over the past fifty years. Just compare the French revolutionary document and the United Nations human rights charter if there's any doubt. Parentage of human rights, and the factors that explain this parentage, belong to ideas and activities that emerged 250 years ago. What happened thereafter is also extremely important, in adding key platforms and eliciting more complex global reactions, but the starting point was crucial.

This said, several limitations and immediate counterthrusts, emerging by 1800, must also be noted. The human rights road would be a rocky one, and a number of problems accompanied the emergence of the new thinking—beyond the kind of birth pains that any innovation engenders. Human rights advocates themselves had some intriguing blind spots. The efforts that did occur roused new kinds of opposition; elements of modern conservatism began to emerge partly based on opposition to human rights programs. Even where initiatives seemed well launched—as with freedom of the press, for example, in the United States—all sorts of slippages were possible, and remain possible even today. There are few stories of unimpeded triumph. Finally, and most obviously from a world history standpoint, the human rights effort in 1800, for all its resounding universalism in principle, was a Western movement, only beginning to hint at wider extensions. Here, as with the other limitations, the prospects for what would happen next, in the 19th century and beyond, were complex.

Blind spots

Hindsight, as all historians know, is a marvelous tool, enabling contemporary people to deploy their values and understandings to criticize the failings of the past. It's certainly easy to marvel at what the human rights pioneers did not discern, how they did not grasp the obvious implications of their own principles, as contemporaries have in more recent times.

What happened was that the level of innovation wrapped up in the human rights ideas was itself so extensive that it proved impossible, with rare exceptions, to apply the ideas fully against all entrenched traditions. It's easy to see the shortcomings, and to lament how long it would take for the omissions to be repaired. It's also important to recognize how difficult it was, in a rapidly changing environment, to think as systematically as advocates now—250 years later—find logical.

Examples are numerous. Did the high-sounding American declarations about all men being created equal in fact apply to slaves? The answer, from the American Revolution and subsequent discussions, was "no." Slavery persisted, which meant that equality under the law was mainly for whites only. Of course there were advocates available who already realized the incompatibility between human rights principles—already being used elsewhere in anti-slavery campaigns—and the new American constitution. But resistance from many slave owners plus some tradition-based confusion about whether slaves were really people prevented logical consistency.

As human rights thinking took shape, new factories were being established in several parts of Britain as part of the first phase of the industrial revolution. In these factories many workers were progressively deprived of traditional rights to determine their own pace of activity or the discipline that would govern the workday. Early factories were notorious for levying fines arbitrarily or dismissing workers without clear cause—including workers who ventured any kind of complaint about conditions, now scorned as "troublemakers." Because these kinds of factories were just as novel as human rights thinking was, it is probably not surprising that advocates did not think in terms of the workplace implications of protections for free speech or freedom from random punishments. This gap would not be clearly noticed for some time, and it is still under discussion today.

Very little human rights thinking was applied to children, a category we have already noted as inherently challenging to the human rights approach. Some philosophers, like Rousseau, did begin to discuss the importance of education and the need for school reforms that would give children clearer recognition as individuals, but the connections were tentative at best, and did not yet spill over into policy.

But the biggest blind spot—in terms of what most present-day advocates would see as obvious logic—was women. None of the main human rights philosophers talked about women as a specific category that would need attention if universality and common humanity were going to be realized. The propensity for referring to the rights of man, or all men being created equal, resulted partly from a habit of using "man" where we today would use "human," but partly also from the fact that men were the target of choice. Some human rights values might apply to women nevertheless: they could in principle benefit from protections for religious freedom, and they were often used as examples in the anti-slavery pamphlets. But many of the specific inequities facing women, in traditional societies, passed largely unnoticed, including their unequal access to property rights in many Western countries, or their subordination to fathers or husbands in many legal matters. The long-term results of the great French Revolution actually worsened women's legal situation in many respects, tying them more closely to male-dominated families.

This blind spot, however, was too blatant not to be noticed at the time—though notice produced no concrete results for many decades. By the end of the 18th century, several female writers had emerged who proudly proclaimed the applicability of human rights thinking to women's conditions. In France, Olympe de Gouges penned the *Declaration of the Rights of Woman and the Citizen* in 1791, urging a revolution in gender relations to match the political revolution going on around her: "Woman is born free and lives equal to man in her rights." "Perpetual male tyranny" is responsible for the unnatural limits on women's rights, and it should be abolished. Women warrant the same freedom of speech or protection from arbitrary punishment that men do. Following quickly on this initiative, Mary Wollstonecraft, in Britain, issued her "Vindication of the Rights of Women" in 1792. Here, too, the claim to equal rights, and in this case also, equal education sounded strongly. These were important statements, with a rich future before them; the basic principles of feminism were enunciated as part of the birth of human rights more generally. But there is no question that, in fact, a huge gender gap overshadowed mainstream human rights efforts, and would do so for some time. Major remnants of traditional social arrangements had yet—save for the few pioneers—to be thought through.

Opposition

The human rights agendas that did emerge, by 1800, generated increasingly articulate resistance, and a new kind of conservative politics, backed by some important efforts in political philosophy, arose as a result. The abolitionist campaigns, not surprisingly, produced counterthrusts by slave owners, bent on defending their property and eager to claim that slaves were too childlike to be entrusted with anything like equal rights. More durable still was conservative resistance to the new claims about freedoms of religion and expression.

For many religious leaders, defense of religious truth and protection of the position of established churches easily outweighed upstart claims to religious freedom. The definitions of human rights in this area were dangerous to the social order and to human salvation alike. Many religious spokespeople upheld this aspect of conservative reaction, but for many decades it was the Catholic Church that took the lead. As late as 1864, the Pope explicitly condemned as false, in what he termed the "Syllabus of Errors," propositions such as "in the present day it is no longer expedient that the Catholic religion should be held as the only religion of the State, to the exclusion of all other forms of worship"; or "every man is free to embrace and profess that religion which, guided by the light of reason, he shall consider true"; or "it has been widely decided by law, in some Catholic countries, that persons coming to reside therein shall enjoy the public exercise of their own peculiar worship." This was, to be sure, an unusually stubborn statement, which antagonized even many Catholics, but various forms of resistance persisted in many Western societies, with traces visible even today.

For many political leaders—regardless of their views on religion—other elements of the 18th-century human rights platform were dangerously subversive. The clear association of bills of rights with revolutionary attacks on the monarchy and aristocracy was proof positive that political rights were inconsistent with a stable social order. Here, too, resistance was fierce and articulate. Soon after the French Revolution died down, a conservative leader in Austria, Prince Metternich, orchestrated a European agreement in the Carlsbad Decrees of 1819 that explicitly attacked key human rights. Freedom of university professors and students was abolished—professors would be fired who "abused their legitimate influence over the youthful minds" by "propagating harmful doctrines hostile to public order or subversive of existing governmental institutions." No associations would be allowed without state authorization. No publication could appear without "the previous knowledge and approval of the state officials." No writer was allowed to appeal a censorship decision. The needs of society—as determined by established rulers—must take precedence over any kinds of claim to individual freedom.

Over time, in most Western nations, this kind of conservative resistance was overcome, though it sometimes took renewed revolution to break through. A new rising in 1830 in France, for example, was partly motivated by explicit efforts by a conservative government to limit the freedom of the press. But conservative resistance, and the alternative values expressed in conservative thought, by no means disappeared. This was in itself an important product of, and limitation on, the human rights breakthrough of the 18th century.

Barriers of routine

Human rights progress, even in some of the most supportive contexts, was often slow or halting. Partly this was because of outright resistance. And unevenness sometimes reflected blind spots on the part of advocates, and certainly the disagreements over exactly what constituted progress in the human rights domain. But the course of human rights, by 1800 and well beyond, was also affected by political routines and by the fact that other issues and priorities so often seemed to intrude.

Thus, in the new United States, in 1798, worries about contagion from the French Revolution spurred the Alien and Sedition Acts, which in turn banned as "false, scandalous and malicious writing" anything that criticized the government or its leaders. The fact that, as Thomas Jefferson noted at the time, this specifically contradicted the Bill of Rights was ignored, and the act would be cited again in the 20th century in times of national fear.

More subtly, in both Britain and the United States, principled devotion to freedom of speech and expression constantly warred against a belief that the public must be protected from sexual provocation or obscenity. The British government, while proudly proclaiming its defense of free speech, exercised prior censorship over stage productions well into the 20th century. Deeply concerned about sexual morality, which he thought might be undermined if people could use birth control devices, the American Postmaster General, Anthony Comstock, in 1873 banned any kind of writing that might encourage or arrange "the prevention of contraception," with substantial fines and imprisonment for five years at hard labor. And American courts did not begin to rule the effort unconstitutional until 1936.

French revolutionaries, in the 1790s, started to undermine the earlier commitments to freedom of expression out of a concern for protecting the Revolution itself against enemies. Many people were arrested and killed as political prisoners, in the radical phase of the Revolution. And the guillotine, ironically introduced as a more humane method of beheading prisoners, became a new symbol of cruel punishments—though it was retained in France as the sole method of execution until the abolition of capital punishment outright in 1981.

Examples could be multiplied. Even in areas where human rights seemed most clearly defined by 1800, with religion and speech, and in obvious initial havens like France, Britain, or the new United States, human rights advances were often slow and sometimes reversed outright as a result of a variety of forces quite apart from outright opposition. Other issues could intrude, including competing reform interests that might even preempt a human rights concern like freedom of expression. Sheer routine-mindedness, in areas like censorship offices, could run against the implications of the human rights. Changes and adjustments in reality were messier than the principles involved might suggest. This was already an issue by 1800 and it would continue to constrain the process of change thereafter.

Regions

The most glaring gap in the human rights effort by 1800 was of course its regional base. The effective birthplace of the new thrust around human rights centered in Britain and France, with important resonance also in North America, the Low Countries, Scandinavia, and parts of Italy, plus some intellectual contributions from Germany. Even the anti-slavery campaign focused mainly on influencing Western governments, responsible for colonial slavery and the slave trade, and plantation owners of European origin. This was hardly a global foundation.

Human rights arguments, both philosophically and in terms of some of the most ringing proclamations, referred to the whole of humanity and to universalism. Yet, by 1800, few (if any) human rights advocates had thought clearly about how to bridge the gap between geography-in-fact and geography-in-principle.

And it was also clear by 1800 that human rights innovations were going to face heavy sledding in some places, at least under current regimes. Catholic officials were hostile, thanks to the attacks on church position during the French Revolution. In Russia, Catherine the Great, though long a friend of Enlightenment thinking, actively turned against human rights ideas once the French Revolution began threatening monarchies, imposing active censorship that prevented the publication of reformist writings, and exiling key advocates for change.

Even where interest in Western ideas emerged, reformers did not necessarily feature a human rights emphasis. In the Balkans, for example, various leaders in business and other pursuits were drawn to new ideas of nationalism, seeking independence from Ottoman control, far more than to principles of individual human rights. Wanting a nation to be free was not necessarily the same thing as urging protection of freedoms within the nation—a tension that would show up more widely later on.

For most of the world's people, though, particularly in Asia and Africa, the main point was that, in 1800, the new approaches to human rights had simply not penetrated at all. No programs had been sketched to carry the message more widely, and obviously no responses had been necessary either.

Key questions for the future, then, involved learning how human rights principles might be presented to the rest of the world, and how they would be received—and how the kinds of opposition that had already surfaced in a few centers might be handled as well. There was an agenda here, though not at all clearly formulated as yet, that would help usher in the next, and very messy, phase of human rights history during the 19th century and beyond.

Further reading

Good surveys on the emergence of human rights thinking in the 18th century include Lynn Hunt, *Inventing Human Rights* (New York, NY: W. W. Norton, 2008); Gary B. Herbert, *A Philosophical History of Rights* (New Brunswick, NJ: Transaction, 2002); Thomas Haskell, "Capitalism and the Origins of the Humanitarian Sensibility," *American Historical Review*, 90 (1985), pp. 335–369; and Chester James Antieau, "Natural Rights and the Founding Fathers—The Virginians," *Washington and Lee Law Review*, 17(1) (1960), pp. 43–81.

On women's rights, see Gisela Bock, *Women in European History* (Oxford, UK: Blackwell Publishers, 2002); Kathryn Sklar and James B. Stewart (eds.), *Women's Rights and Transatlantic Antislavery in the Era of Emancipation* (New Haven, CT: Yale University Press, 2007).

On slavery and abolition, see Seymour Drescher, *Abolition: A History of Slavery and Antislavery* (New York, NY: Cambridge University Press, 2009); and Robin Blackburn, *The Overthrow of Colonial Slavery, 1776–1848* (New York, NY: Verso, 1988).

Also see Michael Zuckert, *Launching Liberalism: On Lockean Political Philosophy* (Lawrence, KS: University Press of Kansas, 2002); Knud Haakonssen, *Natural Law and Moral Philosophy: From Grotius to the Scottish Enlightenment* (Cambridge, UK: Cambridge University Press, 1996); Amitai Etzioni, "Individualism—Within History," *Hedgehog Review*, 4(1) (Spring, 2002); Peter N. Stearns, *Global Outrage: The Origins and Impact of World Opinion from the 1780s to the 21st Century* (Oxford, UK: Oneworld Publications, 2005). A broad historical perspective on pain can be found in Roselyn Rey, *The History of Pain* (Cambridge, MA: Harvard University Press, 1998).

4 Human rights on a world stage

The 19th century and the interwar decades

Given the surge of human rights interest in the 18th century, it would be logical to imagine a 19th century in which what began as a European innovation quickly conquered world interest, as well as advancing further in the West itself. Philosophical proclamations of universal validity might give way to a genuinely multinational commitment to this new definition of human progress. The innovations involved, as against earlier political traditions everywhere, including the West, guard against setting expectations too high: surely there would be details to clarify still by 1900. But an ascending trend should be clear.

This is not what happened, overall. Some striking gains for human rights can be registered in the 19th century, including unprecedented abolitions of slavery and harsh serfdom. The definition of rights began to expand, at least in some quarters. New regions were drawn into a number of rights-based reforms. Gains of this sort were important in themselves, but also helped serve to link 18th-century origins with the further flowering of rights efforts in the later 20th century.

But the limitations are striking as well. New arguments developed against human rights principles, even in the West itself—despite the fact that formal conservatism actually began to adjust to some elements of a human rights approach. More important: even as contacts around the world accelerated, with growing trade and more rapid transportation, a global commitment to human rights did not emerge. Some regions simply ignored this aspect of the Western message. Others made lukewarm gestures, with little practical effect.

The most fundamental reason for what was at best a checkered global response lay in the ambivalence of Western leaders and publics themselves. The universality of human rights was not entirely lost, but for many Westerners the apparent inferiority of most people outside their own society inhibited a consistent message. Nationalist beliefs, and the excitement of a new round of imperialist conquest, often triumphed over any vigorous human rights agenda. Even when a human rights note did sound, it might reasonably be interpreted as another Western claim for superior values and rejected on those grounds. Above all, new levels of racism, sometimes combined with "scientific" arguments, severely qualified human rights approaches. Many Westerners believed that some peoples were too inferior to be included in a common human rights agenda. They needed permanent oversight, or at least a long period of tutelage, before the privileges of common rights could apply.

A revealing result of the combination of Western ambivalence and substantial global neglect was a startling array of problems, often widely known, that drew no clear human rights response at all. There was no international outcry, and scant domestic reaction, over the slaughter of Indians as the United States pursued its westward expansion. No organizations formed to protest the rise of pogroms against Jews in late 19th-century Russia. European imperialism, trampling rights of many native peoples often beginning with massacres of native troops, generated no systematic international opposition. The miseries of "freed" slaves in the Americas and Caribbean, often impoverished and not infrequently forced into debt peonage or other legal traps, did not inspire global activists. A huge bloodbath in mid-19th century China, around the Taiping rebellion and its repression in which over 20 million people were killed, was not seen as a human rights issue by either the Chinese government or the world at large. The list is considerable, in a century that had at least its share of brutalities. Sometimes, silence reflected in part a lack of dramatic news stories: with the telegraph, international news began traveling faster by the later 19th century but it still could lag behind events. Sometimes silence reflected human rights ambivalence: imperialists, for example, could argue that, while they had to override local opposition, they would ultimately install new protections for human rights in "backward" parts of the world—as when they moved against slavery within the new African colonies of Europe. Most commonly, however, silence reflected a lack of active commitment to the sense of common humanity, a belief that the troubles of distant groups were too remote, involving too much "otherness," to bother with.

Then, after the 19th century itself and one of the world's great wars early in the 20th century, the human rights picture dimmed still further. The 1920s, and particularly the 1930s, saw one global setback for human rights after another, a dismal, even frightening end to a complex chapter in human rights history.

Amid many disappointments and outright failures, the human rights story from 1800 to 1940 remains a mixed one. There was genuine global involvement, in contrast to the 18th century: specific human rights reform had touched many different parts of the world and voices were activated in diverse regions. The rights agenda also grew, and again to some extent on a global basis. Both gains and, then, clear failures would provide the basis for a much wider and at least apparently more positive surge after World War II.

The globalization of human rights: some first steps

We begin with the most positive trend, visible early in the 19th century and at many points thereafter: the clear signs that human rights interests and impacts were going global, picking up on the universality theme previously established only in principle. The fact that globalization would prove incomplete must not be ignored, and we will return to the gaps. But there was change.

The first signs emerged in the Caribbean and Latin America, picking up both on the anti-slavery campaigns and on the political agendas that had infused the French and American revolutions. Larger anti-slavery efforts would continue to resound throughout the 19th century. From the 1830s onward, human rights concerns would mesh with larger reform currents in places like Russia and the Ottoman Empire. And finally, human rights criteria would begin to affect evaluations and policies in war and international diplomacy, beginning to establish an intriguing new category quickly dubbed "crimes against humanity."

Haiti and Latin American wars for independence: the human rights components

The Haitian revolution against slavery and French colonial control, after 1810, and a series of largely successful independence wars against Spain established new and independent nations throughout much of Central and South America, were major developments in regional and world history. Both developments effectively extended the revolutionary mood to new parts of the Atlantic world. They had many facets, but high on the list were the impacts of human rights thinking and the obvious extensions of this thinking to important new regions.

Haiti and Latin America, around 1800, offered two features ideal for a new articulation of human rights interests. First, leadership elements had extensive contact with European thinking on the subject. Second, human rights measures could help frame key demands, about slavery or about grievances against the colonial state.

Haiti's revolution broke out in 1791, the result of a brutal system of slavery combined with access to French human rights ideas. French anti-slavery leaders had been active in the 1780s, among other things predicting trouble in places like Haiti unless the institution was abolished. Their thoughts were echoed by free Haitians of color, some of whom spent time in France but who were not granted legal equality with whites within Haiti itself. Leaders like Julien Raimond had been appealing for equal rights even before the French Revolution broke out. The French rising itself both distracted the colonial government, creating a sense of opportunity, and frustrated the Haitian majority because no concessions were granted. This was the context in which slaves themselves rose in violent revolt. Warfare raged on the island off and on for a decade. In 1801 a Haitian leader, Toussaint L'Ouverture, was briefly able to form a government and issue the first of many Haitian constitutions. It was there that the link to human rights principles became official—but amid some interesting constraints.

It should be emphasized that the slave rising was not caused by explicit human rights ideas. There had been major rebellions before in Haiti, stemming from the harsh oppressiveness of the slave system. New ideas played at most a

minor contributing role. But the expression of the revolt, in the 1801 constitution and subsequently, clearly reflected the new principles. "There cannot
exist slaves, servitude is therein forever abolished. All men are born, live, and
die free French." The document stipulated legal equality for all races. Other
human rights notions gained less attention, despite a reference to a guarantee
of "freedom and individual security." Religious freedom, for example, was
not installed, in favor of declaring Catholicism the "only professed faith."
Later constitutions, in a volatile political climate, might do a bit more. In
1805 a new document proclaimed religious freedom, while repeating that all
citizens are "brothers at home." A new version in 1816 urged that "liberty
consists of the power to do that which does no harm to the rights of others,"
adding "no one can be barred for speaking, writing and publishing his
thought." Clearly, human rights thinking deeply informed Haiti's new political
leaders, at least in principle, starting from the rejection of slavery and legal
inequality but sometimes moving beyond. In fact, unfortunately, poverty and
tensions between former slaves and former free people of color marred Haiti's
political future after the revolt ended. There were many periods of strongman
rule and heavy dependence on military repression. Haiti stands, nevertheless,
as the first instance outside Western Europe and North America where the
spread of human rights criteria can clearly be noted.

By 1810, and the wider risings in Latin America, geographical expansion
moved further. Here, too, was an area, like Haiti, in which some people had
active connections with European ideas, thanks to travel and cultural communication, and in which human rights ideas could both cause and express deep
grievances. Slavery was not, in this case, front and center, but rather a set of
political disabilities which tapped the other major component of human rights
thinking. The French *Declaration of the Rights of Man and the Citizen* was
translated into Spanish in 1794 and widely distributed in places like Bogotá,
Colombia.

The independence wars were spurred by dissatisfaction by the Creole
class—Latin Americans of European origin—who had been substantially
excluded from colonial government in favor of native Spaniards and Portu-
guese, and by the larger restrictions distant monarchies placed on local political and economic life. Creole leaders like Simon Bolivar and José de San
Martín were well acquainted both with the Enlightenment and with French
and American revolutionary example. They readily called up a vocabulary
emphasizing freedom and protection under the law, and their thinking was
easily compatible with the political side of human rights.

There were, however, some tensions from the outset, though in the enthusiasm
of the struggle for liberation they were not always realized explicitly. Simon
Bolivar (d. 1830), for example, the leader of the revolt in what is now
Colombia and Venezuela (and the northern Andes region), used familiar
Enlightenment terms to call the people to action. He talked in 1813 of states
"in full enjoyment of their liberty and independence," of breaking the "chains
of servitude." The enemy Spanish colonial regime had violated "the sacred

rights of nations" and was a tyranny pure and simple. It was revealing that the 1812 constitution of Colombia included a section on the "rights of man and the citizen," obviously borrowed from the French experience, with specific reference to "legal equality and liberty." Overall, however, the invocations of liberty could be somewhat vague and general, and although Bolivar undoubtedly in principle supported specifics such as freedoms of press or conscience, he was more focused on national, or collective, freedom from Spanish rule. The Colombian constitution, interestingly, included considerable attention to the social obligations of citizens, and not just to rights. How the collective and nationalist goals meshed with the more conventional human rights was not entirely clear. As a nationalist, Bolivar could also refer to differences between his people and North Americans or Europeans. While undoubtedly inspired by the rights declarations of France or the United States, he was also at pains to note how challenging it would be to adopt a foreign system of "political, civil and religious liberty." As his revolt progressed, the difficulties of establishing a stable new state prompted him to wonder if the people were yet ready for freedom: they might still need control from above. At one point, disillusioned, Bolivar lamented that "America is ungovernable." The only difference now was that controls emanated from a native republican government rather than a foreign monarchy. Late in his career, in this vein, though still professing his devotion to liberty, Bolivar had himself named supreme ruler, and proved ready to crush potential opposition.

Latin American patterns, then, introduced a definite strain of human rights thinking into the political culture of the region. But it was complicated not simply by conservative opposition—from leaders of the predominant Catholic Church, for example—but also by the potential incompabilities between national versus personal freedoms and by the very real political turmoil that quickly followed from independence in many of the new states. Actual political rights were not firmly or durably established, with rare exceptions.

Yet there were important milestones. The constitution of Colombia in 1819 abolished Catholic censorship of the press and established freedom in that category. Equally important, slavery was abolished, and freed slaves were even given some funds to make sure they could survive on their own—an earlier and more generous approach than that ultimately taken in the United States. Many later Colombian constitutions, such as that of 1863, returned to the theme of political rights, stipulating not only a free press, but religious freedom and freedom of association, while trying to assure that education was not controlled by the Catholic Church. Again, it was clear that a human rights tradition was being established. The problem was consistency: conservatives vied for power and disputed many basic principles. Thus an intermediate constitution in 1843 restored the dominance of the Church and also abolished freedom of the press.

Mexico displayed a similar mixture, with definite, but definitely inconsistent, bows to human rights. Slavery was abolished in 1818. The foundational constitution of 1824 carefully provided for the "political freedom of the press" as one of the government's prime responsibilities. Torture, under any circumstance, was explicitly banned, and rights to trial carefully established. But Catholicism was proclaimed the only religion in the nation. Further, scarcely a decade later, this constitution was scrapped in favor of a dictatorship, as Mexico launched its long oscillation between liberal and conservative political systems. Ultimately, after another revolution, the constitution of 1917 would actually stake out important new ground in human rights history, a point to which we will return. But the responses to independence from Spain were checkered.

Several major societies imitated the United States, in defining some human rights but leaving the institution of slavery alone, until much later in the 19th century. This was the case most notably in Brazil. But in all the former Spanish colonies (though not in persisting colonial regimes like Cuba), slavery was abolished by the middle of the century. The move toward legal equality was less clear cut concerning Indians, where disproportionate taxes and other controls often persisted into the 20th century.

Soon after its independence revolt, in 1813, Argentina moved to assure freedom of the press. Slavery was not abolished outright, but the children of slaves were to be freed. Fuller constitutional development fell victim to the characteristic liberal–conservative quarrels. The main military leader in the Argentine liberation, José de San Martín, defended the idea of freedom in the abstract: "liberals of the world are brothers everywhere." He actively used slaves in his armies, and abolished the slave trade—though not the institution outright. Even more than Bolivar, however, San Martín was deeply convinced of the dangers of disorder. He referred once to the fact that the "unenlightened parts of the community are so numerous"—meaning particularly slaves and Indians. More fully than Bolivar, he preferred to endorse strong government and stability over any particular commitment to human rights. He also supported an authoritarian successor in Argentina itself—one of the first of a long string of strongmen, or *caudillos*, in Latin American political history. Still, ideas about rights took definite root in Argentina as well. After the authoritarian period, the reformist constitution of 1853 offered a clear bill of rights, assuring freedom of religion and the press and carefully stipulating equality under the laws. Citizens were given the liberty to do whatever was not proscribed by law.

Overall, developments in Latin America from the early 19th century onward showed the power of human rights ideas for people in active contact with European and North American political culture. Important reforms occurred under the banner of legal rights and legal equality, and a constituency formed that would defend a liberal legacy in the future. The translations, however, were neither smooth nor complete. Problems of post-independence stability, as well as outright conservative opposition, diluted or even negated human rights efforts in key areas. Concerns about population segments—racial minorities, sometimes the poor more generally—qualified human rights commitments as well. Many advocates of national independence were not sure that freedoms should apply across the board within the national unit. Even more than in Western Europe—where many complications also arose—human rights agendas in Latin America proceeded in fits and starts for many decades, a foretaste of the complexities of human rights globalization more generally.

The emergence of a global campaign against slavery

Though focused initially on the Americas and the Atlantic, the efforts to attack slavery, which had been such an important part of the emergence of human rights agitation in the 18th century, ultimately helped extend human rights thinking even more broadly. By the end of the century, slavery—that age-old human institution—was on its way out on a global scale, the victim of what in essence was the first worldwide human rights movement. What had begun as a Western innovation, though triggered in part by Western responsibility for a particularly dreadful form of slavery, anti-slavery campaigns ultimately created a larger global platform, an important step in the world history of human rights efforts more generally. A vital part of this process also involved expanding the agenda from slavery alone, to other systems that subjected workers to unjust exploitation.

By the 1830s, anti-slavery forces had produced Britain's commitment to end the Atlantic slave trade, a commitment that involved not just ceasing shipments but devoting considerable resources to patrols. It had generated emancipations in the northern states of the United States, of course in Haiti, in several of the new Latin American nations, and, in 1833, in the British colonies themselves. Progress after this point, to reach areas where slavery was particularly deeply ingrained, came more slowly, and involved a combination of steady pressures from anti-slavery advocates in Western Europe and the northern American states with increasing conversions to human rights thinking by leaders in other areas.

In 1823 a major anti-slavery society formed in London, initially to press for full abolition in the British colonies. This goal achieved, in 1839 the group changed its name to the British and Foreign Anti-Slavery Society, intending now to attack the institution worldwide. An unprecedented Anti-Slavery Convention occurred in 1840, drawing people from various parts of the world, including the United States. The meeting was intended to be all-male, but women abolitionists also arrived and went on to form their own group, as well as to begin to extend their interests to women's interests—one of many instances in which one human rights cause would begin to spin off additional implications.

The Anti-Slavery Society persevered, and today (its name changed in 1990 to Anti-Slavery International) stands really as the oldest global human rights organization. The group played a significant role in ongoing agitation against the slave system in the American South, among other things sponsoring a powerful publication by the American abolitionist John Brown. Once the Civil War began, public opinion in France and Britain was one of the factors that impelled Abraham Lincoln to issue the Emancipation Proclamation in 1863, eager to win support from the powerful European nations.

Global agitation also helped apply human rights thinking to the slave question in other important areas, such as Brazil. Here, reformers professed themselves eager to "imitate every European progress, and possess each new material, moral, intellectual, or social improvement of civilization." Slavery was fully abolished in this huge country by 1882, and soon thereafter was eliminated throughout the Americas. Equality under the law became widely established, at least in this regard.

Attention turned also to Africa, where slavery had actually spread early in the 19th century in the interests of producing more cash crops for export. Again, global opinion, and the Anti-Slavery Society itself, pressed for new gains, persuading rulers like the Sultan of Zanzibar to accept abolition (in 1873). Elsewhere in Africa, European colonial conquests brought more direct moves to end the institution.

Agitation also affected the Ottoman Empire and other parts of the Middle East, as well as South Asia. Final gains came slowly. Nepal accepted abolition only in 1923, with a royal decree, and Saudi Arabia acted similarly in 1963. By this point official slavery had effectively ended everywhere, thanks to pressure from the moral convictions of global advocates and at least reluctant agreement from leaders in virtually every region.

Of course a number of caveats must attach to this impressive human rights triumph. It is not clear how much leaders in certain areas really embraced new principles, as opposed to finding it convenient to end one institution and look for less embarrassing substitutes. Many countries and corporations in the world today find ways to reduce labor freedom, for example, through the process of holding the passports of foreign workers so that they will face expulsion as well as loss of job if they raise any protest against harsh material conditions. Anti-slavery advocates themselves had important blind spots. They often focused so narrowly on slavery that they paid little attention to desperately poor conditions among former slaves once the institutions had ended. This proved true to some extent, for example, in the American South during and after Reconstruction. In many regions, certainly including the United States, a rising tide of racism often limited the real human rights gains that resulted from slavery's demise.

On the other hand, global anti-slavery advocates proved capable of expanding their targets, even during the late 19th century. In the 1880s and 1890s, for example, a British shipping employee, Edmund Morel, helped organize a massive public opinion campaign against forced labor in the Belgian Congo, where many workers were violently intimidated into taking dangerous mining jobs. As with outright slavery, vivid stories of abuse and torture helped fuel moral outrage, with support for the cause from many regions, though particularly Europe and the United States. The campaign was an important link between classic anti-slavery efforts and more contemporary human rights attacks on exploited labor.

The British Society itself sponsored attacks on debt peonage in Peru, where a European company used worker indebtedness to force low pay and inhumane working conditions in the rubber industry. The Society also worked against a Chinese practice of selling young girls into domestic service for extended periods during their youth, again with some positive results from the effort.

Agitation continued after World War I. The new League of Nations asked the Society to draft provisions to protect labor in those portions of the League Covenant dealing with "backward territories." The League subsequently conducted several studies of unjust practices, such as debt bondage, purchasing children for work, and forced marriages for women. A variety of new international agreements resulted. And campaigns would continue from World War II onward—for example, against child labor or prostitution.

The point is clear. Global anti-slavery efforts proved capable of extending human rights principles more broadly, into other areas where people were being forced into activities against their will. The same expansion applied geographically. For many parts of Africa and Asia, anti-slavery efforts, broadly construed, provided the first contacts with explicit human rights thinking. Many leaders were prodded into acquiescence without much personal conviction, and certainly many abuses continued under slightly different garb. But the process could also lead some reformers in these new regions to take up the cause, and to begin to think about human rights implications in other categories as well. The results constituted a genuine, if limited, globalization of the whole effort.

Russia and the Ottoman Empire

Even as the movement against slavery spread in the 19th century, some important regions were more fully and directly drawn in to human rights considerations through their wider interaction with Western Europe—in a pattern somewhat similar to what happened in Latin America during the independence period. Here was a next stage—beyond the Atlantic world—in the geographic extension of human rights. Russia and the portions of the Middle East/southeastern Europe under Ottoman control shared with the Americas a network of active contacts with Western Europe, through trade, travel, geographical proximity, and historical exchange. Many upper-class Russians, particularly, had considerable experience in dealing with Western culture more generally, some even speaking French in preference to their own language. Individual Russians, in this context, became at least as enthusiastic about human rights, by the early 19th century, as were many of the Latin American independence leaders. A strong Ottoman interest in human rights also emerged, at least in principle. European pressure and an awareness of the need for some reforms, if only to preserve independence from Western intrusion, created a climate in which key human rights ideas were discussed. Both the Ottoman Empire and Russia were also affected by anti-slavery ideas.

Neither Russia nor the Ottoman Empire, however, was yet in a revolutionary situation—in contrast to the independence turmoil in the Americas. A few revolts surfaced in Russia, but they were quickly put down. Protest in the Ottoman domain tended to focus more on group issues than on individual rights. In both regions, human rights claims had to contend with a welter of established interests, and also with larger cultural traditions that in some cases pointed in quite different directions. Opposition to human rights thinking went beyond knee-jerk efforts to protect social privilege, though this was involved; it could include extensive critical commentary based on quite different values and preferences.

Human rights interest developed in Russia and the Ottoman lands, in sum, but amid many hesitations and counterpressures. Clear interests emerged, but on the whole a bit later than was the case in Latin America. The human rights foothold in these regions was also, on balance, considerably less well established than in Latin America. Here was a different set of globalization experiences from 1800 onward, with a distinctive mixture of change and resistance.

The Russian experience

Russia's official response to human rights interests during the first half of the 19th century can be summed up quite simply: frontal resistance. Beginning with Catherine the Great's tightening of controls over publications, including imported materials, in the late 18th century, the Russian regime was dead set against the currents of reform bubbling up in Western Europe. It even partici-pated actively in several efforts to put down uprisings in other areas, intervening for example against a Hungarian revolt as late as 1848–1849. Russians who advocated change were jailed, sent to Siberia, or exiled. At the policy level, human rights were actually in retreat.

Complete suppression, however, proved impossible. Individual writers (risking imprisonment) railed against the institution of serfdom, arguing both that it was contrary to human rights, an inherently unjust system, and that in practice it held back the Russian economy by generating the only grudging work performance from the oppressed peasantry. In 1825 a movement of liberal army officers, strongly influenced by Western ideas, rose against a new Russian emperor, seeking legal equality and an end to serfdom, and advocating limita-tions on the government and other reforms. Their political platform was vague, beyond the legal equality point, and their rising was firmly quashed. But this Decembrist revolt created lasting memories in Russia, keeping interest in political justice alive. Exiles like the poet Alexander Herzen (often based in London) kept up a steady stream of criticisms of the regime. Herzen at one point launched a newspaper, in exile, pointedly entitled the *Free Russian Press*.

Then, in the 1860s, reform finally arrived. The trigger was the issue of serfdom. An exceptionally severe rural labor system had developed in Russia over several centuries. Landlords wielded disproportionate control of the best land, but beyond this, they also exercised extensive rights over serfs to impose labor objections for their estates while exacting various payments. Further, they had substantial powers to punish serfs, not infrequently imposing stark physical discipline. The overall system was one of the harshest in world history short of outright slavery.

Obviously, Russian serfdom was an easy target for reformers concerned with legal equality and other rights. This is why it drew criticism from many individual Russians, including members of the upper class, who had been exposed to Western values. Even before 1800, Aleksandr Radishchev had attacked the "inequality of treatment" that serfdom imposed, while noting that many serfs—"dead to the law"—had no legal protections of any sort. Decembrists and other reformers, including the exiles, also blasted serfdom through the language of legal rights. Various writings attacking serfdom began to circulate extensively among the upper and middle classes, evading government censorship efforts and building a larger audience for ideas about social justice. By the 1850s, however, serfdom was vulnerable to other criticisms as well. It generated recurrent social unrest, which gave even an authoritarian government reasons for concern. The system also seemed inefficient, constraining the mobility and motivation of labor at a time when the Russian economy was measurably falling behind levels of industrializing Western Europe. Military defeat at the hands of Britain and France in the Crimean War, in Russia's own backyard, put the icing on the cake: Russia had to consider reform out of national self-interest. When the tsar finally decided to "emancipate" the serfs, in 1861, human rights concerns were not the primary cause.

The Emancipation document did, however, promise serfs, over time, the "full rights" of rural inhabitants, creating conditions for legal, though not economic, equality. This was not a ringing proclamation of human rights: serfs continued to suffer from special conditions until they paid nobles back for lost property, and they were urged to be properly grateful to their social superiors. The document itself was full of traditional phrases, like the tsar's reliance on divine guidance and the importance of the nobles' special property rights. And the measure by no means satisfied Russian peasants themselves, who continued to struggle for greater access to the land. But this was a major reform, introducing some language relevant to human rights. By abolishing nobles' local political control, it also required additional steps. The result was a roughly fifteen-year period of additional reforms in Russian society, further reflecting the impact of human rights thinking and helping to create a somewhat broader constituency for this thinking as well.

A major judicial measure in 1864 established equality under the law officially, which also set up an independent judiciary and rights to trial by jury. The era of private, unregulated proceedings drew to a close, at least in terms of the law.

One additional change, during the reform era, was particularly striking, in reflecting the widening geographical scope of some of the most central rights concerns, whether or not relevant language was specifically invoked. A series of reforms of the Russian law codes not only promoted greater equality under the law, and provided more standardized legal procedures, but also dramatically cut back the number of crimes subject to drastic physical punishments, including the death penalty. At one point over 100 crimes had been subject to capital punishment, at least in principle, but opinion began to turn against this pattern from the 1820s onward. The reform era completed a process in which the death penalty could be applied only to a few crimes, beginning of course with murder; and by the 1890s, officially at least, imposition of capital punishment even for murder had become relatively rare.

Changes of this sort had drawbacks. A traditional regime that had offered protections to groups—such as ethnic groups or social categories—now yielded to a more individualistic approach which placed people in more direct contact with the state. Many ordinary peasants, antagonized in any event by the compensation payments required of them, showed little interest in their new legal status, preferring instead to rely on more customary village procedures. But the most obvious limitation of the reform era was that it came to an abrupt end, after the assassination of the reformist tsar in 1881. State censorship and policy surveillance were not only reestablished but stiffened. Political imprisonments (even an occasional execution) and exile to Siberia accelerated. A secret police organization expanded, with primary focus on real or imagined political crimes. Enforcement of the Orthodox religion returned, and persecutions of religious minorities, and especially Jews, became far more virulent. Despite some important legal changes, Russia had not converted to a human rights approach.

Yet important residues remained. As late as 1906 the tsarist regime introduced some further ramifications of the legal equality principle, opening state service to all comers and abolishing special access for the nobility. The language was interesting: the decree stipulated "the same rights to state service" for everyone, and the "abolition of all special advantage." Even a conservative, repressive regime acknowledged the validity of rights in certain categories.

Finally, several groups remained deeply interested in advocating certain kinds of rights. An active feminist movement, though centered in the upper classes, readily joined in some of the same demands for greater equality and freedom that were being mounted by organizations in the West—a clear sign, not just of shared sisterhood, but of surviving commitments to promoting rights-based arguments. The Russian regime had turned away; Russian society in general was less interested in rights issues than in protests about economic conditions; but connections to liberal thinking persisted as well.

The Ottoman experience

On the surface, the Ottoman Empire was more quickly responsive to human rights currents than Russia was. In 1838 the Sultan Mahmud II launched a process of political and religious change that would extend into the 1870s—a process collectively known as the *Tanzimat* (Reorganization) reforms. In principle, and to some extent in fact, the *Tanzimat* reforms were not only a bit earlier but further-reaching than what happened in Russia during its decades of change, though some of the same issues were involved.

There were two reasons for new Ottoman interest, always conditioned by extensive contacts with, and knowledge of, what was going on in Western Europe. First, the Ottoman Empire was reeling from a series of military defeats, losing significant territories, along with internal pressure from local military strongmen. Like the Russian tsar a bit later, the sultan realized that some serious changes were essential to rejuvenate Ottoman society and to reduce internal grievance. But, second, the Ottoman rulers—and here, far more than their Russian counterparts—were able to recall political traditions that had some correspondence to human rights thinking. The idea of rule by law, and an interest in a certain degree of legal equality, touched base with Islamic political culture. The new connections made in the *Tanzimat* period involved real change—this was not just tradition restated—but also served as an important reminder of how earlier efforts to protect people against arbitrary power could connect with the newer human rights concerns.

Thus the Gulhane Proclamation, of 1839, referred specifically to earlier days of the Empire in which "the glorious precept of the Quran and Laws of the Empire were always honored." But with this tradition invoked, the Proclamation went on to install new principles of judicial action, whereby "every accused person shall be publicly judged ... and so long as a regular judgment shall not have been pronounced, no one can, secretly or publicly, put another to death by poison or any other manner." This new principle of protection from arbitrary punishment explicitly extended to all religious groups, not just Muslims. Property rights were also firmly guaranteed. At the same time, the government sought to ban favoritism in state appointments.

The Proclamation was followed, in 1856 (after new military losses to Russia), by an outright bill of rights, further enshrined in a constitution twenty years later. The new statement more explicitly assured religious freedom and legal equality: "Every distinction or designation tending to make any class whatever of the subjects of my Empire inferior to another class, on account of their Religion, Language, or Race, shall be forever effaced"; "All forms of Religion are and shall be freely professed in my dominions, no subject of my Empire shall be hindered in the exercise of the Religion that he professes ... No one shall be compelled to change their religion." People of any religion had equal access to government posts. Police were enjoined to observe "the strongest guarantees" for the persons and property of all peaceful subjects, again regardless of religion. Tax differences among various religious communities were abolished.

These were revolutionary measures, designed to replace not only earlier inequalities, but also the traditional impulse to define communities rather than individuals as the primary source of interactions with the state. The effort to revise and regulate punishments also warrants attention, as another important connection with human rights thinking more generally.

And the measures had consequences. There is no question that religious minorities, particularly Christians and Jews, gained new freedom of operation, and began to develop new public presence, particularly in the area of business. Freedom of travel and rights to privacy were more widely respected, as Ottoman courts generally observed the rights of non-Muslim subjects. Ordinary Muslims were affected as well, always remembering that Muslim courts even earlier had sought to protect people from arbitrary treatment. A crowd could gather after a careful judicial verdict in the later 19th century to shout: "This is justice! This is law!"

The *Tanzimat* reforms, however, did not have the desired effect of stabilizing the empire itself. Various minority groups, defining themselves increasingly in the new terms of nationalism, used new freedom to agitate for national independence—particularly in southeastern Europe. Many Muslims opposed the reforms that weakened the hold of Islamic Sharia law, and that reduced, if not eliminated, their superior legal status.

In this situation, with a seemingly endless series of internal protests and conflicts, the Ottoman government pulled back—much as the Russian government was doing in the same period. A new sultan in 1878 nullified the constitution and bill of rights, particularly attacking freedom of the press. Many political prisoners were jailed, and some were tortured and killed. Though often responding to violent protest, the government also moved forcefully, sometimes brutally, against various national and religious minorities. As in Russia, reform interest persisted, though now often in secret, and various groups arose to urge the restoration of constitutional rights. Still, the hold of human rights goals in the empire was seriously challenged. And, as we will see, even more than with Russia, Western public opinion eagerly seized on Ottoman policies as a sign that the empire was incapable of living up to civilized standards.

A third zone

Russia and the Ottoman Empire constituted something of a third case in the global human rights panorama, as it developed in the 19th century. Human rights continued to find a primary home in Western societies, despite all sorts of inconsistencies and setbacks. A human rights agenda also gained ground in Latin America, though it faced more obstacles and greater competition from other approaches, particularly given frequent political instability. Human rights approaches also affected the Russian and Ottoman Empires, but without durably defining major goals, save for some relatively small groups like Russian feminists. An important overlap with Islamic political traditions, in the Ottoman realm, proved constrained by conflicting priorities in an empire that was struggling to survive. Conservative resistance to human rights was considerable both in Russia and in the Ottoman lands, generating alternative visions of how social organization should be constituted. Agitations for reform often took channels that differed from the human rights approach—peasant issues, for example, loomed far larger in Russia, nationalist issues in the Ottoman Empire, and, while both could overlap with human rights in some respects, the basic thrusts were different. Developments in both regions showed some genuine global extension of human rights principles, as these helped guide significant reform periods in both societies, periods that introduced important political change. But the complexities and resistances involved differed from patterns either in the West or in Latin America. As human rights gained greater global attention in the 19th century, it was inevitable that different kinds of regional responses took shape.

Global standards: the new idea of "crimes against humanity"

By the later 19th century, the globalization of human rights moved into a further phase, with efforts to define universal standards and rights protections as part of international diplomacy itself. This extension involved, first, a new effort to apply human rights thinking to some of the most recalcitrant areas of human conduct, beginning with war itself. The extension then involved a further attempt to use human rights standards as the basis for shaping a public opinion, across national lines, that could call to account governments or groups that were not measuring up to the new criteria. At an extreme, this could involve labeling certain behaviors as crimes against humanity—an important next step in the idea that all people deserved certain minimal protections regardless of nation, race, or religion.

A new human rights chapter opened after 1859, when the Swiss-Italian banker Henry Drumont became appalled at the poor treatment of wounded soldiers in an Austrian-Italian war. He wrote a book urging new international standards in this area, winning support from a variety of public figures, including the author Victor Hugo and Florence Nightingale, the British nurse. An early result was the first Geneva Convention, in 1864, which set minimum standards for the treatment of wounded soldiers (from whatever side), but also prisoners of war. These were people, in other words, who now had rights. A variety of countries signed on, initially primarily in Europe but within a few decades from other areas, including Japan (in 1890). The Geneva Convention would be periodically revised and expanded, through the 20th century, with new rules about weapons or war or the use of torture, but basic principles remained constant.

The same kind of thinking could now apply to the treatment of other groups, across international lines. In the 1870s a Bulgarian nationalist rising was put down by Ottoman troops, with considerable force. Press stories spread of up to 30,000 people killed and whole villages destroyed (the actual total in deaths was probably about 4000). Tales of torture also circulated widely in outside newspapers. Seemingly sober accounts detailed pregnant women disemboweled, "with their unborn babies carried triumphantly on the point of bayonet and sabre." West European journalists covered the whole incident extensively, and many prominent figures expressed their outrage. Russian intellectuals mobilized widely as well. British politicians, pressed by public opinion, denounced the Ottoman government, claiming to speak on behalf of the "moral sense of mankind at large." A former prime minister, William Gladstone, issued a pamphlet claiming that "Turkey" had committed a "deep and lasting crime against humanity," perhaps the first time that phrase had been used. Many leaders called for the Ottoman government to step down or at least punish the perpetrators.

The incident had many sides. The episode clearly reflected the new international communication capacities of the press. The indulgence of exaggeration, particularly in the case of an Ottoman government long criticized as decadent by the West, is obvious—this was a serious incident but it was embellished greatly. It's also important to note that Bulgarians were Christian, which tapped Western sentiment as well. But the notion that people in various parts of the world (admittedly, at this point still, primarily the West) could judge repressive behavior within another society according to standards presumably aiming at protecting innocent life constituted an important further step in a broader human rights effort. In principle, some offenses, even by established leaders in other societies, could be designated as unacceptable, an affront to civilized standards.

The same passion could be roused even outside the West, and it could also be directed against Western practices. By the late 19th century reformers in many societies protested lynching of racial minorities that were occurring in the southern United States. Both governments and bearers of public opinion were involved, noting the killings as "brutal" and "atrocious." While Europeans participated extensively in these criticisms, so did Mexico (in part because Mexican Americans were often victims), and so, after 1900, did the Japanese press. A Japanese paper commented that "the United States, which loves to win the world's best, has the world record in lynching as well." American reformers, in turn, organized international tours to push this feeling of outrage to higher levels, and cited the results in letters back home. Thus Mary Church Terrell, after a conference in Berlin in 1904, wrote that "even the most intelligent foreigner" finds it appalling that "colored men, women and children are still being lynched in the United States."

Most of these early efforts, to extend human rights into national domains where official or unofficial repression was involved, generated few results. It would be decades still before the United States was moved to take firm action against lynching, and post-reform Ottoman nationalist policies changed little in face of outside criticism. But the notion of articulating minimal global standards was beginning to gain traction, another example of how this thinking could expand on the world stage.

Constraints on human rights in decades of globalization

Thus far in this chapter we have been discussing the various ways in which human rights activities fanned out to additional regions of the world. Special contacts and historical ties with the West promoted this process. So did concerted campaigns, beginning with the geographical expansion of the efforts against slavery. So did new efforts to apply human rights calculations to international activities themselves, such as war and diplomacy. All of these developments made human rights by 1900 a far more global topic, in fact, and not just in principle, than had been the case a century before. The fact that different regions responded variably was an inevitable part of this expansion process.

Global extension was not the only 19th-century story, however. New impediments and contradictions also emerged, helping to explain why, in some human rights histories, the 19th century is often largely omitted or regarded simply as part of a hostile past. The most obvious issue stemmed from the expansion of European imperialism, which trampled rights in many regions while also, at times, importing a few more positive reforms. But it was also true that some regions largely stood apart from human rights initiatives, sometimes even while eagerly courting other types of change. The results of both patterns—both imperialism and diffidence/resistance—not only added to the regional variety in human rights responses, but positively limited the whole category as a global phenomenon.

Imperialism

The mid-19th century launched a new round of Western imperialism, based on the West's growing military and economic strength, both derived from the growing industrial base. Many nations participated, including new additions to the imperialist list such as Germany and the United States. New conquests gobbled additional territory in Southeast Asia and the Pacific. China remained technically independent, but huge coastal regions were seized as leases. Africa, both northern and sub-Saharan, was almost entirely carved up.

These were conquests by force or threat of force. Imperialists were adept at negotiating some local support, but military pressure, and often some bloody, one-sided battles, underwrote the whole effort.

Historians have debated the causes for the new surge. Imperialists were stirred by economic factors, seeking secure markets and resources for an increasingly competitive world economy and by opportunities for personal profit as well. Diplomatic maneuvering also played a crucial role, with countries like Britain seizing new colonies to guard against German or French pressure, with the latter responding in kind. Human rights played no real role in the basic causal equation.

The human rights consequences, however, were another matter. Imperialism seriously compromised the globalization of human rights, in several ways, though some standard historical complexity must be added to the mix.

Several categories require attention. In the first place, imperialists often spoke of their civilizing mission—what poet Rudyard Kipling famously called the "white man's burden." Many advocates of empire talked of bringing backward races up to more progressive standards. Much of this was self-serving nonsense, designed to put a more graceful face on the use of force and the new opportunities to exploit subject peoples. Victims of imperialist conquest in Asia or Africa could not fail to notice the hypocrisy gap between Western assertions of progress and the scorn with which many local demands were treated. Imperialism was not a good advertisement for human rights or for serious Western commitment to any idea of a common humanity.

Yet there were some reform moves that reflected elements of human rights thinking, and some imperialists probably did believe at least part of their own publicity. Colonial administrators, often supplemented by Christian missionaries, did press to end formal slavery in Africa and elsewhere. Newborn twins gained new protection in West Africa, against a traditional impulse to put them to death as a sign of evil. In India, the British took action against another tradition, *sati*, in which some Indian women committed suicide after their husbands' death, throwing themselves on funeral pyres on grounds that, with a husband gone, there was nothing else for a woman to live for. More widely, imperial administrations brought some new attention to education for children, though never at the level of establishing a general right. There were, in sum, a number of positive or potentially positive moves. Even in China, Western influence helped spur an unprecedented effort by local reformers to move against the longstanding practice of foot binding for women.

Programs of this sort, importing new standards, could challenge practices that were certainly open to question in human rights terms—even when formal invocation of "rights" was not part of the mix. Equally important, they could even motivate individuals and groups within the colonial society to think in terms of a relevant commitment to further reform—and possibly to the idea of human rights itself. Several Indian thinkers by the mid-19th century, though resentful of British domination and reluctant to accept even one sampling of British standards, did conclude that they, too, needed to speak out against *sati*, because of its hideous unfairness to widows. The Chinese campaign against foot binding could link to wider women's rights efforts later on. Imperialism, in these senses, positively furthered human rights globalization, particularly in parts of Asia. Seeds were planted for later advocacy within the region, and from the region on larger human rights issues worldwide.

But reform was not the main thrust of imperialism, and imperialist reform itself presented some obvious downsides, limiting its impact in building new constituencies for human rights. Reform ideas often created resentment at foreign pressure, even generating backlash against the standards involved. Proposed new rights for women might seem far less important, even to many women themselves, than reassertions of traditional identity against outside criticism from the West. Imperialist language often introduced reforms in terms of presumed inferiorities of regional cultures and the backwardness of colonial races, requiring Western enlightenment—an approach that hardly moved large populations to embrace new rights language or concepts. Racist assumptions, not classic human rights arguments, too often framed the reforms that were presented. New moves in education, for example, were frequently qualified by doubts that "natives" could meet serious intellectual standards anytime soon.

Imperialist regimes were also hesitant and inconsistent, another limitation with their effective involvement with human rights. Traditional practices that were clearly at odds with rights standards were often left untouched by administrators fearful of rousing local opposition to their foreign rule. We have seen, for instance, that female circumcision was largely ignored in north-eastern Africa, at least until after World War II. The British in India did little to raise questions about the caste system, despite its incompatibility with any idea of legal equality—the topic was simply too hot to handle for governments intent, above all, on maintaining their claims to authority. Imperialism was not, at base, a human rights mission, which helps explain its limited impact in encouraging change in regional cultures.

Imperialist governments also undermined some traditional community protections for certain categories of the population, creating new human rights issues that the administrators themselves, as foreigners, could not easily perceive. In Africa, for example, Western legal standards tended to treat women as subordinate members of individual nuclear families, which wea-kened important regional traditions in which extended families and villages had exercised considerable responsibility for women's wellbeing. In India, imports of British legal principles, and assumptions that traditional Indian family practices were uniformly "barbaric," had similar unsettling con-sequences. For example, new rules about widows' control of property, based on the models back home, actually undermined wellbeing when compared to the shared control within an extended family that had been part of earlier Indian tradition.

The huge clash between imperialism and human rights, however, lay in imperialism's ultimate reliance on force and compulsion. The new regimes were not only typically imposed by force, but maintained by force as well, against any commitment to political rights or rights of expression for local populations. The result blocked many groups from any awareness of new human rights standards at all, while convincing others of the absolute hollowness of Western claims in this area.

Political repression could be extensive. In 1904, the Herero people, one of the main components of the population of German-held southwest Africa (now Namibia) rose in revolt against German control, killing about 150 German set-tlers. A hastily imported German army defeated the rebels, but the German administration insisted on going further. The Herero were denied rights as German subjects, forced to leave the colony or be killed. Many fled to the desert, where they died of thirst—in all, half or more of the population was exterminated. Colonial leaders proudly proclaimed that, thanks to the army and the desert combined, "the Herero nation is eliminated." This was a drastic case, but it illustrated the ferocity with which imperialist governments could punish, with no consideration to legal processes of any sort.

In many colonies, outright force, again including harsh physical discipline, drove local workers into Western-owned mines and other operations. Practices in the Belgian Congo were particularly vicious, but similar abuses occurred elsewhere without rousing widespread international protest. More widely, economic pressure, often exacerbated by European seizure of local lands, pushed workers into activities that undermined local economies and increased the hardship of work itself. Late 19th-century imperialism trumpeted its opposition to slavery, but to many colonial populations new compulsions obscured any human rights principles.

Many imperialist regimes used flogging routinely to punish locals, at a time when back home this approach was being rejected for its cruelty. In Kenya, for example, British officials even whipped natives for, ironically, their cruelty to animals.

Equally obvious, especially to potential leadership groups, was the clash between imperialism and open political expression. Protests against imperial rule were put down with violence, but there was more. Dissident political and religious groups were carefully watched, their leaders periodically arrested. As these repressive practices continued into the 20th century, few of the people who would ultimately form national governments—when imperialism finally crumbled after World War II—had not spent significant amounts of time in colonial jails; hardly a favorable exposure to the political rights that Westerners might espouse in other contexts. Even when trials were involved, they were frequently rigged against local defendants, designed to show the dire consequences of expressing any but the most timid sentiments on political issues. Here, too, imperialism constituted a contradiction of human rights standards, seriously compromising their status in the vast colonial territories and preempting much local interest.

In principle, local leaders seeking to resist imperialism might well have taken up human rights arguments on their own behalf, as had occurred in the independence movements in Haiti and the Americas a century before. And there were some gestures in that direction. By the 20th century, leaders of Indian nationalism, headed by Mohandas Gandhi, developed tactics of nonviolent mass protests against British rule, convinced that British public opinion, shaped in part by human rights values, would prevent excessively repressive responses. Gandhi, heartily aware of British political culture through his own education, also espoused values of religious tolerance and greater legal equality, seeking to rally different religions, women, and lower caste Indians to his cause. In the main, however, resistance to imperialism, even in India, did not focus primarily in terms of classic human rights values. The fundamentals of imperialism itself constrained any such response.

Rather, from the late 19th century onward, most resistance leaders turned to nationalist rather than human rights rhetoric to justify their cause. Each people had a right to national self-determination, according to the argument that was gaining ground—but this was a collective right, rather different from the bundle of individual rights that defined the human rights approach. To most leaders in the struggle against imperialism, nationalist goals at the very least came first. Some would indeed argue that self-determination should be seen atop the human rights list itself, with greater importance than religious freedom or a free press. Prioritization was not, however, the only issue. If nationalist goals came first, what about the status of religious or racial minorities within the nation—including groups that might well have sided with European imperialists for their own protection? Should a consciousness of human rights standards restrain the curtailment of political rights for groups that had not supported the resistance cause, or that for other reasons opposed the nationalist definition of government? Serious tensions emerged in many anti-imperialist campaigns, and they would easily survive into the post-empire era, compromising any new commitment to human rights even when the contradictions of imperialism itself had ended.

For whatever combinations of reasons, including the difficult issue of combining national rights with human rights, many anti-imperialist leaders were not very interested in human rights, because of their sense of more important national traditions, their experience at the hands of Western colonialists, or other factors. The criteria seemed irrelevant—far less important than nation-building— or foreign, or both. The Indian experience is instructive here. Gandhi himself preferred an emphasis on the social obligations of individuals to any quest for protecting individual rights and refused to join human rights organizations. Another vital nationalist leader, Jawaharlal Nehru, ultimately the first leader of independent India, took a seemingly different stance. He recognized the importance of the Western human rights tradition and saw that it might be used to protect nationalist agitation. In this vein, he formed an Indian civil liberties association in 1936, based closely on the model of a similar United States organization. At the time, 55,000 nationalist leaders were in jail, and Nehru urged the importance of freeing up public opinion to criticize the imperialist government. Not many other leaders joined in, however, and the organization died off fairly quickly. It soon became clear that, as nationalists gained power, initially in some provincial governments, they sought to use their new position to stifle opposition. One regional leader thus proclaimed that it was impossible to have civil liberties in a "surcharged" atmosphere. Many opposition newspapers were shut down, and Nehru himself largely turned against the human rights movement in favor of building a more unified national government with his political party (the Congress Party) in charge. Civil liberties were not extinguished in newly independent India, but it became apparent that many of the new nationalist leaders largely accepted the repressive policies that imperial Britain had imposed—simply to sustain a different regime.

Overall, the explosion of 19th-century imperialism, revealing as it did that lack of a full human rights commitment in the West itself, both delayed and impeded the globalization of human rights. Imperialism contradicted human rights principles, in the eyes of many colonial groups, while preventing access to the principles for masses of people exposed to new levels of economic exploitation. The resulting complexities continue to affect world history even today.

Cultural resistance: a second barrier

Along with imperialism, another set of developments, becoming more obvious by the later 19th century, also contributed to the confusing patterns of human rights geography. Several regions, though open to some change, found human rights arguments relatively unattractive, and in some cases political and economic leaders mounted explicit counterarguments as part of their process of response. The result was not as serious as the complications that imperialism introduced, but it contributed to a durable set of regional diversities from this point onward.

Japan was an intriguing case in point. Prior to 1868, Confucian culture had gained particular influence in Japan, with its important statement of social responsibilities; we have seen that a word for "rights" was introduced to the language only in 1870. With 1868 and the Meiji era of reform, Japan entered a period of active imitation of all sorts of Western initiatives, from public health to military organization and technology to the early stages of industrialization itself. New discussions of human rights were part of this process but, crucial for an ongoing understanding of regional diversity, not a dominant part.

Spillover did occur, and it was significant. The Japanese imported law codes from France and Germany, though adding local traditions. The government formally provided for religious toleration in 1873. Individual Japanese scholars and reformers went further still: Nakae Chomin, for example, after spending several years in France in the 1870s, returned to Japan as an ardent advocate of blending Confucianism with natural rights philosophy. He translated Rousseau into Japanese and founded the Freedom and People's Rights Movement. Support for human rights in Japan had an eager, if limited, local base from this point onward. We have seen also that the Japanese were particularly concerned about contradictions between Western racism and human rights standards, in the world at large.

But great emphasis continued to be placed on the importance of community and responsibility to society, rather than undue interest in individual rights and protections. In the 1880s the government specifically turned away from undue Western influence in these matters, urging the primacy of loyalty to society and emperor. Yamagata Aritomo, a former samurai who backed the Meiji regime, urged against too much indulgence of individual opinion—what he called "unproductive political debate"—in favor of obedience and adherence to group norms. "Self-respect and self-restraint" were vital to any real freedom. A business leader noted, similarly, that real citizenship consisted of putting society first and the self second. Too much competition or individualism would destroy society: "in order to get along together ... and serve the State, we must by all means abandon this idea of independence and self-reliance and reject egoism completely." Any particular emphasis on human rights was simply irrelevant in this dominant view.

A new constitution, in 1889, tried to put the pieces together. It confirmed equality under the law. It worked to "respect the security of the rights and property" of the people. A specific section on "rights and duties of subjects" specified freedom of speech and the press, and protected individuals against arbitrary arrests. Petitions to the state were permitted so long as they "observed the proper forms of respect." But this important, if modest, section was balanced, in the constitution as a whole, by repeated emphasis on the supreme authority of the emperor—"sacred and inviolable"—and the importance of duty. "We doubt not but that Our subjects will be guided Our views," as the emperor intoned, adding also people would work for "harmonious cooperation" and the glory of the country at home and abroad. Human rights existed, but in a context that gave far more attention to collective identity. Japan formed a culture open to genuine change, but actively committed to values that placed human rights in a subsidiary position.

Voices in other regions similarly worked for alternatives to a human rights approach, without falling back merely on traditionalism or unvarnished repression. We have seen that Russia moved into a period of retrenchment, following the brief reform era after 1861. This was accompanied by elaborate conservative statements that held Russian political culture up as a desirable alternative to chaotic Western individualism. The nationalist Nikolai Danilevsky, for example, wrote about the need for a strong and expanding state to assure freedom. He claimed that true freedom was deeply ingrained in the Russian character thanks to the people's:

> ability and habit to obey, their respect and trust in the authorities ... and their loathing of interference in matters where they do not consider themselves competent. If we look into the causes of all political troubles, we shall find their root not in the striving after freedom, but in the love for power and the vain cravings of human beings to interfere in affairs that are beyond their comprehension.

Freedom, in other words, consisted in letting authorities run a strong state and spontaneously going along with their decisions. Strong community life, which Danilevsky painted for the Russian peasantry, provided a further basis for a successful society. This was simply a different, more collective version of political success, with no explicit human rights involved. Danilevsky warned Russian reformers against "the cancer of imitativeness and servile attitude toward the West"—and small wonder, for his vision was very different.

By the early 20th century, Russian politics, beneath the level of tsarist repressions, divided increasingly between conservative advocates on the one hand, for whom political order and authority were paramount, and a growing array of Marxists and other social revolutionaries on the other. Neither group valued a classic definition of human rights, with Marxists for their part pointing to the need for power to the working class and massive economic restructuring over the distractions of individual political rights. Liberal agitation continued as well, for example, in the pressures for further legal gains for women, but the effort was crammed between quite different agendas both on the right and on the left.

The geography of human rights grew increasingly complicated as more and more regions were exposed to some aspects of human rights thinking, but amid very different traditions and conditions. For the many regions bound by imperialism, human rights were typically dwarfed by other issues and counter-examples. Other regions had experienced a relevant reform period but, at least at the official level, turned away by the end of the 19th century. Still other regions, like Japan, made some modest accommodations to elements of a human rights program, but saved predominant attention for a new–old emphasis on order and authority. China, disrupted by Western incursions but also a host of internal problems, found little opportunity to consider human rights options save in limited areas such as the campaign against foot binding. Serious discussion began only in the 1920s, when in fact a human rights association did form (1925), but by this point nationalist passions pushed many leaders to claim that only people who supported their definition of the nation deserved rights of any sort. The West itself was divided between real human rights commitments and the deep drive to gain and maintain authority over the rest of the world. Human rights issues of some sort had emerged almost every-where, thanks to a combination of contacts and the efforts of groups such as the anti-slavery organizations; to this extent, a real globalization had occurred during the 19th century. But there was no global conversion yet, as opposed to a confusing mixture of exposures, counterreactions, and other reform options.

Lengthening the list

A final development added to the rich but complex history of human rights in the 19th century, though it had been foreshadowed earlier: the list of basic rights began to grow. Crucial innovations in this area occurred mainly within the West, but the changes found wider geographical echoes soon, including the wave of revolutions that helped open the 20th century. The new human rights list certainly reflected the continued dynamism of the movement as a whole, despite the complexities of global response.

Three areas particularly generated the wider application of standards, along with the growing effort to reshape war and diplomacy through some minimal humane principles. Children's education gained steadily greater attention, along with regulations limiting child labor. Innovations followed from the rise of factory work, but spread more widely as other societies realized the importance of redefining childhood. The results were not yet framed in terms of children's rights, but they were leading in that direction. The idea of extending rights to women, a minority current in 1800, won increasing support and new breadth—the most clear-cut addition to the rights list overall, though still incompletely implemented. Finally, various commentators, and especially socialist critics of the capitalist industrial order, began adding material rights and labor rights to the list of basics. This was a category that had not been clearly suggested in the classic Enlightenment statements, but industrial conditions seemed to require the wider purview.

From the middle of the 19th century onward, a host of nations adopted measures to require school attendance from children, initially at the primary level, and to limit children's work. Britain, France, and Prussia passed child labor laws by the 1830s, as evidence mounted that factory work was dangerous and taxing at least for children under 12. Initial enforcement was weak, but it gradually improved; and many worker families themselves decided that children were best served through more traditional types of labor or even schooling. Gradually, in the cities, work for younger children did decline, even beyond the hard-driving factories. In place of work, reformers increasingly urged the importance of education. School requirements blossomed in the northern states of the United States from the early 1850s onward, and also in several European countries. They were becoming standard by the final decades of the century. Challenges remained: the United States saw its peak amount of child labor (mainly by teenagers, not the younger children) early in the 20th century, which spurred new reform efforts that contended that any formal work for children, traditional or novel, was wrong and should be stopped—and, of course, replaced by more effective oversight for school attendance. The effort paid off, as American rates of child labor began to sink rapidly and school-going became the norm even beyond the primary level. And other countries, convinced that the new patterns for children were essential to economic development, began to join the parade. Japan passed a compulsory education law in 1872 and, by the 1890s, attendance became standard at least for several years. Japan and Russia both introduced regulations in principle limiting child labor.

By 1900, in other words, patterns had been set that radically transformed the experience of childhood and offered protections from exploitative work while furthering opportunities for educational development. The patterns were not, usually, framed in terms of rights. To be sure, an initial book, Thomas Spence's *Rights of Infants*, had appeared in Britain in 1796. But it was only in the 20th century that further thinking about children began to translate reform efforts into the language of human rights. World War I played a key role here, in prompting new attention to the plight of children during conflicts; a determined Englishwoman, Eglantyne Jebb, spearheaded relief efforts for children and set up a larger "Save the Children" movement. By the 1920s, this impulse, and more general support for education, was translating into formal rights campaigns. A Polish educator, Janusz Korczak, issued a book, *The Child's Right to Respect*, in 1929. Jebb herself developed a statement of children's rights in 1923 that was endorsed by the League of Nations the following year. The statement was somewhat vague, urging provision of necessary food and health care, appropriate remedial efforts for delinquents, and overall a commitment to provide each child with "the means requisite for its normal development both materially and spiritually." League endorsement provided no legal sanction, and obviously many areas of the world were not yet deeply affected by significant children's rights action. International advocacy continued, however, with backing from a number of countries, including Switzerland, where the International Save the Children Union now centered. Officials in the Belgian government also pressed for children's rights, though other countries, like Britain, fearful of international interference in the treatment of children, held back. A trajectory was established that would carry on to more far-reaching efforts after World War II.

Attention to women's rights, as an essential component of human rights more generally, emerged far more firmly than was true with the complex category of children. Meetings and associations to promote women's rights surfaced in several places by the 1840s. In some cases, anti-slavery agitation led directly to the formation of women's rights groups, where arguments about the equality of all humanity could have comparable bearing and where male efforts to exclude women from anti-slavery meetings provided a more specific spur.

Women's rights initiatives developed a number of key targets, in addition to general arguments about the need to include women in the various protections applied to humanity as a whole. Property rights loomed large. In Britain, the United States, and elsewhere, legal changes from the mid-19th century onward, under the heading of Married Women's Property Rights, gave individual women firmer control over property, independent of their husbands. Access to schooling was another issue. While most of the new education measures applied to girls as well as boys, women had to work hard to gain rights of admission to professional schools in areas like law and medicine. Sexual exploitation drew attention, with women's groups urging protection for women from the various pressures that might induce prostitution. Governments that sanctioned prostitution (while also sometimes providing some oversight) were urged to step back. Fears of organized international trafficking of women, or what was called "white slavery," generated great concern at the end of the century. While programs drew particular support in Western society, they often gained wider attention. Burned by a widely publicized incident in 1900, for example, Japan passed a measure specifying that any individual woman had the right to leave prostitution, without permission of a brothel owner. Many Latin American countries stepped up to restrict the importation of sex workers.

Great attention, of course, focused on the right to vote, a key area where women argued that gender constraints should not apply. New Zealand became the first nation to grant voting rights, in 1893, and a number of Scandinavian societies followed soon after 1900.

Agitation for women's rights generated a number of budding international organizations. Marie Gregg, a Swedish woman, formed the first International Association, in 1868. Three groups were operating by the 1880s. Global conferences became common, claiming to provide a voice for the "women of the world" in the name of the "great ideals of civilization and progress." Clearly, by the early 20th century, a powerful feminist movement had taken shape, in many regional centers, dedicated to the definition and promotion of women's rights as a core component of any larger efforts.

Disputes persisted, of course, even as more and more countries granted measures such as the vote. A number of organized groups, including women's groups, sprang up to oppose the idea of equal rights for women, arguing that special functions such as motherhood should be the focus of attention. Some reformers themselves were tempted to urge particular measures for women, rather than treatment as part of common humanity. An interesting issue arose on the labor front: should women be given the right to special protections in terms of hours and safety different from those of men, given their family responsibilities and health needs, or should labor rights be genderless? Reformers in the 19th century tended to emphasize special protections, but this would need to be revisited later on. Even with disputes, however, it was clear that women's issues had gained a durable place on the human rights agenda, and awareness of many of the leading concerns spread to many regions of the world.

Finally, there was the question of rights bearing on labor and material conditions, potentially for all people, regardless of age and gender. By the middle of the 19th century a cluster of socialist leaders, repelled by the miserable conditions of the industrial working class, called for a rethinking of human rights. Some, like Karl Marx, were suspicious of the human rights agenda, seeing it as irrelevant to the need for improving material conditions and challenging the capitalist order of the economy. On the whole, however, socialist spokespeople, including Marx, touched base with human rights in several ways. The French leader Louis Blanc thus noted, "The poor man has the right to better his position ... but what difference does that make, if he has not the power to do so." Rights, in other words, were irrelevant unless the power of business owners over workers was modified—but, if redefined, they could push in the proper direction. Marx himself noted the relationship between the fight for a new economic system based on workers' power and the battle against slavery. Workers, after all, though not legal slaves, were in many ways the equivalent, for they had to "sell themselves" to capital.

Socialist voices did not triumph in the 19th century. But their agitation, combined with efforts by other worker organizations such as trade unions, combined in turn with the growing evidence of severe material dislocations under industrial capitalism, did begin to add an important economic dimension to discussions of human rights. We have seen that presentations of children's rights, by the late 19th century, routinely addressed economic issues as preconditions for children's opportunities for development. Women's rights (spurred by the largely middle-class orientation of most feminists) often stayed more in the political realm, except for attention to sexual exploitation. More generally, however, a sense of the need for societies to pay some attention to problems of poverty, unemployment, and the material conditions of later age began to work its way into human rights discussions. By the 1880s, some countries, headed by Germany, were actually introducing preliminary versions of welfare reforms, offering some unemployment insurance and pension funding; measures of this sort might translate more general beliefs that, without some minimal protections for workers, other human rights lacked real meaning. Even non-socialist reformers increasingly added attention to "social questions" of this sort as part of any discussion of social obligations.

And there was a very specific issue as well: the question of workers' right to form organizations to protect their wages and working conditions—the right to unionize. Most Western societies, early in the industrialization process, had actually outlawed worker groups, believing that they would merely sow disorder and hold back the industrialization process. With time, however, the same societies began to relax their restrictions. Britain, for example, altered its approach to trade unions in the mid-1820s, though many tensions remained. Extending rights to unionize touched base with earlier human rights criteria, around freedom of association, so the category was in many ways an easy extension in principle. But given the resistance to worker groups by many employers, and ongoing government concerns about potential centers of resistance, a commitment to worker rights to organize, and related rights of protection of union leaders from job dismissals or imprisonment, became an important measure of the adjustment of human rights statements to current economic realities.

The reworking of the human rights list was still a work in progress as the 19th century drew to a close. None of the additions was firmly established beyond a narrow band of countries, with Scandinavia interestingly in the lead. New rights could also complicate geographical response. Including women on the basic list might raise issues for particularly patriarchal societies like Japan, already a bit hesitant about the whole approach. Particularly capitalist countries like the United States were less interested in extending rights ideas to the realm of material conditions. Mixed responses of this sort added to the global indeterminacy of human rights discussions by 1900—and, of course, even further confusion might result from nationalist references to collective rights of self-determination. It became increasingly easy to debate which set of rights deserved top priority, or to worry that the basic principles were being pressed too far, in too many different directions.

1914–1945

The human rights balance sheet for the 19th century was decidedly mixed. There were real gains, especially in the realm of legal equality. Global outreach clearly expanded, though amid varied regional reactions. The range of defined rights expanded as well, which inevitably created further agendas for the future: for example, even in areas where classic rights categories like religious freedom and freedom of the press were fairly clearly established by the late 19th century, new questions about women's rights would not be resolved for several decades at best. But a variety of resistances even to the initial definitions of rights emerged as well, blocking much change in key regions or even reversing the results of an interim reform period. Many regimes experimented a bit with rights but then pulled back, and some others were simply uninterested in the first place. On another front: imperialism seriously compromised the human rights message from the West, making it easy to see even positive reform efforts as unwanted foreign imports. Even more directly, the imperial surge led to a variety of repressive efforts by colonial systems, based not only on self-protection but on assumptions of the inferiority of colonized peoples.

But if the 19th century record was mixed, the human rights patterns of the years between the world wars were truly disastrous, with only modest silver linings in sight. Many new regimes turned against human rights, while few additional regions opened their doors any further. New bouts of civil strife and persecutions defied any definition of humane standards. War itself frequently engulfed civilians, again violating any commitment to a common humanity. Additionally, some of the passion that in the past had supported human rights claims now turned more fully to the cause of national independence against imperialism. This was not a new tension, but it became more acute, again reducing, at least for a time, potential support for human rights, or at least for such rights as top priority. Overall, human rights interests did not perish during these difficult decades, but they were in retreat.

A rash of attacks

Serious problems began in World War I itself. Contemporary wartime mobilizations turned out to involve huge restrictions on freedoms of the press, even in Western countries. Fears of spies or internal subversion sparked new police activity and political arrests. Organized propaganda offered distorted news about the enemy that blunted any sense of common humanity. Wartime measures provided models for patterns of restriction and manipulation that would define many regimes in the postwar years. Peoples newly exposed to Western values during the war, like Indian or African colonial troops serving in the European theater, learned few human rights messages, as opposed to growing interests in nationalism as the main focus for future struggles against imperialism.

It was also revealing that a new wave of revolutions, before and then during the war, produced complications in the human rights picture somewhat different from the patterns that had emerged in the earlier Western revolutionary wave at the end of the 19th century. There were important gains, but the ultimate vocabulary downplayed or omitted some of the classic components of previous bills of rights. Revolutions in Mexico and Russia did produce new assurances of legal equality—in Russia, now including women; and in Mexico, embracing the Indian minority—and attacks on monopolies by established churches. We will return to these real gains, but the new regimes, once consolidated, also limited freedom of expression and assembly. In Russia, campaigns against religion qualified commitments to individual rights in this area. More broadly, over its first two decades the new communist government in Russia repressed political opposition and quickly reestablished and expanded the secret police, arresting hundreds of thousands of real or imagined dissidents and killing millions of civilians as part of imposing new programs such as collective farms. Revolutionary Mexico, though less fierce, also restricted political activities in defense of its single party system. The new regimes generated many positive changes, in terms of social reforms and, in Russia's case, economic development, but systematic human rights goals were simply not on the policy agenda—some rhetoric to the century.

Even more ominous were the wave of fascist regimes that sprang up in various parts of Europe, beginning with Italy and extending to Nazi

Germany, with analogues or partial analogues in other regions as well. Fascism was explicitly opposed to human rights. Fascist leaders condemned the protections for individuals, in favor of the transcendent importance of the state and of course the dominance of the Leader. Mussolini, in Italy, put it this way: "The state is not simply a mechanism which limits the supposed liberties of the individual," but rather a societal whole that increases human energies by grouping them. Collective strength, not distracting rights, should be the aim. Fascism in practice was even more ruthlessly opposed to human rights than the often vague theoretical statements suggested. To monopolize power, the regimes built powerful secret police forces, with extensive imprisonment and torture of political dissidents. Religious freedom was curtailed through various state controls, and freedom of the press vanished altogether. During World War II, the Nazis effectively reestablished a slave system, with the forced labor of prisoners and others taken abroad. The Nazis, and in their wake other fascists, viciously attacked the legal and personal security rights of Jews, and then in the Holocaust slaughtered millions of them outright. Human rights were trampled in virtually every major category.

Abuses mounted in other societies as well. Japanese forces butchered many Chinese civilians, particularly during the 1930s and then during World War II. The Spanish Civil War, also in the 1930s, brought air attacks on civilian centers. A new round of authoritarian regimes in Eastern Europe and parts of Latin America, as well as Spain, attacked various political freedoms and took many political prisoners, often without trial.

Against these onslaughts, resistance in the name of human rights was feeble and ineffective. Dominated by isolationism, the United States largely stood by, passively. Nazi crimes drew surprisingly weak and scattered international protests. Other issues, including the dislocations of the Great Depression, fear of communism, and anxiety about another world war, took clear precedence.

The devastating setbacks to human rights during the years between 1914 and 1945 had several consequences. Most obviously, many people suffered from the global retreat, and sometimes suffered hugely, in many different regions of the world. Second, precedents set during these decades would find later echoes. Military attacks on civilians or genocidal onslaughts against a race or nationality would be repeated many times and in many places in the decades after World War II. New authoritarian regimes would learn from some of the police tactics pioneered in the 1930s. Recurrent postwar challenges to human rights standards—for example, concerning freedom of the press—fed on the patterns generated between the wars. But the human rights retreat also helps explain the great resurgence and expansion of global human rights efforts after World War II. As leaders and publics in many regions awoke to the horrors of defying human rights, particularly in the context of contemporary technological and organizational power, it became obvious that more systematic definitions and defenses were essential. This was part of the mood that activated the new United Nations and its early commitments in this area. The dark decades helped cause later revival, given the roots that human rights thinking had already planted in various parts of the world but also the clear evidence of the depths to which scorn of key rights could lead.

The positive side

For, finally, amid all the setbacks of the second quarter of the 20th century, human rights standards were by no means obliterated. A few modest victories were even recorded, both in the implementation of certain types of rights and in some specific regional gains. These, too, would feed the wider revival and expansion after 1945. References to human rights began to spread to some additional regions, beyond 19th-century patterns, and the list of rights under consideration continued to expand. At the rhetorical level, at least, there were even some strides toward further globalization.

New geography for human rights

In the years after World War I, several new regimes discussed human rights, in various ways, in their political constitutions. The Mexican revolution, for example, renewed a Latin American commitment to human rights while adding important new interests, in ways that ultimately influenced other nations as well. The constitution of 1917 confirmed many of the classic human rights. As one delegate put it, "no one supported the elimination of individual guarantees, the established rights of man." But the constitution added to this approach a variety of social concerns, seeking broader protections for conditions of work, land reform for the peasantry, and other measures designed to improve economic circumstances for ordinary people. This addition to the list of effective rights focused on "material needs that are presuppositions for the exercise of [human] liberty." In fact, as we have seen, the new Mexican regime faced a number of constraints in dealing with economic issues, while the establishment of one-party rule cut into some of the political assurances for individual rights. But the commitment in principle remained significant, along with the expansion of a social agenda.

The Russian revolution, though less explicit in classic language, showed some similar inclinations to defend human rights in principle while augmenting the definition of what was involved. The Soviet Union, in key constitutions in 1924 and 1936 (and then later, in 1977), spoke eloquently of human rights in many respects. Several main points emerged. First, the constitutions made it clear that Soviet leaders, true to their sense of revolutionary mission, defined human rights differently from the classic statements in the West. Their main goal, in principle, was putting an end to economic injustice—"to exploitation of man by man." The constitutions spoke eloquently of the importance of the "free development" of each individual. This was followed, however, by a focus on improving working conditions and economic standards, giving these clear priority over the political protections of the individual cherished in Western bills of rights. In the process the constitutions proclaimed clear rights in categories like access to leisure, health care, and education. The commitment to human rights, again at least at the level of principle, was genuine but distinctive.

At the same time, certain rights were also defined that overlapped with more standard Western categories. Harmony was greatest in the area of equality under the law, where Soviet and Western conceptions coincided. The constitutions were quite explicit about gender equality, but also referred to religious and nationality groups and other categories. But there was more. The constitutions proclaimed "freedom of conscience," making it clear that this included the right not to believe in any religion. Freedom of inquiry was assured to artists and scientists. People should also have the right to criticize state officials, and "persecution for criticism is prohibited." Most Western observers, and current historians, would quickly note that many of these rights were rather hollow, because supportive laws that actually assured the various assurances were lacking. Further, the constitutions expressly assured the Communist Party of political monopoly, representing the people's will. This context, and the actual operations of the Soviet state, doomed much political freedom, in fact, particularly from the end of the 1920s onward, with Stalin's grip on leadership. And finally, even in principle, certain standard rights were missing from the Soviet statements—notably in categories such as freedom of the press.

We have already noted that the advance of the Soviet system, again particularly under Stalinism, serves as a key illustration of the retreat of human rights. Even so, the Soviet proclamations of principle demonstrated the importance of at least *seeming* to appeal to certain aspects of human rights thinking, even to the point of talking about the "free development" of each individual. A tension existed between the often grim political realities and the kinds of aspirations leaders wanted to claim; and, while realities were more significant, the claims showed that human rights thinking had a certain hold as well. And the alternative definitions of rights—the emphasis on economic and educational conditions—need serious consideration as well. Soviet goals both reflected and furthered a broader definition of human rights than the classic Western versions had generated, and this would be a vital part of the context for human rights discussions after 1945.

The new nation of Turkey, carved from part of the former Ottoman Empire, was another regime that laid important claims to segments of a human rights agenda. Even more than with the Soviet Union, political developments here modestly but definitely altered the geography of human rights. Turkey's new leader, Kemal Atatürk, was keenly attuned to Western political example, and in many ways he also picked up and extended the reform tradition that had been ventured by Ottoman rulers in the middle of the 19th century. The result was an important, if distinctive, furtherance of certain human rights in a key Middle Eastern region.

The new government asserted the equality of religions and the freedom to worship, ending the old Ottoman system of religious communities, including special religious courts, in favor of the protection of individual rights. Equality under the law was also explicitly extended to women, a major development within the Islamic world and well ahead of comparable measures even in many European countries. Atatürk proclaimed that "if henceforward the women do not share in the social life of the nation, we shall never attain to our full development." Kemalist reforms also included a significant reduction in punishments for crimes, incorporating provisions of the Italian penal code. Finally, the regime worked hard to assure greater educational access. In 1928, for example, the regime established the Turkish Education Association to support children in financial need. Overall, Atatürk's government incorporated important elements of the human rights agenda, including the growing concern for children.

There were, however, important limitations as well, and in this case the expansion toward new kinds of social and economic rights, fostered in the Soviet and Mexican revolutionary documents, was largely absent. In the first place, Atatürk's commitment to the conventional human rights agenda did not include vigorous endorsement of components like freedom of the press. In general, the Turkish experience between the wars, like that of Mexico and the Soviet Union, suggested very limited enthusiasm for human rights elements that might challenge state power; there was greater comfort with provisions in areas such as legal equality. Second, like many new regimes, the Turkish state worried greatly about stability, amid population segments that might support various kinds of protest. In fact, the government frequently suspended press freedom, arrested political dissidents, and engaged in other measures that ran counter to human rights.

One final, intriguing tension emerged as well: the Kemalist reform agenda itself included goals that inherently raised complex issues in the human rights area. Atatürk and his colleagues sought some sweeping reforms in the Turkish population, particularly toward reducing the hold of traditional Islamic customs and establishing a more secular lifestyle. To this end, the regime banned certain kinds of dress, such as the traditional headgear for men, in favor of Western-style clothing, and worked to change women's styles as well. A "Hat Law" of 1925 regulated this aspect of men's appearance, while a "Prohibited Garments" law of 1934 banned religiously based clothing such as turbans and veils. Changes of this sort might be seen as desirable, though of course there is ongoing debate, but they certainly attempted to impose change on intimate aspects of behavior on a non-voluntary basis. Reshaping habits and defending human rights were not readily compatible, and the tension set up some ongoing issues in Turkish political life, adding to the need many political leaders felt to defend the reformist state even through illiberal measures.

The regional expansion of human rights posed something of a glass half-empty or half-full conundrum. Russia and Turkey introduced significant and relevant innovations, but without a full embrace of the rights agenda, even at the level of principle. The results certainly did not reverse the human rights retreat. And many regions were exempt even from this degree of change. But there were some new human rights outposts, and support for new definitions of what human rights should involve.

Furthermore, regional change was not the only spur to a new human rights geography. The League of Nations, a major experiment toward more harmonious international relations created in the wake of World War I, also provided some endorsement, in theory at the global level, both directly and through encouraging forums in which human rights issues could be further discussed.

We have already seen, in Chapter 1, that the League did not explicitly endorse a human rights approach in its basic Covenant—in contrast to what happened twenty-five years later in the establishment of the United Nations. So the issue of constraint, in the interwar decades, continues to haunt any discussion. But key founders of the League hoped that the new body would encourage dissemination of human rights concepts, and there were some genuine linkages. President Woodrow Wilson of the United States, for example, proposed that the League include a pledge to respect religious freedom, while this was the point at which a Japanese delegate urged a ban on discrimination on the basis of race or national origin. But different countries objected in one way or another—the United States rejected the discrimination ban—and nothing concrete happened. The League did work hard in its early years, however, to protect minority populations in various parts of Europe and the Middle East, on the principle that all inhabitants of a country deserve full protection of life and liberty, as part of equality before the law. Efforts to assure minorities were not always successful, and they arguably competed with attention to more basic, individual human rights, but there were some successes, and the commitment to the principle clearly reflected some human rights criteria. The League was not able, however, to get members to agree to minority protection commitments that would apply to all nations. Again, the interest was clear, but it was surrounded by contestation.

Human rights discussions proceeded around the League nevertheless, during the 1920s and 1930s. We have already seen some extension of League interests in the area of rights for children. While the results of this and other League endorsements were rarely concrete, the discussions maintained a sense of momentum. They were also revealing, and significant, in reflecting voices from various parts of the world, and not just the West—a key part of a quiet globalization of human rights commitments.

As early as 1917, a Chilean lawyer, Alejandro Alvarez, helped create a new American Institute of International Law, which included a section on "international rights of the individual." A Russian jurist, locating in Paris after the revolution, also worked on human rights scholarship, along with a Greek colleague; one result was a regular series of international conferences on rights issues, which in turn pressed the League itself to commit more clearly to appropriate criteria for civil and political rights and legal equality. In 1929, a new "Declaration of the International Rights of Man" urged that "the juridical conscience of the civilized world demands the recognition for the individual of rights preserved from all infringement on the part of the state." A series of new associations took up these ideas, even as the rise of Nazism began to raise new and urgent issues for the global community around human and minority rights. In this context, in the early 1930s, both Poland and Haiti sent proposals to the League for firm action on behalf of minorities such as the Jews in Germany. The discussions foundered, not just because of German objections, framed clearly in terms of racism, but also because of fears by other countries that League action might stir minority agitation in their own domains. But efforts continued into the later 1930s, with scholars like the British H. G. Wells offering new, often eloquent defenses of the primacy of human rights in any valid international community. Wells, for example, emphasized not only religious and minority rights, but the need for protection against arbitrary imprisonment and torture. On yet another front, a new League for the Rights of Man emerged in Latin America, in 1937. The movement still had life, in several major regions.

A broadening definition

Along with some regional expansion and a new, if not wildly successful, level of global discussion, human rights during the 1920s and 1930s also continued the process of elaboration that had begun to take shape in the second half of the 19th century. For example, a growing number of nations developed specific commitments toward the provision of education for children, at least in principle and sometimes in fact. The 1936 Soviet Constitution was the first such document explicitly to recognize education as a *right*, with the state obliged to respond. The Soviet state worked hard to assure free, as well as compulsory, education to all children, and other socialist societies would do the same. Obviously, these developments built on the growing enthusiasm for education that had emerged during the 19th century, but the conversion to a clear notion of children's rights was nevertheless an important milestone. Revealingly, in a human rights speech in 1944, American President Franklin Roosevelt also referred to adding education as a right—the idea was spreading.

Expanding rights toward fuller assurances about minimal labor standards and economic conditions also gained ground. Again, revolutions played an obvious role, as in Mexico but particularly the Soviet Union. But other societies participated in at least informal discussions of this additional direction for defining basic rights. President Roosevelt, for example, referred clearly to the importance of "freedom from want," as part of the American New Deal. The League of Nations was also involved, primarily through its subsidiary International Labor Office. Formed in 1919, the ILO quickly set to work trying to organize international agreements, or Conventions, on a number of crucial issues. Forced labor was high on the agenda, and the ILO continued and extended older concerns about slavery into this more general area. Prison labor and compulsory work for children provided specific targets. Freedom for workers to associate was another key goal, including protection for labor leaders from arbitrary arrest or economic sanctions. Related Conventions dealt with collective bargaining and rights to strike. The ILO further recognized, as a matter of "special and urgent importance," "the men and women should receive equal remuneration for work of equal value." Supported periodically by regional labor movements (though shunned by communist groups, that formed their own international organization), as the ILO clearly demonstrated that human rights thinking was being extended in the labor arena.

Finally, interest in women's rights as a key component of human rights more generally clearly advanced in the interwar decades. Countries like Turkey and the Soviet Union, adding explicit commitment to gender equality to constitutions and providing women the right to vote, expanded the gender focus geographically. Women's rights expanded in the West itself, with provision of the right to vote in places like the United States and Britain. New international organizations, like the International Council for Women (formed in 1907, but claiming 25 million members by 1925), were aimed explicitly at women "of all races and nations, creeds and classes." International conferences around women's rights proliferated, many of them sending urgent petitions to the League of Nations. New attention turned to Asia, now that rights were gaining ground in some other regions. Western feminist leaders appealed eagerly to Chinese supporters of the right to vote, arguing that "the wrongs of women are common to all races and nations." And, by the 1920s, Chinese feminists were undertaking a major pamphlet campaign on behalf of women's suffrage. Some dissent occurred: at one international gathering, an Arab delegate argued that no progress could be made on women's issues until the West renounced imperialism. "Justice and respect for the rights of the people" came before any specific attention to gender inequality. But new centers of activism opened in Latin America, in South Africa (among whites), and elsewhere. An Estonian delegate to a conference in 1925 claimed that "there are friendly faces in all corners of the World, hands which are ready to help, kind voices calling from everywhere, from Iceland to South Africa." Petitions to the League on women's rights easily gained signatures from dozens of countries. Specific programs targeted practices like *mui tsai*, in parts of China, where young girls were sent as servants to other households with no safeguards for their working conditions. World War I also triggered new efforts to define rape as a clear crime, and larger problems of violence against women were also evoked. Both the geography and the range of issues associated with women's rights continued to grow.

Before the surge

The huge setbacks to human rights during the second quarter of the 20th century ultimately spurred compensatory action. But it is also clear that continued changes—hints of new global effort, the inclusion of new regions and new definitions—helped prepare later momentum as well. As the war clouds gathered, a variety of leaders began to improve their articulation of rights as an international project. Thus, in 1941, President Roosevelt intoned: "Freedom means the supremacy of human rights everywhere. Our support goes to those who struggle to gain these rights or keep them." His speech highlighted the need both for material wellbeing—"freedom from want"—and "the preservation of civil liberties for all," the latter including freedom of speech and religion. He urged that these goals were attainable now, "in our time and generation," but formed a complete antithesis to the world that the new dictators, Hitler at their lead, were trying to create by force. And, in the wake of the Japanese attack on Pearl Harbor, the United States vowed complete victory over their enemies in order "to preserve human rights and justice" not only at home but around the world. Human rights language, in other words, was readily available to help define the Allied cause during the war itself.

A host of organizations sprang up to urge measures like an international charter of freedom, as the basis for rousing wider support for the Allied effort. A cluster of international experts in Chicago, again in 1941, urged the necessity of "New Rights of Man in an International Organization." Groups in various places spoke of the need for an international bill of rights. The Czech president in exile, Eduard Benes, wrote on "the rights of man and international law" as part of his statement of resistance to Nazi invasion. As thinking coalesced about a new "United Nations," many organizations assumed that, not only an international bill of rights, but a permanent international commission on protecting and developing human rights, would constitute vital initial tasks. British and American groups were particularly vocal, around the idea—as a French observer noted—that "protection of human rights should be part of the war aims of the Allied Powers," but voices from many parts of the world added in. The interwar period, with its strange combination of retreat and modest momentum, had prepared the way for much more sweeping commitment, once war itself clarified the need for change.

Further reading

Numerous surveys discuss global applications of early human rights arguments in the 19th century. See Bonny Ibhawoh, *Imperialism and Human Rights: Colonial Discourses of Rights and Liberties in African History* (Albany, NY: State University of New York Press, 2007); Olga Crisp and Linda Edmondson (eds.), *Civil Rights in Imperial Russia* (New York, NY: Oxford University Press, 1989); and Micheline Ishay (ed.), *The Human Rights Reader: Major Political Essays, Speeches, and Documents from Ancient Times to the Present* (New York, NY: Taylor & Francis, 2007).

On the topic of workers' and children's rights, see Peter N. Stearns, *The Industrial Revolution in World History* (Boulder, CO: Westview Press, 2012); Michael F. C. Bourdillon et al., *Rights and Wrongs of Children's Work* (Piscataway, NJ: Rutgers University Press, 2010); and Marcel van der Linden (ed.), *Humanitarian Intervention and Changing Labor Relations* (Leiden, The Netherlands: Brill, 2011).

References on women's rights include Patricia Grimshaw, Katie Holmes, and Marilyn Lake (eds.), *Women's Rights and Human Rights: International*

Historical Perspectives (New York, NY: Palgrave Macmillan, 2001); Arvonne S. Fraser, "Becoming Human: The Origins and Development of Women's Human Rights," *Human Rights Quarterly*, 21(4) (November, 1999), pp. 853–906; and Rosemarie Zagarri, "The Rights of Man and Women in Post-Revolutionary America," *William and Mary Quarterly*, 3rd series, 55(2) (April, 1998), pp. 203–230.

On the spread of human rights globally, see Paolo Wright-Carozza, "From Conquest to Constitutions: Retrieving a Latin American Tradition of the Idea of Human Rights," *Human Rights Quarterly*, 25(2) (May 2003), pp. 281–313; Douglas Howland, "Society Reified: Herbert Spencer and Political Theory in Early Meiji Japan," *Comparative Studies in Society and History*, 42(1) (2000), pp. 67–86; Berdal Aral, "The Idea of Human Rights as Perceived in the Ottoman Empire," *Human Rights Quarterly*, 26(2) (May, 2004), pp. 454–482; Kenneth L. Port, "The Japanese International Law 'Revolution': International Human Rights Law and Its Impacts in Japan," *Stanford Journal of International Law*, 28 (1991–1992), pp. 139–172; and Jeremy Poplin, *A Concise History of the Haitian Revolution* (Hoboken, NJ: Wiley-Blackwell, 2012).

On the interwar period, including the League of Nations, anti-colonial movements, and new attacks on human rights, see: Mark Mazower, *Dark Continent: Europe's Twentieth Century* (New York, NY: Vintage, 2000); Erez Manela, *The Wilsonian Moment: Self-Determination and the International Origins of Anticolonial Nationalism* (New York, NY: Oxford University Press, 2007); Leila J. Rupp, *Worlds of Women: The Making of an International Women's Movement* (Princeton, NJ: Princeton University Press, 1997); Nitza Berkovitch, *From Motherhood to Citizenship: Women's Rights and International Organizations* (Baltimore, MD: Johns Hopkins University Press, 1999); Micheline Ishay (ed.), *The Human Rights Reader: Major Political Essays, Speeches, and Documents from Ancient Times to the Present* (New York, NY: Taylor & Francis, 2007); Jan Herman Burgers, "The Road to San Francisco: The Revival of the Human Rights Idea in the Twentieth Century," *Human Rights Quarterly*, 14(4) (November, 1992), pp. 447–477; Jennifer Jackson Preece, "Minority Rights in Europe: From Westphalia to Helsinki," *Review of International Studies*, 23(1) (January, 1997), pp. 75–92; and Dominique Marshall, "The Construction of Children as an Object of International Relations: The Declaration of Children's Rights and the Child Welfare Committee of the League of Nations, 1900–1924," *International Journal of Children's Rights*, 7 (1999), pp. 103–147.

5   Human rights and global expansion
Surges of growth since 1945

The end of World War II and the forming of the United Nations opened a floodgate for human rights and their impact on international law. More elaborate statements, and more important, clearer commitments on human rights took shape than ever before. These trends were amplified by the formation of a growing array of private groups, or International Non-Governmental Organizations (NGOs), bent on identifying human rights violations. They also included a growing range of regional commitments to human rights principles—for example, in Japan. And they embraced expansions of the lists of human rights themselves, not only to include firmer statements on women and children but also to add other groups, such as people defined by particular sexual orientations.

The expansion of human rights was not a steady flow, but a series of waves—though United Nations (UN) involvement was important in most major stages. The initial burst followed the war itself. Some hesitation or even retreat occurred, then, amid the worst tensions of the cold war and the growing attention to decolonization. The 1960s, however, saw a new phase of international effort, spurred in part by widespread resistance to the South African system of racial segregation—*apartheid*—and the additional enforcement mechanisms required for the global community to attack abuses of this sort. Civil rights agitation in the United States from the late 1950s onward also helped fuel a new phase, with global implications; and it was at this point as well that NGO formation became increasingly significant. Then the end of the cold war and the substantial collapse of communism, from the late 1980s onward, provided a final spur, enhanced by the growing apparatus of contemporary globalization itself.

This chapter focuses on the major steps in the amplification of global human rights. We turn in the following chapter to hesitations, limitations, and regional differences. Obviously, the two patterns must be juxtaposed. Even in dealing with the most important new steps toward human rights it is vital to note that many societies did not go along with the prevailing trends, that many new authoritarian regimes resisted bitterly, that key regions held out for distinctive definitions of what rights should involve. Horrible human rights abuses occurred in some places, often as a result of ethnic conflicts or other civil strife. Even self-appointed paragons of human rights, such as the United States, faltered in crucial respects.

These complexities already raise an important question. With so much opposition, and so many failures, why and how did human rights thinking persist so strongly, for example, at the level of international organizations? Why did human rights advocacy expand in so many directions, rather than hunkering down in self-defense? It's not hard to figure out what caused the initial new push, in the late 1940s. Determining what sustained later stages is a bit more difficult, involving, among other things, some gap between what societies felt they had to profess in international rhetoric and what they were actually willing to implement. Human rights unquestionably gained a new prestige, and this was an important development in itself.

War crimes

An early indication of a commitment to change—though a commitment open to diverse criticisms—involved the decision to bring to trial various Nazi and Japanese leaders, accused of a variety of crimes during the prosecution of World War II. Here was the first instance of actually putting into effect the earlier idea of "crimes against humanity," and it had important implications for the future of human rights.

In Germany, the victorious powers in 1945 cited earlier agreements—the Geneva Conventions but also other international codes dating back to the early 20th century—as the basis for charging various leaders from the defeated powers of fomenting war, attempting to exterminate ethnic and religious groups, and mistreatment both of prisoners and of civilians. An international panel heard the German cases in Nuremberg, beginning late in 1945. A key conclusion was that planning or instigating a war of aggression was a crime under international law. Beyond this, the panel confirmed widespread atrocities under the German government's slave labor policies and through the concentration camps. Several whole leadership groups were declared criminal.

A separate trial opened in Tokyo in 1946, under the War Crimes Tribunal. Again, a variety of accusations were considered by the international judges. Ultimately, severe mistreatment of prisoners of war brought the greatest number of convictions. Several Japanese officials were executed. China also conducted separate trials for Japanese activities in that country, executing 143 prisoners.

At their best, the trials demonstrated that, in a new international regime governed by concern for human rights, certain actions were unacceptable and could be brought to account. The principles involved continue to help guide efforts to enforce humanitarian standards. Yet the approach was also vulnerable. Not every potential criminal was brought to trial, as occupation forces let a number of people off in return for scientific or other information. More important, the whole apparatus smacked of using war crimes principles to legitimize revenge efforts by victors in war. No one from the Allied side was accused of anything, despite many bombings of civilian targets. The Indian jurist on the Tokyo panel explicitly dissented from the whole procedure on this basis.

For all the flaws, the war crimes efforts signaled not only an attempt to put real teeth into earlier statements of human rights principles in wartime, but also the extent to which the experience of World War II, and the realization of massive wartime atrocities, helped spur new thinking about human rights statements and enforcements. The same reactions helped fuel the more systematic efforts attached to the formation and early stages of the United Nations.

The Universal Declaration of Human Rights

The first steps toward actually forming the United Nations, in conferences that surfaced as World War II was winding down, reflected some of the hesitations that had bedeviled the whole human rights field between the wars. Wartime leaders had established some fairly clear, if general, commitments in the human rights areas, making progress in this domain a clear goal. It was widely believed that a firmer international stance on human rights prior to the war might have prevented the rise of Hitler. In this view, not only the weakness of the League of Nations, but its lack of specific capacity to deal with human rights issues, needed to be repaired. The end of the war and the discovery of the full extent of Nazi atrocities against Jews and other groups (including gypsies, homosexuals, and socialists) rallied many people to a new energy on human rights, hoping to assure that such crimes would never occur again.

Yet the United Nations Charter itself, approved in 1945, did not install an effective international system. Several smaller countries pushed for a clear bill of rights, but the major powers—the United States, France, Britain, and the Soviet Union—held back. Each of these countries had human rights issues of its own: the United States suffered from various forms of racial discrimination, the Soviet Union operated prison labor camps, and France and Britain maintained colonial regimes in many parts of the world. They balked at coming on too strong in the human rights domain, and this resulted in statements that were deliberately weak and vague. The outcome not only angered a number of smaller countries eager to see a stronger human rights commitment—headed, interestingly, by Latin American states including Panama, Cuba, and Chile—but a variety of anti-imperialist leaders in Africa and India, concerned about human rights but more particularly eager to win international attention for the rights of people under colonial rule. Australia and New Zealand also pushed for a fuller embrace of human rights.

There was, nevertheless, relevant language, partly because the great powers came to realize that they could not duck this issue entirely, given a mounting level of international concern. A key provision of the Charter recognized that one of the purposes of the UN must be international cooperation in solving various problems, including "humanitarian" issues and "in promoting and encouraging respect for human rights and fundamental freedoms for all without distinctions as to race, sex, language, or religion"—provisions that already advanced over the criteria for the League of Nations. The coverage was amplified by an additional article pledging respect for "the principles of equal rights" and "universal respect for, and observance of, human rights and fundamental freedoms for all without distinction as to race, sex, language, or religion." The definition of rights, however, was left unclear (among other things, in deference to the Soviet Union, any specification of rights to private property was deliberately omitted). And member states were not obliged to guarantee or observe human rights, beyond offering "joint and separate action" in cooperation with the United Nations.

The Charter did, however, introduce several changes. First, it made it clear that human rights were a legitimate international issue, not merely a matter for separate actions by individual nations or governments. This put flesh on a principle that had been proclaimed as early as the French revolutionary "Declaration of the Rights of Man" but had never been explicitly adopted by an official international body. Second, despite the vagueness concerning obligations, member states did pledge to work to advance the purposes of the Charter— now including human rights. And there was an explicit commitment, at least in principle, to avoid any kind of discrimination: if rights were not clearly defined, the long-term assumption of human rights thinking, that people should be treated equally under the law, was now a matter of international law.

And the Charter turned out to be only a first step, inviting the new organization to move further to define and codify what was meant by human rights. This resulted, in turn, in the proclamation of the Universal Declaration of Human Rights in 1948. Passed as a non-binding UN General Assembly resolution, the Declaration intended to provide "a common understanding" of the rights referred to in the Charter and to serve as a "common standard of achievement for all peoples and all nations." This pushed further toward setting obligations that would bear on all UN member states. From this point onward the Declaration became a global foundation for human rights work, by the United Nations but by a variety of other international bodies as well.

For the Declaration restated most of the central principles that had been part of human rights thinking for more than a century and a half, along with portions of the expanded list developed more recently, but now with unprecedented (though not unanimous) international endorsement. Spearheading the discussions that led up to the Declaration were an American stateswoman, Eleanor Roosevelt, along with a Chinese, a Lebanese, and a French scholar. The United Nations had also set up a philosophers' committee to draw opinion from other regions, calling, among other things, on Gandhi. As had been true in discussions of the UN Charter, human rights pressure from a number of Latin American governments was crucial in moving forward on the Declaration. Correspondingly, in the Declaration, the United Nations professed confidence that many regions shared common convictions on which a set of shared principles could depend. To be sure, debates featured some clear disagreements as well: Soviet representatives attacked the "psychology of individualism" which they argued had long favored the "ruling class," urging attention to social and economic rights and duties, while Americans preferred a focus on political rights. Roosevelt was able to persuade the American delegation to accept some socioeconomic clauses, while the communist countries ultimately abstained (along with Saudi Arabia and South Africa) in the vote approving the Declaration.

The Declaration emphasized human dignity as well as key rights and equality before the law, and it cited the "barbarous acts which have shocked the conscience of mankind" as a result of the disregard for rights. Distinctions of race, gender, religion, or national status were proscribed. The Declaration prohibited slavery and also torture or inhuman or degrading punishment, along with arbitrary arrest or imprisonment. Reference to gender was amplified by insistence on the need for consent to marriage. Freedom of thought, religion, expression, and assembly completed the classic agenda. Social provisions were vaguer, but several articles explicitly referred to a right to social security, a decent standard of living, and the "economic, social and cultural rights indispensable for ... dignity and the free development of personality." A following item insisted on fair job conditions and equal pay for equal work, and the right to form and join trade unions. Article 26 specified the "right to education" for everyone, including both free and compulsory elementary education. A final major article, picking up on wider traditions, referred to everyone's "duties to the community." This was a sweeping statement, though with varying degrees of specificity depending on category.

Wider outreach: the 1950s

Furthermore, the Declaration was only part of a series of developments in the years after the war that confirmed a new level of international attention to human rights. Within the United Nations itself, a Human Rights Commission had been established (even before the Declaration), to promote human rights internationally and to assist members in establishing human rights provisions. The mandate was somewhat loose, and no clear enforcement mechanism existed for United Nations principles in this area, but at least there was an ongoing body beyond a single document.

Regional units chimed in. A group of European nations launched a new Convention for the Protection of Human Rights and Fundamental Freedoms in 1950. An inter-American association offered a similar declaration two years earlier. The International Labor Office issued an attack on any discrimination in employment, and another organization did the same for education. More important still, right on the eve of the Declaration, was a United Nations convention on preventing and punishing genocide, attempting to prevent a recurrence of anything like the Holocaust, making it clear that it was now a crime under international law to attempt to destroy all or part of any ethnic or religious group. Reactions to the human rights retreat of the 1930s and World War II continued to generate not only new statements of commitment, but new efforts to shape international law on the basis of humane standards.

The same mood translated human rights provisions into a host of new national constitutions, from the late 1940s onward. The list is considerable, as more and more states freed themselves from colonial status but also as a number of established nations, including those defeated in World War II, revised their political structures.

Constitutions in the Philippines, for example, even before full independence from the United States, routinely included a long section providing a bill of rights. The section assured all citizens of rights to due process of law, against any arbitrary arrests or detention. Freedoms of assembly, speech, and religion were explicitly established. After independence, Philippine constitutions went on to speak of the state's obligation to provide a decent standard of living and "adequate social services" in areas like education, social security, welfare, and housing. They also spoke of equal opportunities at work, regardless of gender, and the rights of workers to organize and bargain collectively. Interestingly, a short section also discussed the duties of citizens, including respect for rights of others but also the obligation to engage in "gainful work" and cooperate with the state to assure the wellbeing of society as a whole. This was in sum a fairly comprehensive statement of rights, with a bit less attention to issues of legal equality and the addition of provisions about obligations—overall, an impressive indication of Philippine adherence, at least in principle, to human rights standards as now internationally defined.

India's new constitution, completed in 1949, included a long section on "fundamental rights." Six rights were emphasized: equality before the law, which included the unprecedented prohibition of discrimination on the basis of caste but also more conventional categories like gender and religion; freedom of speech and association, including, interestingly (another reference to earlier caste history), the right to practice any profession or occupation; rights against forced labor and compulsory child labor; freedom of religion and conscience; the right to education; and the right of "any section of citizens to conserve their culture, language or script, and the right of minorities to establish and administer educational institutions of their choice." Here again was a document that expressed standard rights definitions, including freedom from arbitrary arrest. Beneath the conventions, however, the commitment to abolition of legal castes was a huge change in Indian society, in favor of contemporary human rights criteria—and "untouchability," the status of the traditionally lowest caste, was officially eliminated. The final criterion again showed the capacity to blend standard lists with particular national needs: in the case of India, the multiplicity of regional languages and cultures, in a highly decentralized traditional state, called for the addition of a special right that other societies might have found either unnecessary or undesirable. At the same time, provisions of guarantees for social welfare, which were being added to many common lists, were largely absent, nor was there explicit mention of freedom of the press. Here, India's constitutional effort opened to a number of criticisms, despite its alignment with standard statements in most respects.

Pakistan, split from India after the end of British rule amid considerable tension and bloodshed, generated its own constitutional document in 1956. Interestingly, with a few important exceptions, the human rights statements were virtually identical to those of its larger neighbor, reflecting again the extent to which the language had become a standard part of any contemporary constitutional exercise. Freedom of assembly and opinion was assured, but also freedom of religion and the right to establish independent religious activities and organizations. This was, however, an Islamic republic, with provisions that laws could not contradict the principles of Islam and that the president must be Muslim; the constitution itself reflected this, for example, in the prohibition of the sale of alcohol. Left unresolved was the issue of how to combine the religious commitment with the conventional human rights professions.

As African states began to emerge a bit later, their constitutions largely maintained the trajectory established by most of the new nations in Asia. Cameroon, for example, declaring independence from France in 1960 and issuing a constitution, included a provision on the "inalienable rights" of citizens, with specific reference to the United Nations Charter and the Universal Declaration of Human Rights. This would turn out to be the only part of the constitution not seriously altered from that point to the present day.

Constitutions in several former British colonies in West Africa—notably Ghana, with an independent document at the end of the 1950s and Nigeria, in 1963—included careful protections for most standard individual rights, including religion and speech. They were able to build on prior British documents that, while restricting regional participation in politics, had offered some assurances of other rights; this, along with the wider international context, helps explain the duplications in language. Both Nigeria and Ghana (rather like India) initially also introduced elaborate assurances for the protection of minority groups, cultures, and regions. This created divisions and tensions that rather quickly led to civil strife, as in the Nigerian case, followed by military rule that suspended constitutional guarantees. Or, with Ghana, nationalist leadership quickly turned against these restrictions in favor of greater centralization of power. The issues of blending rights language, effective government, and regional diversities were a challenge that was not easily met. Again, however, at least at first, the impulse to replicate common assurances about human rights applied to these important cases as well.

Finally, the turn to new interest in human rights also guided some established nations that had moved away from earlier interests during the difficult decades between the wars. In one sense, human rights commitments in the new constitutions of countries like Japan and Germany were unsurprising, since they were heavily influenced, if not imposed outright, by the victorious powers— who sought to vindicate their own human rights values and also to restrict any revival of authoritarian impulses in the conquered territories. Japan's 1946 constitution, for example, the "Showa constitution," was essentially required by American occupations forces, and correspondingly reflected Western values. But this artificial start could lead to an impressive and thorough integration of human rights principles, and even an effort to provide some new leadership in international efforts. Some prior precedents on human rights; a real openness to outside influence, after a traumatic historical experience; and some desire to see human rights as one way to reestablish standing in the international community, severely damaged by wartime behaviors—a combination of factors could play a role in solidifying change.

American control gave Japan a new and strongly Western constitution, but it did not erase important traditional elements. Under the constitution, for example, the Japanese Supreme Court continued to emphasize the importance of community rights, including the right to safety, which might take precedence over individual rights—thus police might legitimately enter a home without warrants, in order to reduce the danger of crime. Flexibility of this sort made constitutional protection of human rights more palatable to the Japanese. Nor did the constitution erase the strong Japanese respect for authority, which at points can lead to assumptions that police behavior is automatically correct, as against protections for individuals. It also turned out that Japanese courts normally authorized only modest compensatory payments when arbitrary arrests did occur—another sign of the distinctive balance between the social and the individual. Nevertheless, the Showa constitution introduced real change, including much more sweeping guarantees for freedom of expression even when social traditions or hierarchies were criticized. Indeed, twenty-six different categories of rights were identified, and given primacy over older conceptions of social duties. (Only three categories of duties were specified: payment of taxes, provision of education, and the need to work.) The constitution established a strong judiciary, charged with protecting the law against incursion by other segments of the state; it also provided for careful protections against arbitrary arrest or detention, though with exceptions where social interests seemed to justify action. ("No person shall be deprived of life or liberty, nor shall any other criminal penalty be imposed, except according to procedure established by law"—quite a new concept compared to provisions in the earlier Meiji constitution.) Stipulations against torture, though officially introduced in the Meiji era, were strengthened, though many observers continue to worry that attention to public safety still informally gives the benefit of the doubt to the police. Overall, however, Japanese society quickly internalized acceptance for many of the new human rights criteria. Even where police actions seemed to violate individual rights, a free press was usually alert in offering criticisms. The nation subsequently became active in signing a number of the international conventions of human rights, including covenants on social rights and on the elimination of discrimination based on gender, plus of course the Universal Declaration. In more recent discussions of an "Asian" approach to human rights—to which we will return—Japan strongly insisted that basic rights are universal, as against Chinese arguments, for example, that each nation must define its own approach.

Overall—on human rights as on other key issues—postwar Japan emerged as an intriguing example of a society capable of change, adjusting toward not only accepting, but advocating, international standards, while preserving (as an imposed constitution was actually interpreted) the capacity to shape some rights distinctively. The result was a strong regional extension of basic human rights commitments, but not precisely on the Western model.

The problem of the 1950s

The years after World War II witnessed an unprecedented international surge for human rights. Western guilt over the human rights retreat of the 1930s and the war itself spurred important new measures. A variety of new leaders in many countries emerged to press for clearer articulations, beginning with the Universal Declaration. Assumptions that human rights statements should be a standard part of constitutional development and of the creation of new or reformed nations were widespread, touching every major region.

Variety persisted, but at one level this was an inevitable—arguably, a desirable—concomitant to the geographical spread of human rights. Some societies seemed ready to emphasize further steps in the movement, such as the explicit identification of non-discrimination on the basis of gender, while others held back. Important divisions emerged over the protection of minority cultures with a national context, and this could have significant implications for human rights more widely. As the cold war began to take shape, from the late 1940s onward, the ongoing debate between the Soviet Union and the West over the nature and priority of social welfare rights, compared to individual civil liberties, remained unresolved. Some new nations were readier than others to include economic criteria in their bills of rights. Again, debates over issues of this sort could be taken as a sign of health. Both sides in the cold war, after all, advocated for human rights and their internationalization. And, while their disagreements about definitions were substantial, they could also agree—if only in principle—on certain categories such as gender discrimination in law. It is certainly valid to see the postwar years as a major inflexion point in the overall world history of human rights. International commitments and regional geographies both underwent substantial change.

Yet, as the 1950s proceeded, the human rights agenda faded considerably. There was no measurable retreat at the international level—previous agreements were not pulled back—but priorities shifted. And, in some regions, new levels of acceptance of human rights turned out to be rather hollow, as other problems gained precedence and, in many cases, initial constitutional arrangements were rescinded. The fact was that the two great global forces of the 1950s—the cold war and decolonization—both had negative implications for human rights, while presenting some interesting ambiguities as well.

Growing military tensions and political competition between the Soviet Union and its allies and the United States and its allies—the cold war— damaged human rights on both sides of what popularly became known as the Iron Curtain. On the Soviet side—now involving east-central European countries as well as the Soviet Union itself—the role of secret police expanded, with extensive monitoring of civilian behavior and a great deal of domestic spying. Many people were arrested for real or imagined dissidence. Competing political units were repressed, in favor of Communist Party monopoly. In the Soviet Union itself, pressures eased somewhat after the death of Stalin in 1953; outright executions for political crimes declined. But tensions in other areas increased. Construction of the Berlin Wall, for example, was part of a massive effort to prevent much travel outside of the Soviet sphere itself, and many people were killed for trying.

Western nations, headed by the United States, took delight in pointing out the civil rights deficiencies of the communist bloc—this was a standard part of the international cold war competition. But the West itself suffered from new levels of policing and political repression. In the United States a wave of anguish over the threat of communism justified a host of new efforts to regulate real or imagined subversives. Many people lost jobs because of federal investigations of their loyalty; new blacklists prevented some of these from gaining employment, and there were some outright arrests. The Federal Bureau of Investigation stepped up secret inquiries into a variety of organizations. A new law, the McCarren Internal Security Act of 1950, set up a "subversive activities control board" to provide further scrutiny. President Truman, unsuccessfully opposing the law, did argue that "in a free country, we punish men for the crimes they commit, but never for the opinions they have." And later, in 1965 and 1967, key provisions of the McCarren Act were declared unconstitutional. For a time, however, the state of effective political freedom in the United States was under siege.

The impact of decolonization was harder to chart. We have seen that many former colonies seemed to embrace human rights ideas, even copying constitutional provisions from countries like France or Britain that had sponsored imperialism in the first place. Growing disengagement from imperialism in the long run simplified human rights commitments in the West, particularly by reducing or eliminating the need for repressive tactics against colonial agitation. Over time, even older imperialist staples, like the belief that non-Western peoples were somehow inferior, began to decline, removing some of the tensions from human rights arguments about a common humanity.

During the decolonization process itself, however, there were a number of complications. In the first place, while many former colonies gained independence relatively peacefully, there were huge clashes that, in some cases, brought new levels of repression at least until the colonial regime relaxed its hold. In Kenya, local attacks on white settlers generated forceful British response. Many nationalist leaders, including independent Kenya's ultimate first president, were arrested, often on trumped-up charges of criminal activity. The long war for Algerian independence, against France, brought mutual violence and many arrests, not only in Algeria itself but in France as well. A number of new nations, in other words, were born amid new restrictions on political rights, and this could color their own early years.

A more subtle issue involved the relationship between efforts at national independence and human rights more generally. The issue was not new, but it gained new articulation. On the one hand, many nationalist leaders urged that the "self-determination of peoples" was a prime human right. In 1946, the Nigerian activist Mbonu Ojike stated simply, "The right to rule oneself is a natural right." The Vietnamese leader Ho Chi Minh similarly urged that national independence was an "inalienable right" on the scale of Thomas Jefferson's list. In 1952, Asian and Latin American nations, backed by African leaders as well, made respect for the "self-determination of peoples" part of the United Nations human rights program.

A number of Western rights advocates objected, worrying that the fervor over national rights could easily eclipse more conventional human rights criteria. Western nervousness about loss of imperial power may have fueled concern as well. One of the French leaders who had helped craft the Universal Declaration argued that "Arab states" had derailed the whole United Nations program, by forcing "self-determination" onto the agenda. Some British leaders also contended that national independence did not belong on the list. In other words, while decolonization reduced some of the contradictions Western leaders had faced in simultaneously trying to support human rights while defending empires, it opened new arguments. Many Westerners began to use human rights criteria to scrutinize and to criticize some of the newly independent nations, a pattern that continues to the present day in certain instances. While overt racism was declining, it remained possible for some Western spokespeople to feel quite self-righteous about their society's superior priorities in the human rights domain.

And there were some real issues. The fact was that many nationalist leaders did place a far higher premium on establishing their own independent government than on any other human rights criteria. Some turned out to be willing to trample political dissent in the process, once they gained the opportunity to do so. Self-determination itself was not always a clear category. We have seen that some new nations began with considerable recognition of minority cultures, but then turned out to prefer a dominant national state; attacks on the position of minority groups resulted in some cases. Some minority groups, in turn, began to argue for their own self-determination rights and to point to repression on the part of new national governments. Human rights principles, as the decolonization process unfolded, were not always easy to define. Western critics might easily seize on the problems that resulted. Local leaders, in return, might feel that human rights critiques constituted a new version of outside, neo-imperialist, interference.

Finally, many new nations quickly encountered problems of political stability that challenged the observance of human rights, whatever the initial views of the new leadership. Some of the issues resembled those that had quickly troubled Latin American nations early in the 19th century, and that had in some cases obscured initial human rights commitments. In some extreme cases, like Nigeria, outright civil war broke out among different regions or groups. Social and religious unrest placed pressure on many new national leaders. In many cases, responses involved imposition of more authoritarian regimes, sometimes under military control; initial constitutions, with their human rights provisions, might be rescinded in the process. Freedom of the press was a common victim of reactions of this sort. Not all new nations fell victim to these problems— we have seen that, in several cases, human rights provisions have survived since independence. But problems were widespread. Along with cold war repressions, the results constituted the clearest sources of human rights retreat during the later 1950s and beyond.

Both the cold war and decolonization brought some new support for human rights as well; trends were often complex. The decline of imperialism really did reduce certain categories of repression, and opened the way to new regional human rights statements. As Western critics maintained a commentary on human rights abuses in some new nations, they might annoy local nationalism; but they might also spur remedial action. The process increased international discussion of human rights at least in some respects.

The cold war certainly offered some support, though particularly after the worst tensions eased from the early 1960s onward. Both sides in the struggle frequently sought to claim human rights successes and, while the results were sometimes purely rhetorical, they could heighten international awareness of the principles involved. The Soviet Union liked to boast, for example, of what it claimed was a superior record on gender equality—and this might help convince other countries that gender was a valid component of human rights. Soviet criticism also increased United States awareness of domestic racial issues. Already, in 1946, some African American groups had appealed to the United Nations for support against ongoing discrimination, and cold war rivalry increased official American sensitivity. One result was a much more aggressive federal stance against lynching, a practice that finally began to decline. The United States also created a new State Department policy of offering annual reports on other countries' human rights performance, under legislation enacted in 1961. The idea was to determine the "status of internationally recognized human rights"—partly to determine eligibility for foreign aid, partly to provide the United States with arguments against opponents (beginning, of course, with the Soviet Union itself). The result might annoy other countries—and this remains true today—but it could also provide one more reminder that better human rights performance might boost international standing.

Certainly, human rights impetus was not lost by the end of the 1950s; there was no retreat to compare with what had happened in the 1930s. This in turn helps explain why, despite some new problems and loss of momentum, a new surge of international human rights activity, with many different facets, began to develop in the 1960s and 1970s.

The second contemporary surge: new organizations and new rights

The next phase in the recent history of human rights involved additional geographical shifts but particularly a new surge in relevant international organizations and a new round of expansion of the rights list itself, both internationally and in key countries such as the United States. Changes in international organization, ultimately interrelated, featured the emergence and expansion of dedicated NGOs, beginning with Amnesty International in

1961, and important alterations in the United Nations approach, fueled in part by growing international revulsion at the racist apartheid system in South Africa. The organizational changes in turn created new receptivity to the expansion of rights areas, with both the United Nations and non-governmental groups picking up and disseminating new signals.

Amnesty International and the NGOs

Amnesty International was a product of the new human rights tensions emerging in the 1950s, played out against the vitality of basic ongoing principles. The group plausibly claimed to be the second oldest human rights organization in the world, after the Anti-Slavery Society, and it embraced a wider rights agenda from the outset.

As with earlier human rights activity, Amnesty took its initial roots in Great Britain, spurred by a socialist lawyer, who was also a convert to Catholicism, and several colleagues, including a Quaker advocate. A newspaper article announced the new organization:

> Open your newspaper any day of the week, and you will find a report from somewhere in the world of someone being imprisoned, tortured or executed because his opinions or religion are unacceptable to his government ... The newspaper reader feels a sickening sense of impotence. Yet if these feelings of disgust all over the world could be united into common action, something effective could be done.

Amnesty International was based on assumptions that there were universal standards of political freedom, that there were people in every region actuated by these standards, and that rousing world opinion was the way to gain greater acceptance for the standards.

Amnesty started by establishing a London office to collect information on "prisoners of conscience" anywhere in the world: "Any person who is physically restrained (by imprisonment or otherwise) from expressing (in any form of words of symbols) an opinion which he honestly holds and which does not advocate or condone personal violence." The organization recruited volunteer members, and sent missions to many places to investigate abuse. Considerable attention focused on cold war problems, but Amnesty was careful to balance criticisms of communist regimes with identification of repression in the West; and it reserved a third effort for reports from new, developing nations. In the West, early campaigns focused on issues like British treatment of prisoners in the Protestant–Catholic conflict in Northern Ireland.

By 1977, when Amnesty won the Nobel Peace Prize, it had identified over 15,000 political prisoners and had assisted in the release of over half of them. (By 2004, the group took credit for over 40,000 released prisoners.) A trade union leader in the Dominican Republic described the process, after Amnesty had organized a global petitioning campaign on his behalf:

When the first two hundred letters came, the guards gave me back my clothes. Then the next two hundred letters came and the prison director came to see me ... The letters still kept arriving and the President called the prison and told them to let me go. After I was released, the President called me to his office ... He said, 'How is it that a trade union leader like you has so many friends all over the world.'

Other prisoners wrote of how the international publicity Amnesty generated protected them from execution or managed to bring torture to a halt. Various regimes, in other words, though not committed to human rights, feared to have too much unfavorable international press, accepting at least part of the persuasive power now available on behalf of global standards. Amnesty defended some high-profile prisoners, like Nelson Mandela in South Africa, but it worked on more routine cases as well.

Amnesty steadily built up a membership base, avoiding dependence on any government for financial support. By 2004, it had over a million members worldwide. Western nations led the list, but by the 1980s important chapters flourished in Latin America. By 1989, over 150 countries were represented. Leaders came from various regions as well, including leading human rights advocates from nations like Senegal in Africa. The group managed to press other groups to take action, beyond its reliance on active public opinion. In the 1960s it roused the Council of Europe to move against torture in Greece, while in the 1970s its campaign against people who "disappeared" under authoritarian regimes in Latin America prompted the formation of a special United Nations working group. The organization could move fast. In 1981, six members of a human rights chapter were arrested in Buenos Aires. The wife of one called Amnesty, which organized an international telegram blitz, and the prisoners were released in about a week. Over time, Amnesty added a number of policy efforts to its continued commitment to publicize individual abuses. Thus it took on violence in the African diamond trade and ethnic conflict in the Balkans, while ultimately deciding to press against the death penalty every-where. By the early 21st century its agenda expanded still further, to include domestic violence against women and the use of rape in civil conflicts.

Basic principles, however, remained consistent. A 2001 statute repeated the message:

Amnesty International's vision is of a world in which every person enjoys all of the human rights enshrined in the Universal Declaration of Human Rights and other international human rights standards ... Amnesty International forms a global community of human rights defenders with the principles of international solidarity, effective action for the individual victim, global coverage, the universality and indivisibility of human rights, impartiality and independence, and democracy and mutual respect ... In addition to its work on specific abuses of human rights, Amnesty International urges all govern-ments to observe the rule of law, and to ratify and implement human rights standards ... and it encourages intergovernmental organizations, individuals and all organs of society to support and respect human rights.

Important as it remains, Amnesty turned out to be just the first of a growing crescendo of organizations devoted to supporting human rights and rousing global awareness. One, Human Rights Watch, was the direct product of the ongoing evolution of the cold war. In 1975, nations in the Soviet Bloc and the West met in Helsinki to reduce cold war tensions. The resulting declaration included a specific provision to guarantee human rights, including rights of expression and freedom of religion. Predictably, the two sides interpreted this provision differently. Western groups were quickly established to monitor Soviet human rights behavior, and in the communist bloc itself the declaration ultimately encouraged dissident groups seeking greater political freedom. The Western monitoring process, in turn, ultimately gave rise to Human Rights Watch, based in the United States but, like Amnesty, quickly eager to develop an international clientele. For example, it soon founded an Americas Watch division, to cover the important conflicts in Central America, which were leading to widespread violence against civilians.

Like Amnesty, Human Rights Watch generated a mixture of professional investigators and volunteer supporters, tracking situations in many different countries. It also expanded its reach to include women's and children's rights as well as political repression. Its commitment to "international standards of human rights" that "apply to all people equally" rested centrally in the movement's traditions. The goal was mobilization of public opinion but also pressure on governments, such as that of the United States, to move against systematic abuses by other states. The organization, again as with Amnesty International, frequently called for international tribunals to deal with war crimes, for example, in the conflicts in the Balkans during the 1990s. It also turned to issues in the West, attacking United States policies on prisoners and on immigrants, and it moved against the death penalty. In 1993, the group's new Women's Rights Division joined other associations to win 240,000 signatures on a petition to the United Nations to do more on discriminations against women, under the heading "women's rights are human rights." Other causes included political arrests in China and the treatment of members of the former untouchable caste in India—again, a substantial topical and geographical range.

Other organizations played a role as well. The International Justice Mission was a Christian group working against genocide and other forms of violence targeting civilians. Another group, Interrights, was based in Britain. Still other organizations included Physicians for Human Rights, the Index on Censorship, the International Commission of Jurists, and the International Federation for Human Rights. All were committed to reporting abuses and rousing attention toward their remedy. Collectively, the organizations increasingly moved discussion of abuse of prisoners and unjust punishments from restrained diplomatic discourse among governments toward a more passionate confrontation with crises.

Finally, these global groups—with wide participation, though usually based particularly in the West—helped spur the formation of local human rights efforts, which were crucial to reporting actual problems and generating attention from the parent bodies. A good bit of the creation of these wider local networks awaited the 1990s and beyond, and we will return to them. But a foretaste took shape in the 1970s and 1980s in Latin America, providing one of the most important non-governmental campaigns against abuse and signaling how important wider efforts in the same direction might become. By the 1970s, Latin American opinion was coalescing against a new series of human rights abuses, including torture and arbitrary detention, by authoritarian regimes such as the Pinochet government in Chile. A number of regional NGOs mounted publicity campaigns, both locally and internationally. Considerable support emerged both from Catholic groups, increasingly friendly to many human rights issues, and from labor movements, including union leadership in the United States. Attention focused especially on growing problems in Central America. Clashes involving conservative militants, often backed by the United States against presumed leftists, occasioned many brutalities, particularly in the nation of El Salvador. Immigrants from the region, often fleeing the violence to destinations in the United States and Canada, provided an additional voice, while larger organizations, headed by Human Rights Watch, took up the cause. Both newspaper accounts of local atrocities (some of them targeting Catholic clergy) and international petitions mounted. The European Commission and the United Nations were both drawn in, attempting to implement more humane political ground rules. The end result, from the mid-1980s onward, was a series of regime changes, ushering in more democratic governments, and a quiet retreat by the United States from its partisan policies.

An activist in Guatemala put it this way:

> If it were not for that international assistance, principally from Americas Watch, Amnesty International, the World Council of Churches, solidarity organizations from democratic countries, Canadian organizations, organizations of Guatemalans working in the US, Canada or Europe, without the moral and political help of those organizations, I believe that we would have been dead many years ago, the army would not have permitted our organization to develop ... If you don't have the contacts, if the people who are doing the killing know that nobody is going to do anything if you disappear, then you disappear ... It was vital to have contacts so that information could go outside.

The combination was clear: local activity was required, to generate data and outrage about repressive policies; but the international network of NGOs was also essential, dedicated to human rights principles and capable of rousing substantial public opinion against atrocities. It was not a foolproof formula: during the same decades, brutal repressions occurred in some societies, like Cambodia, with far less effective outcry. Overall, however, the rise of private organizations was a vital new step in the further global articulation and defense of human rights.

United Nations and international law

A second series of shifts, emerging at about the same time, involved the United Nations and affiliated groups. The trigger was the apartheid system in South Africa, and growing international outrage about its principles—founded on gross racial inequality under the law—and about the violence directed at resistance activities by black South Africans themselves. The system itself had taken shape from 1948 onward, as Afrikaner-led governments had segregated the black majority with a series of laws restricting residence and work and educational access, along with basic political rights. Here was a set of issues that proved ideal fodder for international attention, as they involved both classic human rights claims, from freedom of expression to legal equality, but also the rights of national self-determination that were part of the anti-colonial struggle. Meetings of newly independent Asian and then African nations, from the early 1950s onward, routinely condemned apartheid, noting among other things that it directly violated United Nations Charter commitments to fundamental freedoms "without distinction of race." Even cold war competition helped a bit, as the Soviet Union provided eager support for the anti-apartheid cause and the United States, though hesitant, worried about antagonizing African opinion.

Pressure mounted further by the early 1960s. Most of the major colonies of the world were now free, which helped funnel attention to remaining centers of abuse, South Africa in the lead. Local clashes, including a massacre of protesters in Sharpsville in 1960, drew further global outrage. As the United Nations General Assembly became increasingly dominated by nations from Africa, Latin America, and Asia, it opened opportunities for discussion of measures against apartheid, including economic sanctions, though strategies were initially diffuse. By this point also, some groups in the West were beginning to highlight apartheid as well, even though, for some time, Western governments themselves held back. The first anti-apartheid group in the United States formed in 1953 (the American Committee on Africa) as a coalition of African American and white civil rights leaders.

A key question was what the United Nations could do, as it became increasingly clear that there was wide agreement that apartheid constituted a pervasive violation of all basic human rights. The Charter, after all, urged member states to promote fundamental freedoms; South Africa was a member state, clearly not engaged in this promotion but rather the reverse; what was to happen when such a violation of Charter obligations was identified? After much inconclusive debate—many governments were worried about giving the United Nations any power to criticize internal policies—a decision was reached in 1967. The UN Human Rights Commission was charged with making "a thorough study of situations which reveal a consistent pattern of violations of human rights, as exemplified by the policy of apartheid as practiced in the Republic of South Africa." With this move, the Charter was shifted by a mere statement of principle to an instrument in international law, with United Nations enforcement. A second measure followed in 1970, authorizing another UN group to receive communications from individuals and groups that revealed "a consistent pattern of gross and reliably attested violations of human rights." Here was a mechanism by which local and global NGOs could now ally with the United Nations, in common cause against human rights abuses.

It was at this point also (1966) that the United Nations crafted a new International Covenant on Civil and Political Rights, charged with receiving regular reports from signatory states on how human rights were being implemented. Now-standard rights were defined once again, including the right of all peoples to self-determination—to "freely determine their political status"—and the application of all basic rights without distinction of race, sex, or religion. Basic rights included expression, religion, movement, political action (including the right to vote); stipulations against arbitrary and excessive punishment now involved limiting the death penalty to the most serious offenses only, and also prohibition of arbitrary killings by security forces. A number of countries signed the treaty, which took effect a decade later, though many held back. Some signed but with specific "reservations": the United States, for example, insisted that it could impose capital punishment on anyone other than a pregnant woman. By 2010, all but twenty-seven countries recognized by the United Nations had accepted the treaty at least in principle. While some jurists argued that individual reservations, like those by the United States, limited the treaty's effectiveness—domestic laws were often not adjusted to take account of the new obligations—others cited the importance of the new measure in providing regular United Nations oversight of human rights conditions. Supporters also singled out important protections for the rights of association, seen as covering the activities of human rights NGOs—though here, too, there were qualifications, allowing societies to limit associations in the interests of national security or public safety.

On balance, the new statements about United Nations responsibility for implementing and monitoring, and not simply stating, human rights standards represented an important shift. A United Nations human rights committee now met regularly. A series of regional actions also followed. The Organization of American States formed a new convention on human rights in 1978, and a resultant Commission for oversight. European courts became more active, and a bit later (1986) the organization of African states also issued a Charter on Human and Peoples' Rights.

These various developments provided new bases in international law for new responsibilities in the human rights field. While apartheid triggered the changes in the United Nations, and continued to command considerable international attention, the new apparatus was available for attention to human rights abuses elsewhere, and new targets emerged from the 1990s onward.

Apartheid itself ultimately collapsed, a result that constituted a real victory for the combination of human rights principles and international pressure, always based on passionate, often heroic, local resistance. By the late 1970s concern was certainly mounting. In the United States and Western Europe, various religious and labor organizations, as well as human rights groups themselves, passed resolutions condemning the apartheid system. On American campuses, students organized to press university administrations to end investments in South Africa, and agitation spread directly to some corporations as well. Several city governments pointedly reviewed their investment policies. Marches on Washington, against apartheid, occurred in 1981 and 1982. In Britain the main union movement persuaded several retail chains to stop carrying South African goods. Canadian concern ran high: as one academic put it, "in few other cases of political repression is the situation so morally unambiguous." In South Africa itself a new Free South Africa movement launched in 1984, triggering many arrests and yet another round of international protests. A variety of foreign leaders, like former President Jimmy Carter, visited the country to bear witness to abuse. By this point over a thousand organizations were working against apartheid in the United States alone. Public opinion polls throughout the West showed majorities hostile to apartheid and eager for firmer action from their own governments. United States investments in South Africa dropped by 50 percent. Japan joined the parade, thanks to internal human rights pressures there, banning exports to South Africa in 1985 and limiting imports the year after. The European Union also spoke out. Finally, under new leadership at home, the South African government yielded, freeing political prisoners like Nelson Mandela in 1990 and ending the whole apartheid system in 1994. An ensuing new government, under Mandela's presidency, quickly embraced human rights principles.

Civil rights and their ramifications

The final innovative stage for human rights during the 1960s and 1970s involved an expanding range of targets, including renewed interest in rights for women but also some entirely new foci. Pressure from expansion came from several regions, and generated different kinds of efforts, as well as new sources of opposition. Ultimately elements of this expansion affected the global arena, even when initial innovation had occurred within individual regions.

One target involved renewed attempts to win clearer endorsement of social and economic rights. The President of Mexico urged a new international charter in 1972, against the protests of the United States and other wealthy countries. The United Nations adopted a new Charter of Economic Rights and Duties of States in 1974, calling for policies on tariffs or on technological advances that would pay special attention to the poorer nations of the world. The focus here, however, was on governments, and particularly on efforts to speed economic development, not on protections for individuals or standards for their treatment.

The United States proved to be an unexpectedly fertile source of agitation for human rights during the 1960s, including the expansion of range. Initial focus rested on legal discriminations against African Americans, particularly in the southern states. African American activism never ceased after the Civil War and the abolition of slavery, but it oscillated in intensity. World War II galvanized new interest, with the attention to Nazi racism and international resolutions against racial discrimination obviously spurring concerns at home. As we have noted, the cold war itself made American discrimination an international embarrassment. A 1954 Supreme Court decision struck down the idea that separate schools for African Americans could be regarded as equal and, somewhat reluctantly, the federal government began to enforce school integration. Agitation on other issues surged from this point onward, led by inspiring figures like Martin Luther King. African American individuals and groups, often joined by white civil rights advocates, attacked segregation on buses and for swimming pools. Students pressed for integration of lunch counters in North Carolina and elsewhere. Barriers to voting were attacked, as were discriminatory housing arrangements. By the later 1960s, the federal government was actively supporting efforts to break down the elaborate structure of legal and social discrimination. Many elements of de facto segregation remained, but equality in law was more firmly established than ever before.

This important passage in American history obviously involved implementing principles that had long been part of the human rights movement, not only in terms of legal equality but also around the right to protest social injustice without repressive police interference. The energy aroused, however, had larger implications. The American civil rights struggle, the largely nonviolent tactics used, and the successes that were won, could spill over into other efforts to attack racial inequalities—for example, among Australian or Canadian aborigines. They helped fuel the international movement against apartheid. Consequences fanned out beyond the United States.

Within the United States, both the passion and the arguments deployed in the civil rights campaigns also helped to galvanize other groups. Feminist programs, most obviously, developed renewed enthusiasm. The idea of extending rights to women was not new. In the West, however, feminist pressure had eased considerably once legal codes were largely changed to reflect greater equality and governments granted the vote. Various intellectuals, however, began writing about agendas yet to conquer, not so much in terms of formal legal rights as through greater pressures for social and economic equality in what they still saw, quite plausibly, as male-dominated structures. Women needed rights to free themselves from standard assumptions about careers or about family responsibilities. The National Organization for Women (NOW), formed in 1966, vowed "to take action to bring women into full participation in the mainstream of American society now, exercising all privileges and responsibilities thereof in truly equal partnership with men." Basic language for this new feminism revived familiar human rights traditions, in calling for full legal equality and an end to every form of discrimination—in this case, of course, based on gender. But the feminist surge was attempting to stretch the applicability of equal rights beyond government policy—to policies followed by schools or corporations, for instance. They also claimed new rights, for example, the right to abortion (a woman's right to her own body), as a means of protecting women against unwanted pregnancies and children. The expansion had real success, in spurring new thinking and career aspirations among many women, particularly in the middle class. It also provoked new opposition. Huge and ongoing controversy surrounded the abortion issue, for example, with women's rights pitted against a fervently claimed right to life for unborn babies. On a wider front, NOW devoted a great deal of attention to an equal rights amendment to the American constitution, but it failed to win support from a sufficient number of states. The expanded version of women's rights remained a work in progress and a target for continued contestation.

The global implications of the new feminism were in some ways simpler. Women in other Western societies, including places like Australia, easily followed the American lead, expanding their claims for rights and equalities. In France, for example, a new women's liberation movement emerged after popular protests in 1968, copying many features from its sister organization in the United States and urging that women gain freer access to contraception and abortion and greater autonomy from their husbands. Here and elsewhere, feminists also urged more women to run for public office or gain government positions, often surpassing American levels in the process. New feminist organi-zations also sprang up in Latin America, where for the most part women had also already won the vote. The organizations focused on applying greater legal equality to family codes, for example, with regard to rights to divorce, on greater economic opportunities, on rights to claim appropriate child support from fathers (an issue of concern in the United States as well), and on promoting greater political participation. As elsewhere also, Latin American feminists worked hard against negative portrayals of women in the media and other sites of popular culture. Latin American feminists also joined others in supporting a more general human rights agenda, against remaining authoritarian regimes.

New wave feminism, in other words, inspired a wide commitment to fuller definitions of rights inside and outside the political domain, in all the regions where earlier movements had worked to extend human rights thinking to gender issues. While broader definitions roused opposition, the advocacy could also pay off. Larger numbers of women in Latin America went into politics than was true in the United States. After some bitter battles, European feminists managed to win more widely accepted compromises on abortion availability, mainly by focusing on the initial three months of pregnancy, than was true of their American sisters.

The most recent round of feminism also, however, had still wider global impact. American feminist leaders, like Betty Friedan, one of the founders of NOW, worked quickly and actively to establish wider international ties, recognizing that women in many regions needed encouragement to move into an initial phase of rights demands.

This kind of push, along with existing United Nations commitments to legal equality, generated a new level of international sponsorship for women's rights. Beginning in 1975, the United Nations began sponsoring a "year of the woman" with a major international conference every decade (the first in Mexico, the second in Africa). These meetings, drawing international participation including established feminist leadership, in turn generated an unprecedented number of local women's organizations, ready to claim new rights and prepared, like the human rights NGOs, to report on abuses. Not by accident, it was at this point as well that the NGOs themselves, like Amnesty, began adding explicit women's rights programs. In Africa, for example, the African Women's Task Force emerged in 1986, on the heels of the "Year of the Woman" conference in Nairobi. The same push helped generate the first unequivocal international statement against female circumcision, in 1982. Not surprisingly, in this same context, a growing number of national constitutions began inserting clauses about the legal equality of women, in regions such as Egypt where they had been previously missing. Ivory Coast set up a Ministry on women's conditions, while the Organization of African Unity in 1981 offered a Charter that affirmed the elimination of "every discrimination against women" and acceptance of all relevant international standards in this area. New regions of India also sprouted active women's rights groups. With few exceptions, at least a basic level of feminism was going global.

Civil rights agitation and principles, finally, helped generate group rights claims in some entirely new areas. Particularly important was the establishment of the gay rights movement, initially in the United States. Associations to support homosexuals were not entirely novel, but until the civil rights decade they had concentrated, fairly quietly, on mutual support. In 1969, a new wave of protest emerged with the Stonewall Riots, initially targeting police repression of a gay bar in New York City. Wider rights advocacy soon followed, aimed both at promoting greater social and cultural acceptance and at addressing discriminations in law. Targets of specific rights campaigns have included demands for the right to adopt children, to gain access to benefits and hospital visits for gay partners, and most recently to win legal recognition of gay marriage. Eliminating earlier laws that targeted homosexual acts was a crucial goal. Gays should have, in sum, all the legal rights that heterosexuals have—a standard kind of human rights demand, simply applied to a new category of the population. Gay rights promotion roused considerable opposition, and the story is very much a work in progress, though with growing success in American public opinion, particularly among younger population segments. The movement's global status is also tentative, though rights advocacy fairly quickly developed in other industrialized countries on the strength of the American model. In Britain, for example, gays won the right to adopt in 2002 and the right to form civil partnerships in 2005, though the movement for outright marriage moved more slowly than in the United States.

Still other targets spilled out. The United States in 1973 enacted new codes to protect the rights of disabled people to the fullest possible access to jobs and education, another important new direction. In 1969, the National Association to Advance Fat Acceptance formed, claiming the need for civil rights for the obese, particularly to make sure they had equal job access regardless of size. The Western world, at least, began exploding with new opportunities to apply the basic principles of human rights as widely as possible.

Interactions

The expansions of human rights initiatives in the 1960s and 1970s, finally, clearly and significantly interacted. We have seen how new United Nations provisions facilitated collaboration with the growing range of NGOs, providing greater overall visibility to human rights claims for both types of organization. Several of the new UN conventions, along with their binding obligations on members in international law (at least in principle), could also protect the associational rights of the NGOs themselves. Expansion of rights definitions—particularly, but not exclusively, for women—quickly involved both the United Nations and the NGOs, even when much of the initial energy came from new efforts in a single region. Major human rights victories, like the fight against apartheid, involved NGOs, the United Nations, and also the new energies around civil rights causes in places like the United States. Individual leaders gained momentum from several of the new channels. President Jimmy Carter in the United States, serving from 1978 to 1982, had gained deep commitments to human rights causes in part because of civil rights efforts in his native south. In turn, he helped propel greater United Nations attention to human rights issues, actively promoted movements in Latin America to eradicate political abuses, and helped form the new human rights oversight from the Organization of American States. Changes in geography, definitions, organizational structure, and simply levels of energy, intertwined in this important second contemporary phase of human rights development.

The third phase: 1989–present

The most recent phase of human rights expansion in many ways built directly on the achievements of the two previous phases. Networks of NGOs became denser. United Nations programs expanded. While the fervor of the civil rights movements declined somewhat, some of the newer causes, like gay rights, maintained high visibility.

New ingredients were also significant, however. Several factors add up to a real shift in context, with measurable changes in the human rights profile resulting.

First: between 1989 and 1991, Soviet communism effectively disappeared, and much of the Russian empire crumbled. The result was a host of new nations in east-central Europe and central Asia; the further result was the need to devise new, post-communist regimes even in Russia itself. In terms of human rights, these developments, most obviously, allowed a number of nations to confirm a commitment to standard human rights, particularly in the political domain, that had been impossible under communism. Most of the new east-central European regimes quickly adopted constitutions guaranteeing rights in areas like religion and the press, while reducing (if not eliminating) arbitrary arrests and imprisonments. A few countries maintained authoritarian structures, but overall there was a notable expansion of human rights geography.

Additionally, the effective fall of communism simplified international discussions of human rights. The United Nations was less polarized, on human rights issues, between communist and Western camps, which arguably created a freer hand for further global efforts. The change had some downsides: cold war competition had helped prod the United States into human rights leadership, and this pressure was now removed, which could facilitate some slippage. The collapse of communism and the advances of global capitalism without question reduced attention to social and economic rights. These rights had never secured an absolutely fixed place on the human rights agenda, but now they definitely trailed off. Many countries, for various reasons, began to reduce welfare programs—not just in Europe and the United States, but also in India and Latin America. Income inequalities and the levels of lowest-tier poverty almost certainly worsened—yet there was no systematic human rights response.

The fall of communism, in sum, furthered human rights in many ways; it simplified global geography; but it also risked narrowing the human rights list.

Second: partly because of the fall of communism, but also partly independently, the number of countries with essentially democratic political systems began to expand. One-party rule and military governments declined in many regions, though they did not disappear. Most Latin American countries became functioning democracies, with multi-party competition and reasonably free media, by the 1980s. The Philippines installed a renewed democracy in the middle of the decade, and quickly generated a constitution that restored firm commitments to human rights. Obviously democracy spread in east-central Europe after 1989. Big changes occurred in Africa in the 1990s, with twenty-five countries converting to democracy. This included the most populous nation, Nigeria, as well as South Africa after apartheid. In 2011 and the so-called Arab spring, several Middle Eastern countries toppled authoritarian regimes, though what this meant for human rights remained unclear.

Democracy was not yet a uniform global commitment. Different nations continued to define the system in different specific ways. Nevertheless, at least for the moment, there was a substantial trend, and it went hand in hand with greater attention to human rights. Here was another component of further geographical change.

Third: the fall of communism and concurrent changes in business organization and technology vaulted new processes of globalization to the world's center stage. Globalization was not, of course, a new phenomenon. In the human rights field alone globalization had been proceeding for at least a century. But conditions in the 1990s did change in some respects. The power of global corporations—called multinationals—became both greater and clearer. Many businesses were producing parts of products in different parts of the world, seeking the best regulatory atmosphere, the lowest labor costs, as well as favorable resources and transportation. They were able to maintain communication internationally, to oversee their far-flung operations, and they developed greater power and larger resources than many governments could muster. Increasingly, the multinationals were determining working and environmental conditions for large segments of the world's population. Globalization also accelerated on the strength of technological changes. The Internet, effectively introduced around 1990, transformed the speed and volume of international exchange. Along with international jet travel (increasingly available from the 1950s onward), global technologies greatly reduced the impact of distance.

The new aspects of globalization had many implications for human rights, both positive and negative. On the negative side: big corporations, and the competition they offered for other businesses, might worsen labor conditions and make it harder for workers to organize in resistance, simply because of the power disparities. At an extreme, if conditions in one place became too difficult for a multinational, management could easily pack up and move elsewhere. On the plus side, communication among different peoples might be revolutionized, thanks to the Internet, cell phones, Tweets, Facebook—the long list of ever-changing opportunities. There was challenge here: some political regimes, nervous about freedom of thought, became more anxious than ever, seeking new means of repression. But full repression was probably more difficult than before, because so many people, interested in new ideas, also became adept at technological shortcuts. Most obviously, contemporary global communication created new opportunities to exchange information about human rights abuses or about opportunities for positive political change. By the 21st century an organization like Amnesty International could mobilize petition campaigns by email and win hundreds of thousands of signatures in a day or two once a potential abuse had been identified. A religious court in Nigeria sentences a woman to death by stoning, for adultery. Local human rights groups quickly notify the global NGOs, which in turn begin sending email chains to members; within a short time the Nigerian government is bombarded with protests and quickly arranges to overrule the religious court and spare the woman. Not all stories had happy endings, but they became more possible with contemporary technologies. The same technologies allowed protest movements to spread more quickly than ever. Uses of cell phones and Facebook were vital to the exchanges from one center of agitation to another during the contagious popular risings of the Arab spring in 2011—from Tunisia, to Egypt, to Yemen, to Libya, to Syria, and beyond.

Fourth: new problems emerged that spurred new human rights energy. As the cold war ended and the main tasks of decolonization were complete, various areas began to face a new series of issues. Along with growing economic inequalities within many regions, and also environmental degradation, new types of regional conflicts surfaced. Many countries in Africa were torn apart by brutal civil strife, in which different ethnic groups attacked each other, often with massive bloodshed that in some cases reached the level of genocide.

The 1990s saw intense fighting among different ethnic and religious groups in the Balkans, as the former nation of Yugoslavia split apart. Conventional warfare actually declined, at least for the moment, but internal group violence may have intensified as, in several cases, organized governments effectively broke down. Finally, new levels of terrorism surfaced, with organized attacks on several countries—the United States, Spain, Britain, India—but also a great deal of terrorist violence within individual nations such as Pakistan and Iraq. These challenges, and measures taken to try to deal with them, raised a host of human rights issues, spurring some important innovations and certainly creating both energy and dispute.

Along with these major factors, it is worth noting that, compared to the previous phase, the United States leadership role in human rights clearly declined. American politics became more conservative from the 1980s onward. Many newly prominent leaders were not just uninterested in, but positively hostile toward, human rights, like the presidential candidate in 2011 who stated quite simply that human rights were "often nothing more than a front for attacking institutions that teach traditional values." It was also true that new problems, including the confrontation with terrorism after the 9/11 (2001) attacks on several iconic centers, distracted the nation and might in fact prompt responses that curtailed human rights. The nation did not, overall, turn against human rights. Rather, it lost leadership—for example, to the European Union—which pushed more clearly for further steps down the human rights path. And in some cases it took measures that provoked international outcry, becoming again a target for human rights criticism as well as a source of such criticism for others. The State Department continued to churn out annual reports of human rights abuses in other countries, and many NGOs continued to depend heavily on American support, but the national role had changed.

Most important, however, was the combination of effects resulting from new types of problems, the acceleration of globalization, the end of the cold war, and the spread of democracy. Human rights did not change shape in response, but there were impacts extending from geography to a new round of adjustment to the list of basic rights themselves.

The new geography

The expansion of the number of countries publicly committed to human rights was a key development. More and more constitutions embraced human rights clauses. The 1997 constitution of Poland, for example, crafted after the collapse of communism and Soviet control, referred specifically to the nation's commitment to "universal values," while also reflecting on the recent past: "mindful of the bitter experience of the times when fundamental freedoms and human rights were violated in our Homeland." The constitution assured equality of the law regardless of gender or religion; it insisted on freedom of speech and expression and the right to peaceful assembly; it guaranteed respect for all basic rights, and offered important reference to appropriate working conditions and welfare levels; it noted the rights of children, including provision of compulsory education to age 18; and it renounced arbitrary arrest, torture, or any kind of physical punishment. It was, in sum, a classic contemporary human rights document.

And the same could be said for new constitutions generated not only in east-central Europe, but in many parts of Africa and Asia, where more democratic regimes took hold. Never before had so many countries offered human rights guarantees as part of fundamental law.

New geography also meant, however, growing opportunities for local NGOs and reformers to work toward even higher standards. After the collapse of authoritarian rule in Indonesia, for example, local NGOs were relatively free to investigate labor conditions and try to rouse public opinion in instances where labor organizers had been fired for their activities. NGOs in many African countries worked to create greater awareness of the rights of women. In India, a variety of local groups pressed for more fundamental changes in the treatment of women. They documented cases of domestic violence and even murder. They pressed the government to assure greater political opportunities for women, instead of merely allowing women to vote under their husbands' watchful eye; a key result was new legislation requiring the selection of a certain percentage of women in all local elections. Still other organizations worked against child labor. Kailash Satyarthi, a tireless crusader, worked both in India and in contacts with international organizations to urge better enforcement of labor laws and school requirements. He founded the Global March Against Child Labor, the South Asian Coalition on Child Servitude, and the Global Campaign for Education, winning both Indian and international support in the process. Satyarthi claimed that his direct efforts had rescued as many as 66,000 children from work in factories, domestic service, and circus performance.

More and more regions, in other words, not only subscribed to criteria in principle but tolerated and even sometimes embraced ongoing monitoring and reform ideas within their own borders—often in active linkage with international organizations.

And even countries that did not readily tolerate human rights activity almost always had individuals and at least small groups eager to identify problems and abuses. Syria, for example, had a human rights organization in exile (in London) that regularly reported on political arrests, suppressions of newspapers, and other authoritarian measures. The path was not easy. Many activists were arrested—a recurrent problem in China—and some were beaten or killed. No major region, however, was devoid of some significant human rights activism despite the quite varied reactions of those in power. This, too, was a major change in geography.

International organizations

Two developments expanded the role of the United Nations and related groups in promoting human rights, from the early 1990s onward. First came a rededication to the whole human rights cause, through a conference and ensuing declaration—the Vienna Declaration—in 1993. Second, unprecedented instruments were introduced to punish, or attempt to punish, excessive violations of human rights through a new international judicial body.

The Vienna Declaration resulted from a world conference on human rights, called by the United Nations. It was only the second international conference to focus on human rights exclusively—the first, in 1968, had celebrated the twenty-year anniversary of the Universal Declaration. The conference began to be organized in 1989, in the excitement of the cold war's end and a belief that, now, international meetings could really make headway in resolving global problems. The years immediately after 1989, however, saw a fair amount of bickering and outright nervousness among participants, as optimism that a better world was right around the corner faded somewhat. An Amnesty International leader commented bitterly that "it is not surprising that governments are not overenthusiastic. After all, they are the ones violating human rights."

The Vienna Declaration was, however, meaningful in several ways. It reaffirmed the principles and importance of the Universal Declaration. It called member states to action, and committed the United Nations itself to more forceful measures in the human rights domain. And it ratified some extensions of the human rights concepts themselves. The Declaration's basic theme insisted that "the promotion and protection of ALL human rights is a legitimate concern of the international community." It called on all peoples and all governments "to rededicate themselves to the global task of promoting and protecting all human rights and fundamental freedoms so as to secure full and universal enjoyment of these rights."

The Declaration sought to erase distinctions between civil and political rights, on the one hand, and social and cultural rights: all categories were important. It made it clear that effective democracy—the right to vote with freedom of choice—was now a basic right: the endorsement of democracy reinforced what seemed to be a global trend. It urged that economic development and the elimination of poverty worldwide were vital aspects of a human rights agenda. It added environmental protection, for example, against the dumping of toxic wastes, to the list of human rights to life and health. It attacked racism and discrimination, and repeated the United Nations commitment to the protection of minorities (another international convention on this subject had passed just a year before). It drew careful attention to women's rights, including protections against sexual harassment and exploitation. It also noted the rights of children, through assurances of adequate material and medical support and access to basic education and through elimination of at least "harmful" child labor. An explicit section identified rights for the disabled, against any kind of discrimination and for equal opportunities and the elimination of any socially created barriers. The result was the longest list of internationally established human rights ever before produced. The Declaration finally returned to the call for action, by international bodies and individual governments, to assure better defense of rights and appropriate educational efforts to widen understanding. A new position, United Nations High Commissioner for Human Rights, was established to promote better monitoring and fuller compliance.

The rise of new levels of international attention to human rights, along with some specific new issues, also accounted for the reemergence of effort to bring to trial individuals accused of major violations—to put some teeth into claims of crimes against humanity. This had been a response to World War II, of course, but it had then trailed off partly because of the huge international disagreements of the cold war. During the 1990s, the new South African government established a "Truth and Reconciliation" commission to investigate apartheid abuses. The goal was to clear the air, not primarily to punish: individuals who acknowledged roles in enforcing racial discrimination or attacking protesters were granted amnesty, so long as they admitted their guilt. The leniency was not universally popular, but it did help establish responsibility along with making it clear that abuses of this sort were unacceptable. Proceedings were also instituted in several Latin American countries, such as Argentina, for abuses under military or authoritarian rule. The United Nations itself established an inquiry—a Truth Commission—on repressions that had occurred in El Salvador. Other international tribunals investigated war crimes and genocide in the former Yugoslavia and in Rwanda. And the process continued. In 2011, the Egyptian rising against authoritarian rule quickly led to a trial of the former ruler for his role in police abuses against protesters. More widely still, the United Nations began exploring methods to prevent individual states from granting amnesties to protect gross violators of human rights.

Even more sweeping, however, was the establishment of a new International Criminal Court, in 2002. The goal was a permanent tribunal to prosecute individuals for genocide, crimes against humanity, war crimes, and crimes of aggression (though this latter category was not to come into play until 2017). Interestingly, within a decade 116 states had joined the process, including all of Latin America, nearly all of Europe, and about half the nations of Africa, though some major nations, including the United States, held out against this kind of international oversight.

A court of this sort, to deal with crimes against humanity when individual governments cannot or will not act, had been under discussion since World War I. A number of lawyers who participated in the Nuremberg trials urged that a body of this sort was essential, but cold war disputes made action impossible. With the cold war over, and new regional conflicts and attendant abuses emerging in the 1990s, the time finally arrived to act. Human rights NGOs played an important role in advocating for the court, and continue to serve a function in providing accusation and supporting information. The court itself is designed to have appropriate human rights guarantees against arbitrary action, with careful provisions for legal defense and appeal of initial verdicts. At the same time, as with all human rights issues, important disputes surfaced about coverage and definition. Some nations wanted acts of terrorism to be brought before the court, but international agreement on what constituted terrorism was not yet possible. India and some other nations urged that the use of nuclear weapons should be regarded as a crime against humanity, but again insufficient agreement resulted to add this to the court's jurisdiction.

How much the court will actually impact the global human rights situation has yet to be determined. Several accusations have been brought to the court, mainly from situations in combat zones in Africa, although in some cases the accused have not been captured. Several trials were underway by 2011. The first leader of the court, from Latin America, has been vigorous in asserting jurisdiction over potential war criminals. Whatever the uncertainty for a truly novel enterprise, the very establishment of the court, as a permanent opportunity to identify and act on crimes against humanity, represents an interesting further step in human rights evolution and global response. Innovations in international organization, along with renewed assertions of basic principles and responsibilities, continue to be a basic part of the contemporary chapter in human rights history.

Widening the agenda

The final set of developments in recent human rights history picks up a theme that has recurred since the later 19th century, as well as during the 1960s and 1970s; the list continues to grow. Expansion includes areas of substantial agreement, where a new target of human rights thinking quickly seems logical in terms of existing basic standards, and areas that immediately arouse controversy—again, by now a familiar mixture.

Children

In 1989, the United Nations finally was able to issue an international Convention on the Rights of the Child, which was then, of course, referred to as a standard category a few years later in the Vienna Declaration. We have seen that children have often constituted a challenging category in human rights thinking. At the same time, many individual countries had long since resolved on certain rights criteria. What was new, but also surprisingly difficult, was forging a global statement on the subject.

The International Labor Office provided important initiative. Since the 1920s this organization had been passing resolutions against child labor, seeking to extend legislation common in industrial countries to the world at large. Progress was slow. A campaign in 1973 to win global agreement on a ban on child labor under 16 failed, because too many countries still depended on this kind of work, too many parents needed children to contribute to the family economy. India, for example, an important rights advocate in many categories, strongly resisted action in this area. So did the United States, hoping to continue to use child labor among migrant agricultural workers and also characteristically hostile to international oversight. The 1989 Convention was a compromise: child labor was banned by signatories but only in the more extreme cases, with emphasis on sexual exploitation of children, sale of children to pay family debts, and the use of child soldiers. The Convention was able to repeat the standard agreement in principle that children should be provided with adequate material protection and that they had rights to education. Wider efforts continued as well. The Anti-Slavery Society—that old bastion—launched a global march against child labor in 1998. The Federation of International Football developed a "foul ball" program around the same time, trying to ban sports gear made by children. The idea of child rights was advancing, but with limitations.

Important controversy also arose on punishments for children. Most countries signed an agreement banning the death penalty for minors—applying the old human rights interest in limiting extreme punishments to the category of children. The United States long held out, along with Somalia. But in 2005 the United States Supreme Court ruled that children under 18 could not be executed for any crime, citing international legal standards as a crucial reason for the decision. Global standards, once defined, could make a difference.

Labor

New and global human rights interest applied to labor by the end of the 20th century—not an entirely novel area, but one of increasing importance as the economy globalized. Multinational companies sometimes sought greater opportunities for exploitation of labor, in terms of long hours, unsafe conditions, and restrictions on pay. Perhaps even more commonly, smaller local subcontractors, desperate to cut costs, or other local businesses in competition with the multinationals, increased the pressure on workers. Efforts to repress worker protest and punish potential "troublemakers" were part of this package in many cases.

A new set of international NGOs sought to respond, applying the idea of labor rights to additional parts of the world; they helped knit a larger local network of watch organizations, in what was becoming a familiar pattern. A Dutch-based group, Clean Clothes Campaign, with branches in many countries and close ties to union movements, began to issue Urgent Appeal messages focusing on news about individual factories. Students Against Sweatshops was an American-centered association, with units on many college campuses, among other things pressing university administrations to end support for logo products made by exploited labor. A larger Workers Rights Consortium sent researchers to various countries, providing information on factories that should be on a global watch list. Another U.S.-based group, the National Labor Committee, specialized in massive public relations campaigns against sweatshops involving well-known brands or investments by celebrities. A number of celebrities were caught with shares in factories with distressingly substandard working conditions, often in Central America, and some, once publicity surfaced, vowed quick redress. Yet another group, Global Exchange, was founded in 1988 with a focus on factories in Vietnam controlled by famous firms like Nike, and ultimately urging product boycotts that prompted several corporations to set up new fair standards policies. The International Labor Organization itself held a series of conferences after 1990, aimed among other things at drawing attention to harsh working conditions and the need to protect workers' freedom to organize. New efforts were directed informing consumers in affluent societies like the West or Japan that many of the products they purchased resulted from exploitative, or sweatshop, labor.

The global monitoring process that emerged closely resembled other human rights activities. An example: in 2003, over 500 workers walked out of a sweater factory in Indonesia, protesting substandard conditions. They were immediately fired and replaced. A local watch group, the Legal Aid Institute, quickly informed several global NGOs. These in turn petitioned the Indonesian government, which had protective laws on the books in accordance with international standards, and also pressed European investors, who owned the company. Internet stories pictured the workers after dismissal, and also recounted stories of people forced to work despite injury or illness. Consumer boycotts of relevant products surfaced in Europe. And, at least for a time, the company backed down, rehiring the protesters. In another case, again in Indonesia, textile workers in one plant noted frequent injuries from unprotected equipment, low pay, and exhausting hours including compulsory (and uncompensated) overtime. With assistance from a local NGO, they established a website that dramatically proclaimed, "Workers' legal and human rights are not respected in PT Busana [the company involved]." Again, global NGOs took up the cause, noting that the right to unionize was enshrined in the Universal Declaration of Human Rights. Signatures of support poured in, not only from the West but also East Asia, and particularly Korea, plus Australia and New Zealand, and Latin America, along with adherence from local NGOs in Indonesia itself.

While the application of human rights to labor issues was not itself unprecedented, given the globalization of business, both the level of attention and the tactics were new. The result was an important extension of human rights activity, connecting the effort to additional categories of the population, particularly in Southeast Asia and parts of Africa.

Environment

Concern about damage to the global environment grew rapidly by the end of the 20th century, with evidence about global warming, the depletion of the ozone layer, and other problems. A series of high-level conferences, often with United Nations sponsorship, sought intergovernmental agreements on controlling pollution.

The issues involved were important, though they provoked much debate. While much of the furor focused on high-level policy issues and scientific findings, the growing human rights climate of the late 20th century invited connections in this category as well.

As a result, contemporary declarations, like the Vienna document, began to include environmental rights in the expanding catalogue. People had a right, so the argument went, to be protected from extreme environmental damage and the resulting problems in health and reproduction. As with labor, the linkage was applied to individual cases. Thus, in 1990, a Nigerian activist, Ken Saro-Wiwa, founded a group demanding compensation from the Shell Oil Corporation for local environmental degradation resulting from petroleum extraction. Saro-Wiwa was arrested, and at his trial spoke eloquently of the "environmental rights" of local peoples. Saro-Wiwa expressly referred to freedom from manmade environmental damage in the language of rights, explaining how he, as a student, had imbibed global human rights concepts that now required this additional extension. He urged minority groups in Nigeria "to stand up now and fight fearlessly, and peacefully, for their rights"; and he added support from the Quran: "all those who fight, when oppressed shall incur no guilt, but Allah will punish the oppressor." Environmental movements in other regions, such as India, also adopted human rights language.

In 1992, an international conference in Rio de Janeiro established the connection more formally, issuing a Declaration on Environment and Human Rights that put "human beings at the center of concerns for sustainable development" and affirming rights "to a healthy and productive life in harmony with nature." The principles were intended to guide individual governments, promoting an end to environmentally destructive economic practices and providing citizens with access to legal remedies for environmental damage. The Declaration also referred to the special need to protect minorities and indigenous groups that had evolved their own balance with nature but needed help against the inroads of large corporations.

Human rights arguments did not win primary attention in the ongoing struggle to control environmental change. They provided some support, however, and their invocation was a revealing example of how the language of rights was expanding, providing important rationales for a variety of global problems.

Sexuality

Human rights language, historically, had not usually been explicitly connected to areas of sexual behavior. On the whole, however, the logic of rights could be attached to efforts to create greater freedom for sexual activity. Religious freedom, after all, could include tolerance for disagreements about appropriate sexual behavior. Governments might be urged to end enforcement of any single set of sexual standards. Freedom of the press might apply to sexual materials; this was the case for crucial Supreme Court rulings in the United States in the 1950s that dramatically curtailed censorship in various media. The addition of gay rights to the agenda, in many parts of the West, was a specific instance in which human rights efforts sought to expand the range of sexual freedom. Changes in sexual standards always promoted huge debate, but on the whole the human rights linkage was reasonably clear.

Without changing this overall association, new developments in the women's rights movement, by the later 20th century, promoted some interesting modifications. In the West, growing attention was devoted to the problem of sexual harassment, and women's rights to freedom from same. The problem was first identified, at least through formal terminology, in a magazine article in 1976, calling attention to work situations in which people, particularly women, might be intimidated into accepting intimacies that caused them great physical and psychological distress. Increasingly, in the United States, Western Europe and also Japan, new bodies of law, with official enforcement attached, sought to provide protection from unwanted advances particularly in situations of inequality, such as manager–employee or teacher–student. Here was an effort to define limits both to traditional types of abuse and to overextensions of any contemporary commitment to sexual freedom.

At the global level, however, the most important human rights development in the area of sexuality was the categorization of rape as a crime against humanity. This had not been a conventional human rights concern. Within individual countries rapes were issues of national law, and variously treated. In wartime, rape was sometimes acknowledged as a problem, but mainly in terms of relationships between an invading force and a local population. Officials in East Germany after World War II thus worried that rapes by Russian troops might complicate local acceptance of communism. Many military officials paid attention to rapes but mainly as sources of venereal disease, which could affect military performance; this was the stance of British and American armies in post-World War II Germany. The women victimized knew what had happened, but there was no large audience for any sense that crime was involved.

This changed by the 1990s. In 1993, the United Nations added systematic rape to its definition of war crimes. Growing evidence from conflicts such as those in the Balkans, plus the changing standards in the human rights field resulting from growing inclusion of women's rights concerns, combined to generate this important new category. As we have seen, NGOs like Amnesty International quickly picked up the cause, adding attention to rapes as crimes against women not only in wartime but in situations of domestic violence, identifying this as a leading contemporary human rights issue. United Nations resolutions in 2000, and again in 2006, returned to the persistence of sexual violence, urging more effective measures.

Growing international attention also applied to sexual trafficking of women and children. This was explicitly referred to in the Convention on the Rights of the Child. The 1995 "Year of the Woman" conference in Beijing issued an explicit attack on violence against women, which "both violates and impairs or nullifies the enjoyment by women of human rights and fundamental freedoms." The measure sought to encompass rape, trafficking, and forced prostitution, and harassment in a common category of reproval, "incompatible with the dignity and worth of the human person." The resolution specifically noted that both traditional and modern practices needed attention in this area, and that both state policies and private behaviors might be involved.

The death penalty

Finally, one of the most interesting extensions of human rights thinking applied to a new series of debates about the death penalty. Here, as in the other contemporary categories, linkage to older types of human rights discussions was clear and important. Human rights advocacy, from the 18th century onward, had always focused strongly on reducing extreme punishments and avoiding unjust impositions of physical pain. This had always included some concern about the death penalty, often resulting in reductions in the number of crimes to which the penalty applied, a new interest in assuring as painless a death as possible, and increasing belief that penalties should be imposed in private rather than generating public spectacles.

Now, however, some human rights groups went further, arguing that the death penalty in any circumstance was a violation. Reform pleas accelerated after World War II, particularly in many West European nations. A British spokesperson thus spoke of the incompatibility of the death penalty and "the respect for the sanctity of human life," in seeking new legislation in the late 1940s. Many Scandinavian states had already abolished the penalty, after World War I; by the 1950s, Germany, Italy, and Austria made the same move, as did Spain and Britain in the 1960s. By this point public opinion throughout the region largely accepted the argument that the death penalty was ineffective and unjust—ineffective because it did not deter crime, unjust because it was often applied to people later found innocent, and barbaric overall. By 2003 the whole European Union had proscribed the death penalty as a "denial of human dignity," and nations seeking membership, from east-central Europe, readily complied: "The State's actions should not have human beings as victims, but [should promote] the human person as one of the major purposes of criminology." A number of Latin American countries adopted the same stance, and post-apartheid South Africa joined in as of 1995.

The result was not simply a regional change. European and Latin American leaders, often including the Pope, frequently attempted to intervene against applications of the death penalty in other places. State governments in the United States were frequently bombarded with petitions in high-profile death penalty cases, and ordinary members of the public might chime in as well. Amnesty International became increasingly active against the death penalty as part of its global program.

For this whole arena, in specific terms one of the newest human rights fields, surfaced massive international debate. United States trends long countered the European and Latin American pattern, though individual states had moved in a comparable direction. In the 1990s, 80% of respondents to American public opinion polls favored the death penalty, and rates of actual executions went up rapidly. Other nations, favorable to human rights thinking in many respects, also held out, including India and Japan.

Further change did seem to be brewing. While Japanese law did not yet change (the country, in fact, rarely imposed the penalty), public opinion turned increasingly hostile, partly because of the campaigns by various NGOs. In the United States, support for the death penalty began to drop, after 2000, though there was wide variety among states and regions. In 2002, after years of effort by human rights advocates, the Supreme Court abolished the death penalty for the intellectually disabled. Several individual states began to express new concerns, imposing moratoriums while the issues could be more fully explored. As on other key topics, the human rights discussions continued, on a local and a global scale.

Conclusion: contemporary trends

The rapid changes in human rights over the past seventy years leave many loose ends. Key innovations have yet to be fully tested. How widely will gay rights enter into a standard agenda? Will there be greater global agreement about the death penalty? Will a growing number of nations recognize human rights as having the force of law, given the intensification of commitments by international organizations? The list of yet-to-be-answered questions is a long one, precisely because so many recent developments have occurred.

The same abundance raises a new set of challenges more generally. Is the human rights list becoming too long, diluting attention to what should be the real priorities (and who will define the priorities)? The record of recent expansion inevitably provokes not only new disagreements but also some near-contradictions. The clash of rights claims in the abortion field, though particularly vivid in the United States, is one example of an area where a common and passionate commitment to rights can take strikingly diverse directions. Do human rights in contemporary sexuality mean new freedoms from traditional controls, or a new set of legal constraints to restrain impulse? Arguments of this sort are probably inevitable, possibly healthy; but they can also confuse the human rights field as a whole.

Despite complexities of this sort, and many uncompleted tasks, it is easy to see the evolution of human rights in the contemporary period in truly positive terms. Earlier human rights principles have been more widely applied than ever before. Hesitant steps toward greater inclusion, for example, where women's issues are concerned, have blossomed into full embrace. A scattered set of precedents for NGO activity have turned into a welter of organizational networks. The role of human rights in political globalization has become deeply and durably embedded, whether one measures by the amount of attention given by official international organizations or the efforts by individual nations to claim their clear place in human rights listings. While global geography remains an issue, the number of regions that serve as reliable sources of support for major segments of the human rights agenda has unquestionably expanded. All of this would have been impossible without the firm foundations established in the human rights field over the two previous centuries; but the magnitude of rates of change makes it understandable that some observers, impatient of history, date the human rights record itself as beginning in 1945. Even scholars with greater sophistication enthusiastically chart the range of positive steps and look to the future in terms of fuller fruition. The multiplicity of human rights developments has transformed key aspects of world history in little more than two generations.

Further reading

For global framework for human rights after World War II (UN, Amnesty International, expansion of human rights claims), see: Roland Burke, *Decolonization and the Evolution of International Human Rights* (Philadelphia: University of Philadelphia Press, 2010); Stefan-Ludwig Hoffmann, *Human Rights in the Twentieth Century* (New York, NY: Cambridge University Press, 2011); A. W. Brian Simpson, *Human Rights and the End of Empire: Britain and the Genesis of the European Convention* (Oxford, UK: Oxford University Press, 2004); Elizabeth Borgwardt, *A New Deal for the World: America's Vision for Human Rights* (Cambridge, MA: Harvard University Press, 2005); Roger Normand and Sarah Zaidi, *Human Rights at the UN: The Political History of Universal Justice* (Bloomington, IN: Indiana University Press, 2008); Mary Dudziak, *Cold War Civil Rights* (Princeton, NJ: Princeton University Press, 2002); Anthony Pagden, "Human Rights, Natural Rights, and Europe's Imperial Legacy," *Political Theory*, 31(2) (April, 2003), pp. 171–199; Mary Ann Glendon, "The Forgotten Crucible: The Latin American Influence on the Universal Human Rights Idea," *Harvard Human Rights Journal*, 16 (2003), pp. 27–40; and Samuel Moyn, "The First Historian of Human Rights," *American Historical Review*, 116(1) (February, 2011), pp. 58–79.

Good surveys on NGOs include Jackie Smith, Ron Pagnucco, and George A. Lopez, "Globalizing Human Rights: The Work of Transnational Human Rights NGOs in the 1990s," *Human Rights Quarterly*, 20(2) (May, 1998), pp. 379–412; Michael H. Posner and Candy Whittome, "The Status of Human Rights NGOs," *Columbia Human Rights Law Review*, 25(3) (Spring, 1994), pp. 269–290; David Chandler, "The Road to Military Humanitarianism: How the Human Rights NGOs Shaped a New Humanitarian Agenda," *Human Rights Quarterly*, 23(3) (August, 2001), pp. 678–700; David P. Forsythe, "The United Nations and Human Rights, 1945–1985," *Political Science Quarterly*, 100(2) (Summer, 1985), pp. 249–269.

See also Douglas Sanders, "Getting Lesbian and Gay Issues on the International Human Rights Agenda," *Human Rights Quarterly*, 18(1) (February, 1996), pp. 67–106; David S. Tanenhaus, *The Constitutional Rights of Children* (Lawrence, KS: University Press of Kansas, 2011); and Rajendra Ramlogan, "The Human Rights Revolution in Japan: A Story of New Wine in Old Wine Skins?" *Emory International Law Review*, 8 (1994), pp. 127–214.

6   Resistance and response
More globalization, or less

As various humanists and social scientists began writing about globalization in the 1990s (when the term was first introduced to the English language), interest quickly surfaced in defining the qualities of global citizenship. Many commented on the gap between global political structures and behaviors, and the rapid pace of global change in economics or the environment. Greater attention to global ethics seemed to be a vital part of repairing some of the damage that globalization was causing in the world at large.

The conversation was interesting in many ways, but particularly in light of the gains in human rights that had been occurring since World War II. If human rights were improving in so many ways, why was there such a widespread sense that global problems were, if anything, increasing? This chapter explores the lag between real human rights advances and many measurable aspects of the human experience, particularly during the past two decades, since the end of the cold war in principle opened the way for more clear-cut international political progress.

Priorities and impacts

There are at least two ways to frame the problem, though they are related. First, human rights gains may be real but partly beside the point, as key global issues involve other matters. But second, human rights gains themselves have not won as many concrete results as their apparent advance might suggest.

On the first issue: in November 1999, a World Trade Organization meeting in Seattle drew a major international protest against various aspects of globalization, which the WTO seemed to stand for. Over 600 protesters were arrested. From that point onward, meetings of many international economic organizations drew hostile crowds and demonstrations.

A number of grievances were involved. Some protesters simply wanted to stir things up. Many were motivated by hostility to consumer values, which global economic activities seemed to promote: the values were seen as shallow and destructive. Environmental concerns were high on the list. Global poverty was a key target, with protesters convinced that most international economic organizations, including the WTO, were not doing enough to help developing countries. Finally, treatment of workers drew fire, as too many multinational corporations seemed insensitive to safety conditions and appropriate living standards.

The protesters were not, in the main, at all hostile to human rights; but they were implicitly saying that the human rights thrust did not address what they saw as leading global problems. Of course, rights discussions might tackle environmental issues or challenges of economic development, but most rights advocacy did not place these topics at the top of any agenda, and the attention to individual rights was arguably not the best way to win the necessary policy changes in these areas. On another front, the human rights movement had not had much to say about global consumerism one way or the other. Labor issues came closer to the human rights core, with the inclusion of efforts to protect some basic standards on the job, attack child labor, and assure the freedom of workers to associate. Amnesty International, for example, issued a major call in 1998 under the heading "Labor Rights are Human Rights," among other things pinpointing the problems posed by the growing power of multinational corporations. Even here, however, globalization protesters might well believe that the rights approach was not the most relevant focus, as opposed to insistence on wider policy platforms.

Thus, if the definition of current global problems emphasizes the environment and economic development/regional poverty as the top concerns, the fact was that the human rights agenda was not necessarily central. It is also true that human rights activities have, historically and currently, focused more on the activities of governments and quasi-governments than on corporations, yet in many globalization protests it is the multinationals, along with key international economic groups like the Monetary Fund or the World Bank, that need primary attention. Again, there may be a disjuncture between human rights and leading global problems that explains some of the dissonance between human rights gains and other evaluations of the state of world affairs.

The dissonance may have been compounded, at least for the moment, by the very recent troubles associated with global economic recession, from 2008 onward. Loss of jobs, bank failures, slow economic recovery, and unsustainable public debts continue to dominate headlines in many parts of the world, and again human rights are not clearly relevant to the issues involved. It is a challenge to figure out the priority place for human rights in the larger scheme of world history, either recently or over the past two centuries. While many groups and many individual scholars are eager to continue the expansion of the human rights agenda, to make it more relevant to the probabilities of the 21st century, there may well be important disparities.

Problems surface at the local as well as the global level. In recent years several anthropologists have studied what seem to be well-meaning efforts by human rights NGOs among rural peoples in parts of Africa or Latin America. They find that the foreign NGO agents insist on translating local problems and grievances into language about protecting individuals from the state—language that does not necessarily fit the problems the local groups define. The groups, for example, may be concerned about village control over land or the tendencies of modern economic development to ignore this kind of traditional tenure. But the human rights agents often view the local statement as backward and deficient, and simply impose their own goals instead. They are unwilling to redefine their own notions in terms of local values and locally defined economic interests. The situations are complicated, among other things because each locality is different. But the main point replicates the problem that can also be seen at the global level: human rights lists, at least as thus far conceived, may miss the issues that many people in the contemporary world find most important.

The question, then, is inevitable, for anyone looking at the current state of the world: What is an accurate list of pressing global problems, and where do human rights issues fit (if at all) on the list? Or, from the anthropologists' vantage point: What is an accurate list of pressing local problems, and where (if at all) do human rights issues fit?

It is the second kind of issue, however, where measuring impact is central, that becomes an inescapable part of human rights history itself. The challenge is to know how much difference the very real progress of human rights thinking and organization has made in clearly relevant areas, beginning with political freedom and equality. Here, too, precise answers are impossible but there are different levels to sort out.

- Freedoms are difficult to measure, partly because there are so many factors involved. Almost surely there is more freedom of the press in the world today than there was seventy years ago. Yet, of course media have changed hugely also, and it is less clear that press freedoms have kept up with some of the newer developments. Women in many regions enjoy fuller legal and personal rights than they did seventy years ago. There have been some counterattacks, as violence against women has gone up in some areas; and more traditional protections, like tight family networks, have slipped in many places. There can be great debate as to whether women are better off when all things are considered. But, in terms of legal rights, there has been positive change. For better or for worse, to take another category, child labor has definitely declined around the world. It was increasing for a time in South Asia, but even that region has now joined the global trend. In other words, in a number of classic rights areas and some newer ones, there has been positive change.
- At the same time, however, these same rights areas are not as uniformly protected as most human rights advocates might wish—even aside from some regions that resist outright. An organization called Reporters Without Borders issues an annual global index, which suggests how widely press freedoms vary even among countries largely committed to human rights in this area. The measurements include formal restrictions, but also more incidental arrests of reporters and other pressures. Finland currently heads the list as freest; the United States, interestingly, is only twentieth;

Italy is much further down the list. Obviously evaluations here can be disputed, but some real variability seems undeniable, even among countries with long human rights histories.

- Freedom for workers' unions is even more problematic. In terms of legal and other barriers, this is a category that has surely deteriorated in the United States over the last three decades, without any massive conversion to full opposition. Freedom of religion is another variable. Many critics would argue that, over the past decade in the United States, freedom for Muslims has declined somewhat, because of government investigations of Muslim organizations and widespread public opposition to some efforts to build new mosques. Here, too, the nation has not turned against religious freedom, but the category is not a constant.The point is that full commitment to many human rights is not easy to achieve, and can vary over time and among nations even, again, where principles seem widely accepted. And this means that progress, while probable over the past seventy years, or even past two hundred years, is not quite as clear as might be expected.Finally, there are some human rights categories where it's hard to be sure even of qualified progress. Have torture or arbitrary arrest declined? We have no clear rates to go by, either before or after the human rights movement, but they certainly have not dropped as rapidly as might have been expected from the widespread reformist fervor involved. The past decades, with all the human rights progress, have seen widespread slaughter of literally millions of civilians in civil strife in the Balkans and in many parts of Africa, with little or no effective international intervention. Lots of groups in lots of places, in other words, have not heightened their respect for human rights, and if anything the reverse.

There are, then, two problems (at least). One is the challenge of measuring change, ideally on a global basis, which is, quite frankly, extremely hard. As we think about human rights we need to recognize the complexity of impact and consider ways to improve assessment.

The second problem, though, must be confronted more immediately, as part of human rights history itself: Why has realization fallen short of potential—why is the actual record of human rights implementation so different, particularly during the past seventy years, from the more glowing account of declarations and organizational support? Exploring this theme is the purpose of the first main sections of this chapter. There is no intention of covering all the possible permutations in human rights responses, but an indication of several major categories unquestionably clarifies some of the reasons for a persistent gap.

Effective rejection

During the later 20th century and into the early 21st, a few countries, and even more regions engulfed in civil conflict, effectively ignored human rights, with at most a brief nod in their direction. The list of recalcitrant states changed, but it never disappeared. Here was the most obvious type of setting in which the international human rights discourse had little or no effect, with often horrible results in terms of magnitudes of human suffering.

At issue here are situations and leaders who saw no reason for even rhetorical gestures toward international standards. Threats of punishment for crimes against humanity won no response, either because other issues seemed paramount or because of assumptions that consequences could be evaded later on.

Recurrently, civil wars generated informal military forces for which human rights were simply irrelevant. Their goals were personal gain and leadership power, sometimes embellished by a belief that a particular ethnic or tribal group should purge a region of rivals—at an extreme, generating policies of "ethnic cleansing" that bordered on outright genocide. Thus armies in places like the Congo ran roughshod over civilian populations, killing millions, along with widespread maiming, rape, and torture. Conflicts of this sort could extend over many years, particularly where little or no effective international intervention occurred. The several war zones in Africa replicated human tragedies of the sort that had previously occurred in the Balkans, Cambodia and elsewhere.

A few established governments also effectively scorned human rights. The authoritarian regime in North Korea, for example, operated under a 1972 constitution that did offer a standard section assuring protection of freedoms of religion and expression and various other rights, while also noting, more ominously, that the regime was a "dictatorship of the people." In fact, arbitrary arrests and torture were frequent. The government controlled all media and permitted no freedom in this area. International NGOs were banned. As far as could be determined, despite the interesting constitutional gesture, there was simply no interest in human rights, as opposed to bending the society toward support of the regime and its eccentric leader.

Similar neglect or scorn seemed largely to describe the military government of Myanmar, despite some pledges ultimately to restore democracy (though a promising release of many political prisoners occurred in 2011), and the regime of Robert Mugabe in Zimbabwe, where political opposition was rigorously and often brutally suppressed.

Cases of this sort—and particularly the outbursts of civil war—were important, generating the most widespread gaps between international professions of principle and the facts on the ground. They were not, however, typical of most organized states. To get at more common patterns, we need to turn to more subtle and complicated interactions between human rights professions and actual behaviors.

Gaps between practice and principle

Virtually every society in the world, where human rights language has registered at all, can be called upon for examples of agreements in principle that are violated in practice. Most regimes, faced with real or imagined threats to social and political stability, will be tempted to cut into rights such as freedom of the press or assembly. This category covers a considerable range, in terms of the size of the principle–practice gap, but collectively it adds considerably to an understanding of how the recent historical record has continued to fall short of human rights aspirations.

The United States, a genuine defender of human rights in many respects, internally as well as externally, provides important illustrations. We have seen that fears of communism, in the 1950s, prompted clear violations of personal rights through job discrimination and police surveillance. The "war on terror" that responded to the attacks on 9/11 generated some fascinating juggling between principles and the practical desire to punish potential perpetrators or extract as much information from them as possible. The war in Iraq, which opened in 2003, saw military personnel repeatedly violate the rights and persons of Iraqi prisoners, particularly in the Abu Ghraib prison. Exactly what happened at the prison is debated, but there was apparently at least one murder, where a prisoner was strapped up in a way that caused strangulation; a number of rapes, and certainly threats of rape; a wide range of acts of humiliation, many of them photographed, in which guards stripped prisoners and forced them into shameful positions. All of this happened in an atmosphere in which fears of terrorists and, in some cases, more general fears of Muslims, were being stoked, and in which American prison guards were apparently provided with no clear guidelines or instructions, despite the nation's legal commitments to the Geneva Conventions. The abuses were ultimately uncovered by articles in the nation's free press. Several ordinary soldiers were dishonorably discharged and two were jailed, with one more senior officer demoted and reprimanded.

But the story did not end with Iraq. A number of arrested suspects, picked up in military operations in Iraq or Afghanistan, were also tortured in other settings, though given pervasive secrecy it is impossible to be too precise. A huge controversy erupted over the widespread use of "waterboarding" as a means of forcing prisoners to talk. The practice involves tying a person up so that he is immobilized, and then pouring large amounts of water on the face, stimulating a gag reflex and a sense of drowning, with frequent repetitions in case of initial resistance. The practice is an old one, dating back to early modern Europe at least. It was used by the Japanese and others during World War II, by the French during the Algerian war for independence, and frequently elsewhere. Its reintroduction by Americans in the war on terror was hailed by some officials as a means of gaining valuable information. A number of leaders in the George W. Bush administration (2001–2009) attempted to argue that waterboarding did not constitute torture—thus seeking to avoid a direct confrontation with human rights—but many others, at home and abroad, disagreed, and the practice was again banned in 2009 by incoming President Obama. In still other cases, the Central Intelligence Agency sent prisoners to secret facilities in places like Libya, where they might be tortured as a matter of course but without official American knowledge or responsibility. Again, the effort to avoid a direct violation of human rights commitments was intriguing: even in what they felt was a national crisis, officials were loath to take on the principles directly. But the fact was that major abuses occurred, with the blessing of a number of highly placed political and military leaders.

The results, aside from the suffering of the victims involved, were twofold. First, the episodes demonstrated once again—as in French practices during the wars of decolonization, or British practices during the violence in Northern Ireland—that even nations steeped in a human rights tradition might take matters in their own hands when the going got rough. But also, as evidence of the abuses spread worldwide, other governments felt vindicated in their own disdain for many human rights constraints. If the United States perpetrated such abuses, why should my regime hold back? And what standing did the United States have in criticizing the records of other states, when its own was so blemished?

One of the reasons that human rights results have not measured up to the progress of principle is that so many states, even with longstanding commitments, break down in a crunch—whatever their effort to conceal a direct clash—and weaken the larger global effort in the process.

The problem of practice versus principle is compounded, in contemporary world history, by the many other states that adopt key human rights planks with little intention of living up to them in the first place. The obvious point, from 1945 onward, was that tremendous pressure applied to many countries at least to sign human rights conventions; here was a way to measure up to global standards of respectability, possibly to please the donors of international aid, possibly (at least briefly) to silence internal human rights advocates. The fact that human rights became so fashionable was an important shift in its own right. But it hardly assured compliance in fact.

Examples could be multiplied, but Egypt can serve as a case in point—prior to the 2011 rising that was in part motivated by the lack of human rights protections and frequent abuses by the police. The nation was governed, in principle, by a 1971 constitution that among other things stipulated that "individual freedom is a natural right." Following up, the constitution assured freedom of belief and freedom of practicing religious rights (an interesting phrasing); freedom of expression and the press; and freedom of assembly without requirements to obtain prior government approval. It was a good list, fully in keeping with professed global standards, and sincerely intended when it was introduced.

The provisions were, however, quickly subverted. Emergency rule was declared in the 1970s by a new authoritarian government, suspending the constitution without, however, providing any clear alternative or any reasoned argument against the importance of human rights—and pressure increased still further, early in the 21st century, when a new anti-terrorism amendment was introduced that might justify even further repressive measures.

The result was a situation in which few if any of the conventional human rights were consistently secured, according to observers both within and without this important nation; but at the same time some positive responses persisted as well. Religion perhaps fared best: non-Muslim religious minorities worshipped freely, and the government actively supported this openness, even though Islam was the official state religion. Human Rights Watch reported concern that Egyptian law did not recognize conversion from Islam to other faiths, and there were strict laws against "insulting" any religion. Some private violence against Christians also occurred, and Christians encountered some difficulties gaining permission to repair churches. On another front, the government made some effort to protect women's rights, attempting (without full success) to ban female circumcision.

The media domain was complicated. A variety of laws governed the press, making it illegal, for example, to criticize the President. Journalists were recurrently imprisoned, and Reporters Without Borders in 2006 placed Egypt low in its ratings of press freedom (143 of 167 nations assessed). In response (suggesting Egyptian sensitivity on human rights), a new law rescinded imprisonment for opposition reporters, but did permit fines. At the same time, foreign newspapers were allowed, which provided outlets for some educated Egyptians. And, even in the regional press, more critical articles began to surface after 2006—again a sign that human rights criticisms had some impact. Even more important were changes in television fare. By the end of the 20th century educated Egyptians frequently watched news broadcasts on the American-owned Cable News Network (CNN), which had been launched in 1980, or on outlets from the British Broadcasting Corporation. The formation of a new Arab news channel, Al Jazeera, in 1996, was far more influential. This was an outlet based in Qatar and dedicated to providing various vantage points on crucial news of the day—ranging from transmitting messages from al-Qaeda terrorists to featuring commentary explaining the Israeli point of view on the Palestinian issue. Al Jazeera became an increasingly trusted news source, over other foreign networks but also over government-controlled operations. Yet only rarely did the Egyptian government attempt to block its coverage—most notably, when the 2011 rising began in Cairo, by briefly shutting its local office and arresting six of its journalists. For the most part, though particularly by the 21st century, the freedom and range of the media in Egypt constituted a mixed category.

Several other human rights criteria, however, were more consistently rejected. Egyptian homosexuals were recurrently attacked, jailed, and beaten on charges such as "debauchery and defaming Islam." More broadly, many cases of torture were reported, and on this issue the official Egyptian response emphasized either silence or denial.

Egypt also worked hard to limit the activities of foreign human rights organizations, while constraining domestic versions. A 1964 law required all organizations to gain official permission if they wished to operate freely, and this has been denied to many rights groups. Associations like the Egyptian Organization for Human Rights functioned anyway, occasionally meeting with government officials about abuses; but their statements were ignored by the nation's government-owned daily mass newspapers.

Egypt—and many other nations offer similar profiles—thus scores variably on human rights criteria, doing relatively well in some areas, rather miserably in others, despite shiny constitutional principles. Key officials, even before the 2011 revolt, were aware of human rights standards and were not comfortable with too much criticism; and the nation embraced some reform groups eagerly pursuing further goals. But a human rights agenda was not high on the government priority scale, and leaders could also strike back, not only against individuals but through arguments that large chunks of the human rights argument involved importing Western standards offensive to local values. Preservation of the regime, exercising control over some Muslim protest groups whose own human rights interests were mixed at best, and preserving some regional cultural values, frequently motivated measures that ran counter to the most widely preached international standards.

Overall, then, many countries, indeed perhaps most, offered some level of commitment to human rights which was not fully matched by actual practice. The variance between profession and reality helps explain much of the mismatch between the advance of human rights sentiments over the past several decades and the record on the ground—whether the subject is police behavior, or religious policy, or opportunities for free expression. Within this broad grouping, degrees of national interest and compliance varied considerably, as the United States–Egypt comparison suggests. American officials were far more uncomfortable about openly violating key criteria than were their Egyptian counterparts—but violate they did, in some circumstances, just as Egyptian officials periodically both accepted a rights discourse but rarely acted on it. As specific watch groups noted, in the areas such as freedom of the press, it was possible to sketch a rough ratings scale—again, among countries at least professing a human rights interest—and the differences mattered. But crises could push even fairly compliant countries into unexpected levels of repression, while even authoritarian governments usually hesitated to violate professed standards too systematically.

Minority groups

Another problem sector accounts for additional contrasts between human rights professions and actual behaviors. Many nations continued to struggle with internal minorities in ways that might seem to justify departures from normal compliance. In some cases, residual prejudices against a minority damaged actual implementation of full equality before the law. In other cases, minority resistance activities, including outright violence, threatened or seemed to threaten security, prompting repressive measures in response.

We have seen that, in some instances, clashes between groups overturned human rights considerations altogether, as in civil conflicts or ethnic cleansing campaigns. In other cases, deterioration was more limited. In the United States, for example, despite measurable civil rights progress, police forces recurrently attacked members of racial minorities, with beatings and occasional killings. During 2011, fifty-two incidents, mainly involving African Americans, were under investigation, involving varying degrees of excessive force. The good news, of course, was that civil rights laws did exist, under which behaviors of this sort could be prosecuted; the bad news, however, was that incidents persisted and that, apart from the behavior of particular officers, some police departments seemed to lack regulations clearly aimed at inhibiting excess. All this in a national context in which a higher percentage of the population was in prison than in any other country in the world, with pronounced racial imbalance applying here as well ...

Minority challenges were even more explicit in other cases, particularly where groups occupied specific regions in a country and even more particularly when there was organized resistance to the state. Britain's problems with Catholics and nationalists in Northern Ireland, where violence escalated on both sides with many accusations of arbitrary imprisonment and torture, were a reminder of the strain that minority tensions can create for human rights commitments, even in one of the birthplaces of the whole approach. Small wonder that minority clashes have created periodic abuses in places like Turkey, vis-à-vis the Kurdish minority; or Sri Lanka, concerning the Tamil population; or India, concerning minorities in certain regions.

Patterns in Israel offer a specific illustration. Longstanding conflict between Israel and its large Palestinian population has visibly stressed the record in this nation. The creation of the Jewish state, in 1948, involved a set of Basic Laws that included unusually firm endorsement of standard human rights; among other things, the nation's founders assured "complete equality of social and political rights to all its inhabitants irrespective of religion, race or sex" and a "guarantee [of] freedom of religion, conscience, language, education and culture." The initial declarations included explicit pledges to adhere to United Nations principles. Israel continued to stand as a human rights beacon in some respects, as in its toleration of homosexuality.

Problems in other areas surfaced fairly quickly, however. The nation was a Jewish state, and, while freedom of worship was generally maintained there were accusations of discrimination against non-Jews. Israeli law also required a religious marriage (though this applied to any recognized religion), which meant among other things that couples of mixed religion could not legally wed. But it was the growing clash with Palestinian residents (mainly but not exclusively Muslim) that created the clearest problems, as, among other things, Israeli courts backed off somewhat from a firm priority commitment to equality under the law. By the 1970s, reports of arbitrary arrest and torture of Palestinian prisoners surfaced widely. An Israeli commission itself condemned certain widespread practices, but argued that "the exertion of a moderate degree of physical pressure cannot be avoided." Human rights concern led to acceptance, in 1991, of a 1966 United Nations covenant which had banned torture and degrading treatment, but accusations of physical abuse continued—including a claim that 85% of Palestinian prisoners, or 850 people a year, were subjected to torture. Ongoing tensions also produced growing concern that freedom of the press was being curtailed, particularly where complaints about police or military behavior was involved, though there was no formal attack on this aspect of the Basic Laws. In 2011, the parliament even endorsed a plan to investigate human rights organizations for "delegitimizing" the military. The long and unresolved conflict between the Israeli state and its Palestinian population constituted an extreme case in which sincere human rights commitments were partly sacrificed to efforts to control a (large) minority group, with abusive police procedures the first symptom, but with ramifications in other human rights sectors over time. Partisans of the state would quickly point, of course, to the violence some Palestinians used against the Jewish population, but this merely provided further illustration of how deeply minority clashes could jeopardize human rights values, on all sides of the equation.

Category exceptions

Along with recurrent patterns of compromising principles in practice and the special problem of minority tensions, disagreements over sections of the human rights agenda generated further problems of implementation. As the list of rights expanded, areas of dispute could expand as well. The focus here is on a sampling of cases where societies largely committed to human rights carved out some exceptions, or where societies at least somewhat responsive expressed clear hostility to some of the categories that other regions were finding more acceptable.

Some illustrations have already emerged, from a long potential list. The United States simply did not buy into the international push against the death penalty as part of a contemporary human rights redefinition—though the push had some impact. Showcase executions—for example, the punishment in 2011 of a Georgia man convicted of murder despite some contradictory evidence—continued to demonstrate that many Americans simply did not see capital punishment through a human rights lens.

India's hesitancy over child labor reflected both widespread national poverty, at least until recently, plus a substantial commitment, by many families, to the traditional belief that work was what children were for. The nation shied away, as a result, from international conversations about outright bans on child labor. By the late 20th century, the government itself acknowledged 20 million child workers, and some estimates went much higher. In 1989, a law was finally passed banning work for children under the age of 14, but even this law exempted family-owned businesses and, more generally, it was not seriously enforced. This was simply not a domain in which a country fairly interested in human rights overall could accept a systematic extension.

Many African countries carved out de facto exceptions in the area of gender rights, by the early 21st century. A number of nations that had enthusiastically signed United Nations conventions on the rights of women found that their courts of law in practice rejected the legal obligations involved in favor of traditional standards that gave husbands a controlling interest as the basis for family stability. Thus, in 1999, a court in Zimbabwe overturned a ruling on a woman's right to inherit property, arguing that according to "African tradition" only men could own. The African Charter itself, while endorsing legal equality, also held the family as the "natural unit and basis of society" and "the custodian of morals and traditional values recognized by the community"—and family interests might take precedence over those of individual members. Women's rights unquestionably advanced in Africa—and this included a number of court rulings in favor of women's property ownership—but there was ongoing tension with more traditional patriarchal values and the customary primacy of the family unit.

Homosexuality proved to be an even greater challenge, as it surfaced as a human rights concern, again even in many regions that were responsive on other issues. We have seen that Egypt's reactions to suggestions of gay rights were far more categorical than on more familiar applications such as press or religious freedom. At essentially the same time as Dubai (in the United Arab Emirates) was developing new levels of compliance on children's rights, ending a longstanding practice of using young boys as camel jockeys, the police stepped up attacks on gay bars and arrests of foreign visitors who were gay.

Disparities of this sort may prove temporary, in the longer run. India, long opposed to homosexuality, passed a landmark tolerance law in 2011. We have seen that support for the death penalty in the United States was eroding somewhat. Greater familiarity and international pressure may cause wider accommodations in future. In some instances, however, there may be more durable resistances to particular categories even as accommodations to human rights gain ground in other respects. At the very least, for the foreseeable future, active disagreements over the range of human rights constitutes another complexity in the actual record.

Regional alternatives

One of the reasons for the world's checkered performance on human rights, shading off from the disparities already covered, involves regions that simply disagree with substantial segments of the core human rights approach—beyond, for example, disputes over one or more of the specific, newer categories. They do not necessarily quarrel with the idea of human rights, but rather with the way the standard criteria disproportionately emphasize Western values even as they have framed a more global commitment—for example, at the United Nations. The result, as was already explored by way of introduction in Chapter 1, is an intriguing tension between human rights, as conventionally defined, and regional rights in a post-imperialist age.

The category is a challenging one. In the eyes of many critics—particularly, of course, from the United States and Western Europe—these more distinctive regions are simply abusers: China or Russia perform badly on a number of international scales, and that's that. And without question the regions involved do run roughshod over some human rights as part of preserving the power of leaders and the state; in this sense they simply constitute somewhat worse examples of the disparities we have dealt with in some of the previous categories.

More closely examined, however, the regions are not simply scornful of human rights, but rather in search of alternative statements and insistent that, without these, resistance to international pressure is the only reasonable course of action. Condemnation, without more sensitive exploration of the issues involved, risks needless diplomatic tension and does not necessarily constitute the best way to see human rights implementation move forward. A further look is essential.

China (and East Asia?)

As East Asian regions—besides Japan—gained increasing economic prosperity, by the 1990s, their regional self-confidence grew, as did their world role; and with this came a frequent interest in asserting a powerful and distinctive culture that could not be embraced by a universalist human rights approach. The arguments—mounted by leaders in the city-state of Singapore even more than by the Chinese—unquestionably reflected important political and cultural traditions in the region. They gained importance, as well, at a time of receding imperialism: if Western control over world territory was no longer appropriate, perhaps Western influence over global values also should be rethought. Further, the decline of communism (despite China's continued adherence in principle), removing one contemporary alternative to Western human rights arguments, seemed to require a more successful restatement, more attuned to ongoing regional interests. Finally, the new, post-cold-war burst of international enthusiasm for human rights—ultimately exemplified, for example, in the Vienna Declaration but emerging even from the preparatory negotiations—seemed to encourage a regional dissent, to make it clear that there was more than one valid way of defining human rights without scorning the enterprise in principle.

The result was the most articulate effort at alternative response, along with a host of actual measures that separated several East Asian governments from key elements of the conventional human rights agenda as defined by most NGOs, the American State Department, and other agencies. We noted earlier the importance of insistence on a special Asian approach, and this now can be fleshed out against the backdrop of global human rights evolution.

China launched the process in 1991, with a White Paper claiming that "owing to tremendous differences in historical background, social system, cultural tradition and economic development, countries differ in their understanding and practice of human rights." This was furthered by a 1993 regional conference in Bangkok, Thailand, in which East Asian governments agreed that human rights "must be considered in the context of a dynamic and evolving process of international norm-setting, bearing in mind the significance of national and regional peculiarities and various historical, cultural and religious backgrounds."

Other statements made the regional divergence more specific. Singapore issued an official pronouncement in 1991, arguing that "an emphasis on the community has been a key survival value for Singapore." In contrast, and the government claimed this was the "Asian view," human rights and rule-of-law claims, as usually defined in international documents, are individualistic by nature and hence destructive of Asia's social mechanism. Moreover, the argument continued, they led to growing rates of violent crime, family breakdown, homelessness, and drug abuse—by implication, given these outcomes, the West itself should reject the approach, and certainly no respectable Asian society should want to buy in.

A second plank, beyond the community emphasis, reverted to an important older theme, the need to rank "the right to economic development" over individuals' political and civil rights. China's 1991 paper noted that "to eat their fill and dress warmly were the fundamental demands of the Chinese people who had long suffered cold and hunger." It would take an organized, controlled effort by the whole society to mount a successful program of economic development, and this must be the priority, against any potential distractions of the sort political dissent might create. Industrialization—China's great project, particularly from 1978 onward—would be achieved most efficiently if individuals' civil rights were restricted for the sake of political stability. Special distractions—for example, those that might arise from an independent labor movement—must be avoided.

Finally, the "Asian approach" refused to accept the legitimacy of international review. Chinese leaders asserted that "the issue of human rights falls by and large within the sovereignty of each state." National policy predominates. The message was repeated in 1995, when the government protested "some countries' hegemonic acts of using a double standard for the human rights of other countries ... and imposing their own pattern on others, or interfering in the internal affairs of other countries by using 'human rights' as a pretext."

Chinese officials not only defended their national criteria, but also increasingly accused the West (including, of course, the United States) of hypocrisy. (The government began annually reporting on human rights in the United States, in retaliation for the yearly State Department scolding.) The well-publicized abuses of Iraqi prisoners by American troops gave the Chinese ample opportunity to expand on this approach. And other critics, including some Americans, have wondered if State Department attacks on the Chinese record did not have at least as much to do with other aspects of American policy in the face of rising Chinese economic strength as with a real concern for rights; they noted that the abuses in other countries, either weaker than China or more consistently friendly to American interests, were at least as great, without, however, drawing nearly as much attention.

The argument for an "East Asian" approach to rights was not, of course, merely a matter of theory. There were some clear departures from Western-approved international standards, particularly in the area of political and civil rights. Many Chinese citizens—pressed, of course, by state-controlled media and education, but also informed by older national values—welcomed the departures, in the interests of maintaining political stability and fighting crime; Chinese distinctiveness was not a matter of government actions alone. On several levels, there were deep connections between arguments about a distinctive culture, and actual implementation. And, while this applied particularly to China, there was some regional extension as well.

Chinese sensitivity in the area of human rights was greatly heightened by the democratic protest movement, in 1989, that triggered the Tiananmen Square rising which the government forcibly suppressed, with many arrests ensuing. From that point onward, international agencies heightened their criticisms of the Chinese record on rights. Several foci predominated. The Chinese unquestionably kept some political prisoners—probably 130 people from the 1989 protest were still in jail in 2011, though the charges of course referred to specific crimes, not simply to political dissent. Human rights activists were arrested on occasion. Some torture probably occurred, perhaps in about 400 cases per year (though some critics claimed a much larger figure). China led the world in the imposition of the death penalty, though usually after at least formal judicial proceedings. Substantial religious freedom existed, but there were definite constraints by the state that banned certain sects outright and carefully monitored all religious expression; particular tension arose over the new, rapidly growing Falun Gong religious movement, which the government unquestionably attacked. Associations of any sort required official permission for meetings, though in fact many groups gathered informally without repercussion. Press freedom was limited, and the government routinely blocked some Internet sites. Minority agitation drew repression as well, especially, of course, when violence threatened, though the government sponsored some minority cultural activities. As we have seen, human rights critics pointed, finally, to the laws forbidding women from having more than one or (in some cases) two children, a policy aimed at population control but unquestionably boosting the government's authority over private lives.

The accumulation was considerable, though the record deserves comparison with other large societies in a comparable stage of overall development. It was small wonder that China not only bridled at outside criticism but rigorously restricted external human rights NGOs. On the other hand, Chinese promotion of industrial growth certainly responded to an economic rights agenda to some degree. Education spread widely, and Chinese officials themselves were actively concerned about a female literacy gap with men.

In fact, by the early 21st century the government was displaying a certain amount of ambiguity about the rights agenda overall. Already the 1982 constitution had included the now-standard human rights language. Chinese arguments about Asian values could be read as seeking durable differences in regional standards, but also as urging a temporary leniency until the economy developed sufficiently to allow a fuller embrace. The government signed over twenty international rights agreements, including attacks on racism, the document on rights of the child, and a convention against torture. Commitment to gender equality was considerable. The government began to agree that the "development of human rights is an important mark of the continuous progress of the civilization of human society," and that full realization of all the rights was a shared international goal. It proudly claimed progress even on political rights, by 2011, though how much this was aimed at greater global prestige, how much it reflected consistent policy, could certainly be debated.

China, then, stood for a distinctive regional culture, with a rights record that in some areas was arguably deficient, but with an interestingly ambiguous openness to additional goals in future. The record drew protests from heroic rights advocates within China itself—another suggestion that claims of a distinctive regional culture might be overdrawn.

Other East Asian nations displayed some similar complexity. Singapore, sometimes the loudest advocate of the regional "East Asia" alternative, resembled China in seeking to keep external NGOs at bay. The government was certainly sensitive to criticism. A British journalist who had blasted the city-state's use of the death penalty to suppress opposition was arrested in 2010 and briefly jailed (then expelled) for "selective and dissembling accounts of half-truths which could cause the unwary reader to doubt Singapore's rule." Press censorship in general was extensive, and many reporters were intimidated as a result. An Internal Security Act gave the government extensive rights to impose indefinite detention to protect public order, including religious harmony; this was sometimes used against political opponents, with thirty-six men held in this regard in 2005. Corporal punishment, mainly through caning, was routinely practiced. The American Department of State claims to have found no reports of human rights abuses by the police, and other watch agencies reported that "considerable" (though not extensive) freedom existed. The government had signed several international rights conventions, including those applying to women and children. While homosexuality was outlawed, there were in fact no arrests after 1999, and large gay rights rallies have occurred without interference.

Other East Asian countries presented even fewer problems on a conventional human rights spectrum. We have seen that Japan argued outright against the idea of special cultural zones and for a more universalist approach.

The overall result is suitably complicated: East Asian nations vary. Few, however, are immune to considerable interest in and sensitivity to human rights. Many do reflect (whether or not they articulate this point) a regional aversion to too much individualism and a high degree of attachment to community and to social order, which can lead to statements about the need to redefine the rights agenda overall. The mixed picture makes it difficult to predict whether regional factors will continue to prevail, as against fuller accommodation to global patterns with a modest regional twist.

Russia

Russian human rights patterns, after the fall of communism, also present a mixed picture, though with less formal pronouncement than in the East Asian case. The nation's distinctive history, including the conservative counterthrusts of the late 19th century and then communist attempts to define alternatives, undoubtedly influence a partly distinctive path. At the same time, the post-communist Russian state emerged, in the 1990s, with a vigorous commitment to human rights in principle. The constitution of 1993 contains a long section on the "rights of man and citizen," including acknowledgment of all the "commonly recognized principles and norms of the international law." Provisions banned torture, carefully circumscribed capital punishment, assured freedoms of press and association, and guaranteed equality before the law. Interesting provisions also included rights to education and also to health care, maintaining some of the social rights commitments that had developed under the Soviet Union.

Russian leaders frequently talked up their human rights agenda, while noting that it would take some time actually to build a solid foundation after so many years of communist dictatorship. The nation was already a signatory to the United Nations Declaration, and also joined the Council of Europe, which entailed further human rights obligations. The government appointed officials to oversee human rights, and the officials periodically offered fairly candid assessments of what was a mixed record.

The fact was that the average Russian was almost surely freer than at any time in the nation's history. Newspapers offered diverse commentary, though television fare was more strictly controlled by the state. Conversations could range widely, in contrast to the fearful atmosphere of the Soviet era. Religious freedom measurably advanced, though there were efforts to control foreign missionaries. Yet there were deep concerns as well. Prison conditions were bad, and police and army tactics frequently included torture. Complaints about human rights—for example, to the European Court of Human Rights—often led to government prosecutions of the complainants. Violence against dissident journalists and also human rights activities, almost certainly sanctioned by the government, was distressingly common, and sometimes included murder. The bitter conflict with rebels in the province of Chechnya led to particular abuses, but many problems were more widespread. Courts and judges were notoriously dependent on government directions, and gestures toward a more independent judiciary did not advance rapidly.

Again, the overall verdict was mixed (as with China), not entirely negative. Perhaps most troubling was a sense, by the 21st century, particularly under the presidency of Vladimir Putin, that things were getting worse, especially in terms of intimidation of political opponents. Revealingly, in 2006, a new law made it far more difficult for human rights NGOs to operate in Russia.

Several interpretations were possible for the newer trends, all with some plausibility. First, Putin was simply another autocrat, and Russia's serious deviations from human rights standards constitute another case in which constitutional principles yield in practice to the demands of seizing and maintaining power. Second, many Russian leaders, and not just private rights activists, did hope to make progress, though admittedly it was hard to throw off habits and practices from the past. Putin himself occasionally publicly acknowledged that more needed to be done, and that some outside criticism was quite valid. He even vowed periodically to carry out reform recommendations, though he was often rather vague on which ones he would pursue. Correspondingly, his human rights administrators frequently talked about taking further steps "with great enthusiasm." Third, Putin and many other Russians harbored their own distinctive view of human rights, in which the importance of political order overshadowed commitment to some of the conventional civil rights categories. Supporters of the Putin position, including prominent academics, argued that the establishment of political stability and authority had to come first in Russia, with the protection of rights possible only on this foundation and only to the extent the primary goal was assured. Putin himself did not offer quite such a sweeping position statement, tending to prefer pragmatism over theory. He did on occasion visibly bridle at outside criticism, contending that other countries—for example, in the European Union—had their own problems with implementing human rights and should get their own house in order before "talking down" to Russia. None of this added up to a coherent alternative statement on the order of what had emerged in East Asia, but the strong implication of a different set of priorities, in which human rights featured but at a level that differed from common Western assumptions, had something of a similar flavor.

Islam

Human rights groups, mostly Western-based, have often criticized governments in many Middle Eastern countries for their human rights records in recent decades. In many cases—as the earlier Egyptian example suggests—key problems result simply from the machinations of authoritarian governments seeking to keep their power. Often, constitutions officially acknowledge human rights. And many Middle Eastern countries, from the early 1970s onward, signed on to various United Nations declarations, including conventions on women, on torture, and on a variety of other subjects. Yet, in practice, as in Egypt until very recently, authoritarian states either ignored many provisions or suspended constitutions outright in favor of emergency rule. The results, in areas such as political arrests, torture, or freedom of the press, fall well short of what most human rights activists seek. The issues are important, but they follow from the nature of the state (and so are similar to issues in past regimes in places like Latin America), not primarily from a wider regional culture.

This means, in turn, that any analysis of the longer-term relationship between the religion of Islam (as the most important component of Middle

Eastern culture) and human rights involves more subtle components. The authoritarian political systems that have predominated since World War II, until recently, are often fairly secular in nature. The role of human rights interests in the Arab risings of 2011—the "Arab spring"—cautions against assuming too readily that there are huge and permanent barriers between Islam and many aspects of human rights. An approach that emphasizes another set of regional cultural issues is ultimately more fruitful, and probably more significant for the longer run.

In some respects, of course, authoritarian politics and Islamic concerns may blend. It was revealing that the regional political organization, the Arab League, adopted a human rights plank in the 1970s that no member government has ratified—surely the result of political tensions above all, but potentially reflecting cultural themes as well. There is no question, also, that many people in the Middle East, from leadership on down, view human rights efforts with grave suspicion, as outside, Western impositions and pretexts for criticism and interference—again, a symptom of both political and cultural contexts.

Teasing out the cultural component more explicitly involves complexities beyond the standard results of one-man or one-party rule. We have seen vital links between Islamic traditions and some aspects of human rights already, as in the emphasis on spiritual equality or the effort to use Islamic law—the Sharia—to specify certain protections for women and more generally to guard against injustice. At the same time, and obviously the issues require discussion, many reasonably objective observers argue that at least three features of traditional Sharia law clash with human rights, not across the board but in significant measure:

- Traditional Islamic law does not treat men and women equally. Differences in inheritance rights and in access to divorce are two illustrations.
- Islamic laws allow extensive use of corporal punishment, and may apply it to a wide variety of offenses, including not only physical violence but theft or adultery.
- While Islamic tradition can allow for considerable religious freedom, it does not allow for equal status. Most notably, there are severe sanctions for Muslims who attempt to leave the faith, whereas of course conversion from another religion to Islam is perfectly acceptable. Issues here can also extend into domains of free speech and press, when ideas or images offensive to Islam are involved.

In recent decades, and in certain settings, these points of friction have been considerably extended. In a number of Islamic countries, tolerance of other religions has declined, and there is widespread hostility to new efforts at Christian missionary activity. In religiously based regimes such as Iran and, during the 1990s, Afghanistan, morals regulation extended to rigid requirements about women's dress, with severe sanctions for deviance. A number of widely publicized incidents saw decrees of death by stoning of sexual offenders, particularly women. These extensions are not typical, and they go beyond Sharia requirements, but they certainly dramatize the potential gap between commonly accepted human rights standards and key aspects of Islamic law.

Not surprisingly, interest in discussing the regional cultural record is extensive. Some recent Muslim writers have argued simply that Islam and human rights are easily compatible, though critics claim that this contention is often rather vague. A 1981 declaration, sponsored by Saudi Arabia, urged simply that the Quran introduced "ideal codes" for human rights 1,400 years ago. Other commentators, slightly more hesitant, note a great deal of overlap, but argue as well that there are some problems and that much depends on how Islamic tradition, and particularly the Sharia, are interpreted. Still others, not rejecting human rights, contend at least implicitly that a particular Islamic version must be identified, different from Western norms in some respects but ultimately as valid.

From the 1960s onward, a number of Muslim scholars have put a great deal of effort into highlighting those aspects of the Islamic tradition that assure human rights, but implicitly introducing a somewhat different set of priorities from those dominant in the Western rights tradition. The discussions acknowledge that, in fact, some Islamic societies have not measured up to standards. But they also point out that Western societies have often deviated as well, and in some cases (as in the excesses of the Atlantic slave trade) offend far more deeply than Islamic societies have ever done. Elements of this lively discussion have spilled over from scholarly discussions to public conferences and proclamations, such as a "Human Rights in Islam" declaration in Cairo in 1990.

Using the Quran and the wider tradition of the Sharia, the recent arguments emphasize the Islamic commitment to justice, as in making sure that the accused and any victims get a fair hearing and appropriate verdicts. They note that Islam fundamentally protects against any abuses by the state, by stipulating that only God can limit human freedom and that no mere government can require unquestioning obedience. They emphasize a commitment to religious freedom: as the Prophet said, "there shall be no coercion in matters of faith." And, while they acknowledge the reproval of Muslims who abandon their religion, the Islamic human rights advocates note that no particular punishment is stipulated. In some discussions women's right to chastity is emphasized, as an Islamic safeguard against rape. Equality under the law follows from the Quranic insistence that "no Arab has any superiority over a non-Arab": Islam argues against racism or nationalist bias. Frequent Quranic references to "humankind" reinforce the point. On another front, traditional assurance of freedom extends even to prisoners of war, whom the Prophet urged should be liberated as an expression of mercy. Finally, Islam establishes the right to sustenance—the "rights for the needy and destitute"—as a clear commitment to the kind of economic and social categories that some other versions of the human rights agenda have emphasized as well.

These arguments—in essence, a vigorous restatement of Islamic tradition as already fully adequate to provide for human rights—tend not to play up categories like freedom of expression or the press. They do not seek to deny the rights, and commitments to religious freedom have direct bearing here, but implicitly they lower the priority, in favor of the discussions of justice, basic equality, and other categories.

In some cases, however, the arguments are joined with an admission that in a few areas Islamic traditions do need to be rethought, though not in mechanical imitation of the West and its excessive individualism. Notably, some presentations urge much greater attention to the equitable treatment of women and the need to give Muslim women concerned about their rights an Islamic home, a real alternative both to unreformed traditionalism and to Western insistence on treating women without attention to family and community bonds. Some pragmatists suggest that a flexible interpretation of the Sharia will suffice in adjusting Islamic tradition and human rights—for example, downplaying harsh physical punishments in practice. Other reformers, while again insisting that Islam is fundamentally compatible with human rights, urge the need for a more substantial rethinking, particularly in the area of gender. Thus a Malaysian feminist group insists that, throughout Islamic history, traditions have been reinterpreted and that, at present, it is appropriate to bring "our own reading of these past texts" to bear on women's issues.

As with China and Russia, the regional story is ongoing. In the spring of 2011, risings in many Middle Eastern and North African countries reflected a new surge of popular interest in human rights. The first protest, in Tunisia, directly responded to accusations of police brutality. Egypt's contribution to the "Arab spring" involved extensive grievances over police behavior, arrests of dissidents, and restrictions on the press. Human rights issues were extensively involved in protests against the authoritarian regime in Syria. Late in 2011, an activist in Egypt asked passersby on a busy Cairo Street, "Do we have human rights yet?"—a sign of unresolved issues but also of great enthusiasm.

At the least, the Arab spring arguably demonstrated that there is no incompatibility between basic human rights goals and Islamic culture. As the Vice President of the Maldives stated to the United Nations, "The democratic uprisings across the Middle East prove that Muslims yearn for democratic rights just as much as non-Muslims." Citing a similar democratic transition in his own country in 2008, the President went on:

> We must counter the false perception that people must make the choice between devotion to Islam on the one hand, and the full enjoyment of rights on the other. We strongly believe in the compatibility of Islam and human rights and seek to do our part to promote understanding and tolerance.

He pledged a new conference on progressive Islamic law and human rights, to further this understanding.

Prospects for next steps in the Arab world were not, however, entirely clear. Human rights interests were not the only fuel to protest, and only the future would determine whether human rights advocates would win out in regimes that were still being shaped. Amid uncertainty, with advocates for democracy jostling with groups like the Muslim Brotherhood in Egypt, it was virtually certain that the power and validity of an Islamic version of human rights would be further tested and illustrated in the years to come.

Regions and rights

Powerful human rights statements and countercurrents in East Asia and the Islamic world, and complex trends in Russia, demonstrate the ongoing importance of regional factors in assessing the impact of human rights. Various groups, including leadership elements, in key parts of the world, without rejecting human rights, seek a somewhat different set of standards from those current in the West and among most relevant international NGOs. Their concerns affect not only their own region, but also wider international diplomacy: quite frequently, efforts by Western powers to win international agreement on condemning certain regimes for rights violations run aground through the refusal of China, Russia, and some Islamic states to chime in. In 2011, for example, China and Russia blocked an effort to win United Nations support for a resolution against the repressive regime in Syria, which Western advocates saw as a crucial blow to their efforts to promote human rights. The regimes involved, with Russia and China at the fore, dissented from some of the human rights criteria Westerners used to judge other societies, and they worried about international precedents that might be turned against their own rule or might galvanize more internal human rights agitation. This kind of diplomatic discord may reflect other factors, including different assessments of political prospects or desire to gain national advantage—but disputes about the nature and priority of human rights often seriously enter in. Regional variation, then, provides a final explanation for the ongoing gap between human rights gains and human rights realities.

The regional picture is clearly complex, because there is no large statement flatly rejecting human rights, and even disputants periodically seek to brighten their image by claiming progress along conventional lines. Yet the regional challenge is sufficient to motivate one final development in the recent history of human rights: a renewed attempt to define the rights agenda in a more cosmopolitan, less culturally specific manner. Here, too, the process of change is ongoing.

Toward wider definition

As the human rights movement rekindled after World War II, there was an explicit attempt to reach out to scholars in many regions. The effort to assure that human rights are not simply a product of Western culture is thus not new. Equally obviously, the ongoing regional concerns about undue individualism and lack of cultural inclusiveness suggest that the early effort was inadequate, or that at least it has to be renewed. It might be possible, of course, as Chinese leaders have sometimes suggested, that human rights should always be treated as a cultural variable, with acceptance of several different regional versions. But the larger human rights tradition seeks greater universality, so it is not surprising that the last two decades, since the end of the cold war distraction, have seen another round of discussion, now benefiting as well from the fuller efforts in East Asia and the Islamic world to articulate opportunities and concerns.

Three overlapping approaches have emerged, among theorists concerned with returning to the human rights project with contemporary issues in mind. The first involves probing more deeply elements of other cultural traditions—strongly including Buddhism and Hinduism, as well as Islam—to pull out elements that support a large and inclusive human rights project. In some cases, this appeal to an expansive background is joined by a new emphasis on the importance of human dignity in any rights agenda—dignity applying, among other things, to the need to treat diverse cultural traditions with respect.

The second approach, not really contradictory, involves reasserting the importance of a universalistic approach to human rights, a fundamental commitment to a single standard of basic justice. This point, which can also acknowledge the existence of acceptable cultural differences, was already incorporated in the Vienna Declaration of 1993. It can be enhanced by even fuller references to the importance of cultural diversity and the need to maintain tolerance and appreciation, but not in a way that elevates moral relativism. This argument insists that there must be some global criteria, to which governments respond without escaping into claims of distinctive traditions.

And the third approach involves attempts to restate the basic points themselves, but with arguments that take cultural disputes into account. The American philosopher John Rawls, for example, writing in the later 20th century, attempted to posit principles of justice that all people would agree to if they were in a situation in which they could be completely objective, with no personal or specific cultural interests involved. The argument recalled elements of the natural rights approach, though with a different derivation—the idea of objective popular selection—that took the contemporary problem of regional cultural diversity into account. Rawls believed that such a universal definition of justice would include, first, basic liberties for all citizens, here including the familiar list of expression, conscience, and association, as well as rights to vote—all predicated on equal access to the liberties. The second basic principle would involve an assurance of meaningful options for all people—that is, without pretending an assurance of economic equality, everyone should have enough material support to have a life worth living, with protection for the least advantaged. Rawls argued, interestingly, that the first set of liberties would be more important than the second, which has triggered ongoing debate mirroring the older tensions over prioritizing political versus economic rights. Rawls also attempted to deal with cultural issues through an idea of justice as fairness between citizens who hold different religious or philosophical views. He argued that this path opened opportunities for consensus regardless of deep cultural differences. His term here was "overlapping consensus," because different, sometimes conflicting, moral codes would overlap with each other when it came to governance. He believed that this definition would encompass concerns for political and social order. Societies that failed to meet standards of liberty and decency were "outlaw states," with no rights to mutual respect and toleration from others, and, while hoping that peaceful reforms would predominate, Rawls even argued that human rights violations could justify military intervention to correct abuse. All of Rawls' propositions, and certainly the suggestion of military enforcement, triggered massive debate and dissent, muddying any sense that a newer approach to philosophy could transcend regional divisions or some of the other tensions in human rights discourse.

More recently still, a number of theorists have tried to simplify the global picture by restricting the number of rights that must be specified—and Rawls himself had endorsed this kind of thinking. Going beyond Rawls, the idea here was that human rights should not seek perfection, but rather should concentrate on modest improvements in the human condition. As one theorist put it, the purpose of human rights standards should be setting "lower limits on tolerable human conduct." The hope was that this pared-down list would, first, make it easier to effect essential reforms by avoiding an impossible list of demands and, second, would facilitate adjustment to different cultural priorities by reducing the specifics over which conflict might occur. The challenge of dealing with a complex global environment continued to generate restatements.

Most global human rights activity operates within a more familiar orbit, rather distant from ecumenical theory. The focus is on seeking to help local and international groups generalize a fairly conventional set of human rights standards and assist in reporting abuse. Whether the more ambitious attempts to rephrase human rights in more culturally comprehensive terms will affect on-the-ground movements, or seriously reduce regional tensions over definitions and priorities, remains to be seen. While a number of recent developments— highlighted certainly by the Arab spring—point in promising directions for human rights, the endeavor is very much a work in progress, with open questions about serious trends toward closing the contemporary gap between profession and practice.

Further reading

Regarding resistance to human rights arguments, patterns in government responses, and popular concerns about excessive individualism, community and family disruption, see Robert Weatherley, *Discourse of Human Rights in China: Historical and Ideological Perspectives* (New York, NY: Palgrave Macmillan, 1999); Marina Svensson, *Debating Human Rights in China: A Conceptual and Political History* (Lanham, MD: Rowman and Littlefield,

2002); Wm. Theodore de Bary and Tu Weiming (eds.), *Confucianism and Human Rights* (New York, NY: Columbia University Press, 1998); Sarah B. Snyder, *Human Rights Activism and the End of the Cold War: A Transnational History of the Helsinki Network* (New York, NY: Cambridge University Press, 2011); Daniel C. Thomas, *The Helsinki Effect: International Norms, Human Rights, and the Demise of Communism* (Princeton, NJ: Princeton University Press, 2001); Richard N. Dean, "Beyond Helsinki: The Soviet View of Human Rights in International Law," *Virginia Journal of International Law*, 21 (1980–1981), pp. 55–96; Randall Peerenboom, "Assessing Human Rights in China: Why the Double Standard?" *Cornell International Law Journal*, 38 (2005), pp. 71–172; Rhoda E. Howard, "Human Rights and the Search for Community," *Journal of Peace Research*, 32(1) (1995), pp. 1–8; Charles N. Brower and John B. Tepe, Jr., "The Charter of Economic Rights and Duties of States: A Reflection or Rejection of International Law?" *International Lawyer*, 9(2) (1975), pp. 295–318; G. W. Haight, "The New International Economic Order and the Charter of Economic Rights and Duties of States," *International Lawyer*, 9(4) (1975), pp. 591–604; and James A. Gross and Lance Compa, *Human Rights in Labor and Employment Relations: International and Domestic Perspectives* (Champaign, IL: University of Illinois, 2009).

A number of recent studies deal with the complexities of human rights activism in rural areas: Dorothy Hodgson, *Once Intrepid Warriors: Gender, Ethnicity, and the Cultural Politics of Maasai Development* (Bloomington, IN: Indiana University Press, 2004); Sally Engle Merry, *Human Rights and Gender Violence: Translating International Law into Local Justice* (Chicago: University of Chicago Press, 2006); Ronald Niezen, *Public Justice and the Anthropology of Law* (Cambridge, UK: Cambridge University Press, 2010); Mark Goodale, *Surrendering to Utopia* (Stanford, CA: Stanford University Press, 2009); Harri Englund, *Prisoners of Freedom: Human Rights and the African Poor* (Berkeley and Los Angeles: University of California Press, 2006).

For a current comparative analysis, including the dynamic nature of the human rights effort as evidenced in the Middle East in 2011 and the related role of new technologies in human rights debates, see: J. S. Peters and Andrea Wolper (eds.), *Women's Rights, Human Rights: International Feminist Perspectives* (New York, NY: Routledge, 1995); Mahmood Monshipouri, *Human Rights in the Middle East: Frameworks, Goals, and Strategies* (New York, NY: Palgrave Macmillan, 2011); Salma K. Jayyusi (ed.), *Human Rights in Arab Thought* (New York, NY: I. B. Taurus & Co., 2009); Abdullahi An-Na'im, "Human Rights in the Arab World: A Regional Perspective," *Human Rights Quarterly*, 23 (2001), pp. 701–732; Ebrahim Moosa, "The Dilemma of Islamic Rights Schemes," *Journal of Law and Religion*, 15(1–2) (2000–2001), pp. 185–215; and Heiner Bielefeldt, "'Western' versus 'Islamic' Human Rights Conceptions?: A Critique of Cultural Essentialism in the Discussion on Human Rights," *Political Theory*, 28(1) (February, 2000), pp. 90–121.

Good area studies also include Ian Neary, *Human Rights in Japan, South Korea and Taiwan* (New York, NY: Routledge, 2002), and Abdullahi Ahmed

An-Na'im and Francis M. Deng (eds.), *Human Rights in Africa: Cross-Cultural Perspectives* (Washington, DC: Brookings Institution, 1990).

On reconciling human rights and regionalism, see John Rawls, *A Theory of Justice* (Cambridge, MA: Harvard University Press, 1971); Carol Gould, *Globalizing Democracy and Human Rights* (Cambridge, UK: Cambridge University Press, 2004); and J. A. Lindgren Alves, "The Declaration of Human Rights in Postmodernity," *Human Rights Quarterly*, 22(2) (May, 2000), pp. 478–500.

7   Conclusion: human rights in motion

Human rights issues and opportunities today flow directly from a rich history over the past 250 years. Basic ideas formulated in the 18th century—about more humane treatment, legal equality, and greater freedoms for beliefs and actions—have persisted. But their applications have steadily amplified, bringing in additional groups and issues, a process that has made the precise list of widely accepted human rights a moving target.

The globalization of human rights has been an ongoing process as well. Spreading ideas about human rights, and the consequences of human rights principles, was implicit in the whole movement; after all, a common humanity served as one of the core points. Inevitably, however, the actualization of a global reach has proved quite complicated, with many issues still in play today. The diffusion of human rights encountered different political cultures: while human rights can touch base with ideas of justice and law in many different traditions, it meshes more easily with some regional approaches than with others. In fact, also, different regions were exposed to human rights in different ways. We have seen important cases where human rights thinking seemed quickly to respond to local needs and aspirations, but others in which it seemed to be a foreign intrusion or even a basis for unwanted foreign intervention not only during, but after, the formal age of imperialism. Finally, Western presentation of human rights was uneven, depending on Western interests and on cultural intrusions such as racism.

As human rights thinking matured, as it encountered changing conditions (such as the impacts of industrialization), and as it globalized, certain bifurcations within the movement itself opened up, and some persist still. For a time, significant tension developed between claims for national freedom and more conventional human rights approaches. This has eased somewhat, given the range of new-nation formation and the end of most colonies, but traces of the problem remain certainly in the situation of certain minorities and the clashes their aspirations, and resistance to these aspirations, can bring to the human rights field.

Recurrently from the mid-19th century onward, a second set of tensions emerged around the relationship between social and economic rights, amid widespread and (in some cases) growing global poverty, and civil and political rights. While some declarations have attempted to include both categories, in fact the problem of prioritization has hardly been resolved to this day. From the early days, in fact, human rights efforts have generated criticism over the priorities implied. From the 19th century to the present day, some radicals have argued that the whole movement really misses the point, distracting attention from real problems and essentially serving the interests of industrial capitalism rather than real reform. Anti-slavery, in this formulation, really served to mask the evils of factory working conditions. Even today, so the argument goes, the great passion is aimed at governments rather than the real masters of the contemporary work, the big corporations. Obviously, tensions around these issues were greatest during the cold war, when the communist camp could push the primacy of social and economic rights most forcefully. But attacks on human rights as mere window dressing still surface today, and find echoes as well in some of the regional disputes over what issues should come first. In defense, rights advocates may note that attention to corporate abuses is gaining ground and that the oppression that even conventional advocates target is very real, not mere diversion. But some tension here persists, and warrants ongoing evaluation.

A final set of problems has emerged most clearly in fairly recent decades, as international human rights efforts interact with increasingly powerful regional statements: Do human rights principles retain too many traces of their Western, rather individualistic origins, and can they be reconciled with other, more communal ideals? Here again, history helps frame the problem but clearly provides no definitive response.

The history of human rights hardly predicts the future in other respects, but it does frame some ongoing questions. The movement has, as noted, steadily added targets: gender, for example, was barely a footnote on the initial list of concerns, but now it consumes whole chapters. From this process in turn, two questions for the future:

First, will the process of amplification continue? The inclusion of gay rights and disability rights on the agenda, over the past forty years, has been a significant further change. It reflects the application of human rights logic to additional groups, and it also shows how human rights thinking can help awaken demands. Are there other groups or issues on the horizon? Might we expect to see some further flowering of thinking about children's rights—an ambiguous category in human rights thinking thus far? Or the rousing of some other category altogether? The capacity of human rights to stretch has not necessarily played itself out, but precise prediction is difficult.

Second, will we see the same pattern of gradual but growing acceptance for some of the more recent innovations that developed for some of the earlier expansions? For at least a half-century, and in some cases even longer, few (if any) human rights statements have not included serious attention to women, yet in the mid-19th century even fervent human rights advocates might easily have omitted this connection altogether. Women's rights are hardly uniformly assured in the present day; there should be no downplaying of the ongoing issues involved. But there has been impressive widening of attention, in virtually every part of the world. Even Saudi Arabia, a holdout in many respects, in later 2011 granted women the right to vote in local elections—a sign of how difficult it has become not to offer some serious gestures toward change in this rights domain. Will this same process of steady, if uneven, normalization apply to currently disputed categories such as gay rights? Is there a firm historical process at work here that slowly bends resistance to the expanded human rights logic? Or are there some extensions that are so difficult, such cultural hot buttons, that assumptions of a common process will prove misleading?

There may be a different alternative, amid assertions of regionalism. Will international activists decide to trim their sails, contrary to recent impulses, to focus on a smaller core set of rights? Is this the best path toward more successful overall results, as some global compromisers now suggest? If so, tough decisions will be needed to define the core and to determine what happens to the rest of the agenda.

Ongoing globalization raises some additional possibilities and uncertainties. In many ways the spread of global interest in human rights has been an impressive feature of modern world history. We have seen that relatively few regions, by the later 20th century, were unaware of human rights statements as part of standard political discourse—essential features, for example, of most constitutional statements. The global advance has been sporadic, not steady. It is vital to remember that the modern record indicates clearly that human rights agendas can retreat, not just in individual regions, but on a wider basis—as was the case in the 1930s. There's no assurance that reverses will not recur in future. Nevertheless, if one compares the situation in principle, in the early 21st century, with the geography of human rights just two hundred years before—with a Western base, though still somewhat tentative, and the first signs of export to Latin America—the geographical gains are incontestable. Even regions uncomfortable with dominant international statements of human rights, like Singapore, feel compelled to come up with alternative versions; only a few small countries are comfortable in ignoring the topic altogether.

Here the questions are whether geographic expansion will continue—enticing the few remaining complete holdouts—and whether the expansion will move more fully from statements in principle to fuller embrace in practice. Here, obviously, the crystal ball is cloudier, even aside from the possibility of another period of reversal. Uncertain predictions must also embrace the question of whether human rights statements themselves will become more culturally inclusive, successfully meeting some of the concerns that emanate from other regional cultures without dissolving into meaningless generalization. We can note the geographical change over recent history, and its recurrent quality, but we will simply have to watch to determine persistence of trend.

The biggest question, of course, involves implementation. Will we see more progress in moving from acceptance at some level of principle, and actual changes in the behaviors of states, corporations, and other power groups—including more willingness not simply to proclaim, but actually to enforce? The inherent uncertainty of forecasting the future is magnified here by the difficulty even of determining past trends. We have seen that the human rights action, in combination with other factors, has probably reduced the use of torture and the rate of capital punishment worldwide, despite ongoing issues in certain regions. It has certainly expanded legal rights for women, again with important regional variety, though measuring the impact of informal barriers to equality is a harder task. It has probably, along with the huge changes in the media themselves, expanded people's access, overall, to a greater variety of opinions and expressions. But, while religious freedom has gained in some places, it has at best stabilized in others and has actually retreated in some important instances, compared to earlier traditions. In a world experiencing growing income inequality—globally, and within most regions from India to China to the United States—it's hard to talk about clear progress in the economic–social human rights category. And, while child labor has definitely declined, and schooling gained—the results of human rights thinking combined with fundamental shifts in the economy and in relevant technology—it's somewhat harder to be certain that children's human rights have been appropriately defined and implemented. Equality under the law, finally, has certainly generalized in some key respects—there has been real change here—but issues remain, whether the venue involves police behaviors, or the policies of multinational corporations, or patterns of family life.

There may indeed be a few cases where human rights statements, particularly emanating from international groups in ways that smack of foreign interference, have actually made matters worse, provoking new harshness against women, or religious minorities, or other human rights targets. More commonly, as we have seen, the problem is a gap between professions of principles (however sincerely intended at first) and actual practice. Charting the history, much less the probable future, of this gap is truly important but also very difficult. Even most human rights groups, focused primarily on current abuses (as they should be), have hardly undertaken the task of systematic, global evaluation over time.

Another concern has arisen that deserves attention: cases where successful human rights action turns out not to solve basic problems, including problems of security. South Africa may be a case in point, though there are others. The end of apartheid and the careful sifting of related human rights violations constitute a real triumph. But in South Africa today crime problems are rampant, and many people feel the society has deteriorated. Human rights gains, in other words, were not enough, and it's worth assessing other current situations with this warning in mind.

This dilemma, then, remains. At one level the story of human rights over the past two centuries, though complex and uneven, is the story of considerable progress, of changes in the way many people think and behave and in the way states are organized. At the level of actual human experience, the story is surely even more complex, and maybe quite different; it certainly is different in many specific places at key points in time, not only in terms of rejection of principle but in terms of insincere or ineffective acceptance. The result is an ongoing challenge to analysis, historical and otherwise, and a challenge as well to those who strive to narrow the gap between still-novel kinds of protections for human endeavor, and what happens to actual people around the world.

Index